Communications in Computer and Information Science 1649

More information about this series at https://link.springer.com/bookseries/7899

Maria Ranieri · Marta Pellegrini ·
Laura Menichetti · Alice Roffi ·
Damiana Luzzi (Eds.)

Social Justice, Media and Technology in Teacher Education

27th ATEE Spring Conference, ATEE 2021
Florence, Italy, October 28–29, 2021
Revised Selected Papers

Springer

Editors
Maria Ranieri
University of Florence
Florence, Italy

Laura Menichetti
University of Florence
Florence, Italy

Damiana Luzzi
University of Florence
Florence, Italy

Marta Pellegrini
University of Cagliari
Cagliari, Italy

Alice Roffi
University of Florence
Florence, Italy

ISSN 1865-0929 ISSN 1865-0937 (electronic)
Communications in Computer and Information Science
ISBN 978-3-031-20776-1 ISBN 978-3-031-20777-8 (eBook)
https://doi.org/10.1007/978-3-031-20777-8

This Springer imprint is published by the registered company Springer Nature Switzerland AG
The registered company address is: Gewerbestrasse 11, 6330 Cham, Switzerland

Preface

The 27th ATEE Spring Conference: Social justice, media and technology in teacher education was held online during October 28–29, 2021. It should have been held in the marvellous town of Florence, the capital of the Renaissance, in May 2020 but due to the insurgence of the COVID-19 pandemic, the conference was postponed and, finally, took place solely online. The conference was jointly organised by the Department of Education, Languages, Interculture, Literature and Psychology of the University of Florence and the Association of Teacher Education in Europe (ATEE). The aim was to allow researchers and scholars from diverse fields such as education, communication, sociology, psychology and computer sciences, to undertake a public discussion on the interplay between the growing digitisation of our societies and its implication for social justice and access to education. A specific context was privileged, that is the school, particularly referring to the role of teachers and their preparation. The title of the conference embraces these aspects and summarises the main theme of the event, which was relevant at the time the conference was planned but which became even more significant later, that is when the impact of the lockdown on schooling had shown how social and educational inequalities are connected to digital inequalities, and vice versa.

These conference proceedings host a selection of papers that were fully submitted after the end of the conference and went through the process of double-blind review. In total 49 revised paper submissions were received, of which 19 were selected for publication by the Scientific Committee following a minimum of three reviews per paper. The authors of the accepted papers come from different countries, although a major presence of Italian authors can reasonably be acknowledged, having held the conference in Italy.

The 27th ATEE Spring Conference proceedings span three topical areas, which are generally well balanced in terms of contents and contributions.

Seven articles are included in the area on "Teaching critical media/digital literacy in multicultural societies" the focus of which was on exploring the potential of education to foster the critical understanding of the relationships between media, information and power, particularly referring to the media (mis)representation of marginalised social groups. The leading question of this area was as follows: To what extent may teacher education incorporate critical media/digital literacy to prepare teachers to teach in multicultural schools?

Four articles are grouped in the area on "Decommodifying teacher (digital) education". Since many discourses around "digital education" are taking place leading to the reconceptualisation of education as a commodity rather than as a public good, the issue is whether teacher education and training on educational technology and/or media literacy can be critically approached to question the commodification of school education.

Finally, eight articles are collected in the area "Digital technology and equity for inclusive teaching" to go deeper into the understanding of the alleged participatory potential of Information and Communication Technologies (ICT). The main questions were as follows: How to prepare future and in-service teachers to design digital-inclusive teaching? What impact may teacher education about digital technology have on teachers' capacity to design learning for all?

The reviewers' commitment in the review process and their efforts in providing constructive feedback improved the quality of the papers. Comments, revisions and corrections were critically incorporated in the papers with authors greatly appreciating the suggestions received. We are grateful to the referees for their dedication and to the authors for their accurate work. A special thanks is due to the members of the Organising Committee, and to all the bodies that contributed to the success of the Conference.

July 2022 Maria Ranieri

Organization

Scientific Committee

Maria Ranieri (Chair)	University of Florence, Italy
Gianfranco Bandini	University of Florence, Italy
Raffaella Biagioli	University of Florence, Italy
Giovanni Biondi	INDIRE, Italy
Vanna Boffo	University of Florence, Italy
Gianna Cappello	University of Palermo, Italy
T. J. Ó Ceallaigh	Mary Immaculate College, Ireland
Miroslava Cernochova	Charles University, Czech Republic
Cornelia Connolly	National University of Ireland Galway, Ireland
Giovanna Del Gobbo	University of Florence, Italy
Loretta Fabbri	University of Siena, Italy
Floriana Falcinelli	University of Perugia, Italy
Paolo Federighi	University of Florence, Italy
Paul Hopkins	University of Hull, UK
Hanneke Jones	Newcastle University, UK
Hiromi Kawaguchi	Hiroshima University, Japan
Panagiotis Kimourtzis	University of the Aegean, Greece
Sirkku Kotilainen	University of Tampere, Finland
Ersilia Menesini	University of Florence, Italy
Stefano Oliviero	University of Florence, Italy
Mojca Pajnik	University of Ljubljana, Slovenia
Davide Parmigiani (ATEE President)	University of Genoa, Italy
John Potter	University College London, UK
Juliana Elisa Raffaghelli	Open University of Catalonia, Spain
Paolo Raviolo	eCampus University, Italy
Pier Cesare Rivoltella	Catholic University of the Sacred Heart, Italy
Pier Giuseppe Rossi	University of Macerata, Italy
Blerim Saqipi	University of Pristhina, Kosovo
Maurizio Sibilio	University of Salerno, Italy
Clara Silva	University of Florence, Italy

Organising Committee

Maria Ranieri	University of Florence, Italy
Stefano Cuomo	University of Florence, Italy
Michiel Heijnen (ATEE Vice-President)	Marnix Academy, Netherlands
Laura Menichetti	University of Florence, Italy
Davide Parmigiani (ATEE President)	University of Genoa, Italy
Mariagrazia Tagliabue (ATEE Secretariat)	ATEE

Local Committee

Communication Staff

Ilaria Ancillotti	University of Florence, Italy
WooJeon Park	Mathema, Italy

Managing Editors

Laura Menichetti	University of Florence, Italy
Marta Pellegrini	University of Florence, Italy

Editorial Staffs

Luca Bravi	University of Florence, Italy
Francesco Fabbro	Tor Vergata University of Rome
Elena Gabbi	University of Florence, Italy
Cristina Gaggioli	University of Florence, Italy
Damiana Luzzi	University of Florence, Italy
Alice Roffi	University of Florence, Italy

Contents

Teaching Critical Media/Digital Literacy in Multicultural Societies

Media Education and Digital Storytelling: An Experience of University Teaching

Filippo Bruni(✉)

Università del Molise, Campobasso, Italy
filippo.bruni@unimol.it

Abstract. The paper presents a university teaching experience using digital storytelling from the Service Learning perspective. A small group of students in their third year of the degree course in Communication Sciences was involved. The didactic activity included in preliminary research is part of a project agreed with other university sites. This research aimed to collect through a questionnaire the students' satisfaction, the difficulties they encountered and the perceived effectiveness concerning the positive impact from a social point of view on learning new skills and strengthening relational networks. Positive elements emerged as a high level of involvement, an acceptable level of digital skills and interest in social issues. There are also several critical issues related to the different kinds of interaction and social networks activated in the local context.

Keywords: Digital storytelling · Video · Media education · University teaching

1 Media Education, Video and Digital Storytelling

In Media-Education videos were and still are relevant tools in the research and teaching fields [1–3], particularly concerning their production, which is a key element in teacher's digital competencies. It is certainly relevant to be able to analyze videos, but this is only the first level of competence. To operate at the making is much more significant: it allows students to understand the mechanisms related to this type of communication, acquiring, in the perspective of Media education, higher levels of digital literacy. Video production also represents a fundamental element in teaching, including at universities, because it goes beyond transmissive approaches.

We need to highlight the link between video production, media education, and storytelling. Storytelling can use various digital tools, but undoubtedly video is the tool with the biggest potential. Video-based digital storytelling implies strong forms of engagement and seems effective in creating a narrative on such topics as social inequity, discrimination and injustice. Storytelling constitutes a peculiar way of thought that differs from a logical-scientific one [4]. In logical-scientific thinking, the present time prevails in storytelling times has a wide range. In this sense, the relationship between storytelling and digital culture becomes meaningful. Faced with the availability of an enormous amount of information offered by the internet, the traditional balance between oblivion and memory is lost. It becomes hard to find the balance that has allowed the construction

M. Ranieri et al. (Eds.): ATEE 2021, CCIS 1649, pp. 3–12, 2022.
https://doi.org/10.1007/978-3-031-20777-8_1

of narratives that imply an interpretation and selection of what happened. The feeling of «living an eternal present becomes widespread: past and future are flattened in a dimension of disheartening and almost anguished actuality, completely contrary to the natural propensity of the human being to live in a history» [5]. The more important is to find elements within the digital culture that can promote a narrative approach. The digital dimension adds the advantage of facilitating the making, editing, documenting, and sharing [6]; extensive experiences have been accumulated even in the educational field, both in the international context [7–12], and in the Italian one [13, 14]. A peculiar approach is that of digital storytelling in the perspective of Service Learning, as a method that combines forms of community volunteering with the learning of professional skills [15–17]. On the one hand video production is a popular activity among the new generations, one for all, the social network TikTok on the other hand, the challenge is to promote both a link with the territory and a careful approach to difficult situations, giving a voice to disadvantaged groups.

In the university context, making video storytelling gives an interesting perspective in identifying procedures and creating analysis tools, even more if linked to specific targets such as the people with disability, the elderly, the immigrants.

2 Proposed Research

The described research tries to match the narrative dimension by using digital tools, Media-Education, attention to the social context and university teaching. Given the small sample, this research is only at the preliminary stage and aims to test evaluation tools shared with other universities. The challenge is to promote both a link with the territory and a careful approach to disadvantaged social groups. More specifically, the idea is to test the realisation of videos to achieve three objectives: an aware use of digital products (Media-Education); promoting the practice of digital storytelling in the logic of Service Learning and thus with a focus on the social dimension; the promotion within university teaching of digital competences and civic sense (Civic Media).

In proposing the activity of the University of Molise, the methodological design has three phases.

The first is related to the definition of the task: an invitation to create digital storytelling in the logic of Learning Service. In addition to a brief presentation of the proposal, specifying its peculiarities, the link with other universities and other territories was emphasised, also showing examples of videos already realised. The activation or recovery of contacts with associations or persons in the regional context - a small region in southern Italy, with a predominantly mountainous territory, limited industrial development and an ageing population - was then requested. The specific Service Learning activities carried out ultimately fall into two main typologies: interviews with young people belonging to disadvantaged categories, mainly the disabled, and interviews with elder people living in small towns which are gradually becoming depopulated. The latter typology also indicates the main geographical and socio-economic context in which the students operated. To support the project was presented one of the most widely used and easy to use software for editing videos: most of the participants, however, had experience in making videos, but not in digital storytelling. For the first phase, after the presentation and definition of the task, two months were left to make the videos. In a dedicated meeting, the students had: a) to present the video project, indicating the theme, the subjects involved, and the structure b) to show to the professor and other students, if they wished, either parts of the video or an early version of the video to receive suggestions on the technical aspects as well as the structure and content of the video. A second phase was the presentation of the final version of the videos in the classroom for a debriefing: the limited number of final products allowed adequate forms of analysis and discussion at the university. More specifically, for each video, indications were requested/given concerning: a) hardware and software; b) the involvement of people and associations in the area; c) length and editing. They spent approximately 15 h for this second phase, spread over a month. The final phase consisted of a survey aimed at assessing the levels of satisfaction and promoting the self-evaluation of the experience. Overall, all the activities starting from the initial presentation to the questionnaire administration took place over three months.

The survey, consisting of 19 questions, addresses three thematic issues:

1. the level of satisfaction and the reasons why it is satisfactory or not;
2. the difficulties in planning, involving the territory - the associations and institutions - and in the use of hardware and software;
3. perception of effectiveness in (I) the positive social impact in the context, (II) learning new skills and (III) strengthening relational networks.

The questionnaire used is part of a more wide project, which involves the University of Bologna and the University of Padua, the project leader. More specifically, the students of educational sciences used the questionnaire developed at the University of Padua. In a dedicated meeting, they adapted the questionnaire to make it suitable for different degree courses and usable in different Italian regions, leaving open the possibility of a national comparison.

As part of the teaching of Media Education and Digital Literacy, a small group of 13 students from the third year of the Communication Sciences course at the University of Molise were involved voluntarily.

3 Findings

The results of the questionnaire lead to five areas of interests: 1) the characteristics of the students who participated in the activity 2) their level of satisfaction, 3) the difficulties encountered, 4) the perception of the effects on the territory and the people involved, 5) the perception of the effects on the students who joined the research.

In terms of students' characteristics, the largest group (46.2%) felt that they were well informed about the local context (see Fig. 1). Concerning the belief that they can contribute to change, the prevailing view is that they can be more effective in their community than in wider contexts, and the two largest groups are at a medium/high level (see Fig. 2).

Concerning the second area, student satisfaction, the first positive result is the intention to use digital storytelling again: the most numerous groups are at medium-high levels (see Fig. 3). There are two types of reasons for this. The first is.

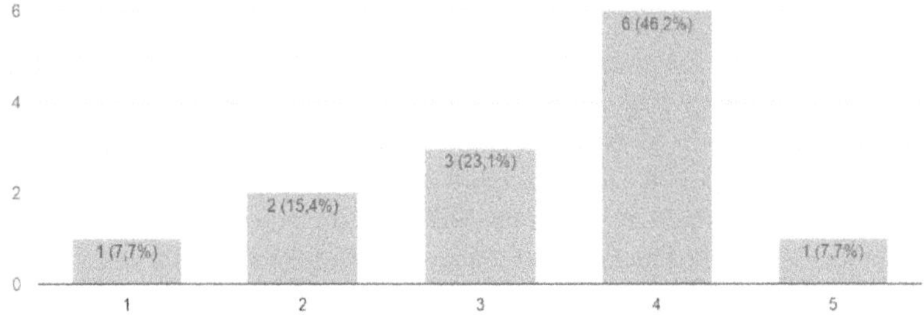

1 at all 5 a lot

Fig. 1. I am informed about the most important issues in my local community.

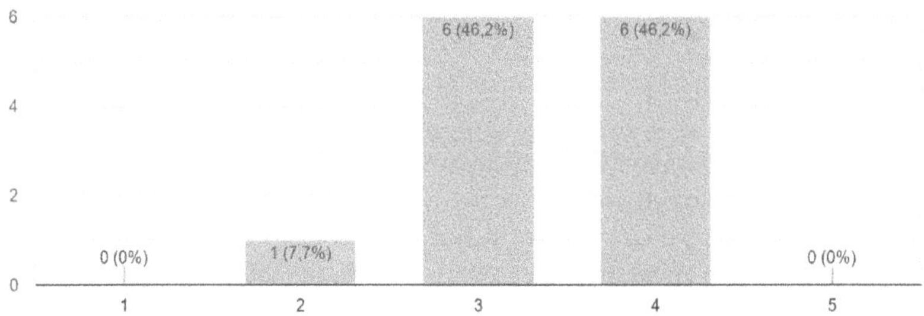

1 at all 5 a lot

Fig. 2. I think my contribution could change something in my community.

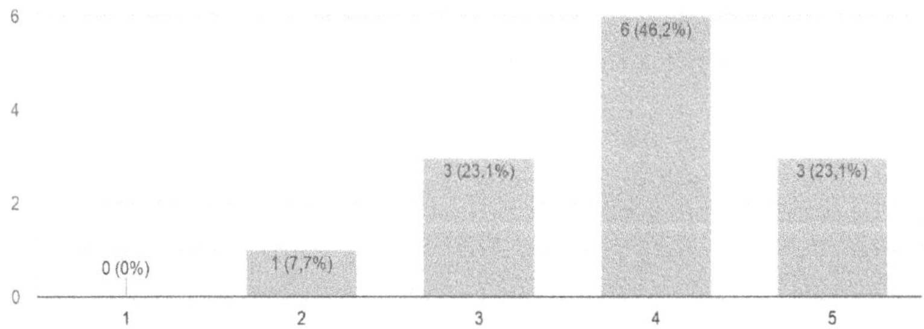

1 absolutely not 5 absolutely yes

Fig. 3. After this experience, do you think you will use the digital storytelling with similar purpose in the future?

The first focus is on the characteristics of the video: it is a multimedia product that attracts attention, and it is persuasive and more effective. The second refers to the subjective experience of the video maker: interest in the local context, professional aspirations, the pleasure of narration, and the desire to meet other people and share their experiences. As a student stated: "It is nice to experience other people's stories and empathize with them". A further specific question ("What did you like the most?") provides additional elements. They liked the making and editing of the video, followed in order of preference by the pleasure of visiting/knowing the local contexts and the satisfaction of interviewing people. And it emerges as a final element of a taste for storytelling and the construction of stories. In short, the technical dimension linked to the design and making-of the video, and the relationship dimension, connected with meeting and interviewing people was ultimately the two most appreciated central aspects.

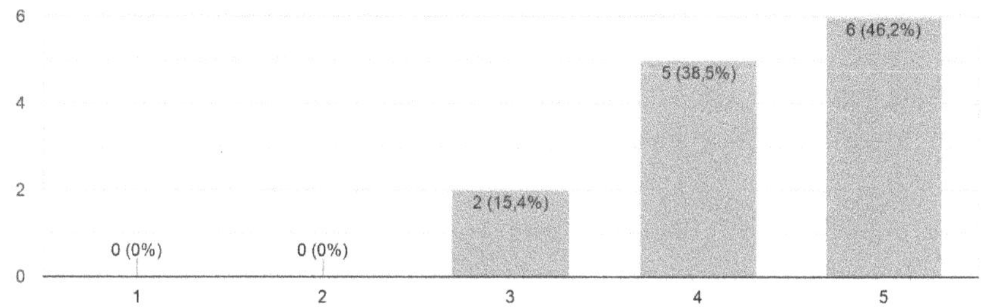

Fig. 4. How do you rate the experience? (1: very negative – 5: very positive)

The overall experience is evaluated by the majority of students as very positive (46.2%) or positive (38.5%), with only a 15.4% group at an intermediate level (see Fig. 4).

Concerning the third area, the difficulties encountered, only a 15.4% cluster encountered significant difficulties in managing relations with the people or institutions and associations involved. A large group was at an intermediate level (30.8%), while the majority (53.9%) reported little or no difficulties. Overall, the result shows a good relationship with the local context (see Fig. 5). Considering the technical realisation of the video, the majority group (76.9%) makes an intermediate evaluation between difficulty and ease (see Fig. 6). It is a sign that some skills are necessary and not strong enough among the video-makers sample. We should also consider that, ultimately, the technical making of the video seems to be both one of the most engaging elements and the cause of some difficulties.

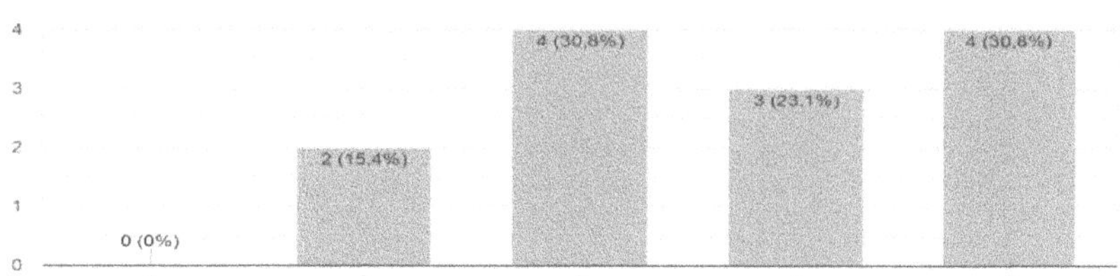

Fig. 5. Have you encountered issues with the people/organizations involved in the project? (1: no difficulties – 5: many difficulties)

With regard to the perception of the effects on the territory and the people involved, there is a gap between a general belief in digital storytelling and the perception of the effectiveness of its vision. On the one hand, the vast majority of students (84.6% are on the two highest levels) believe that digital storytelling is effective to improve people's

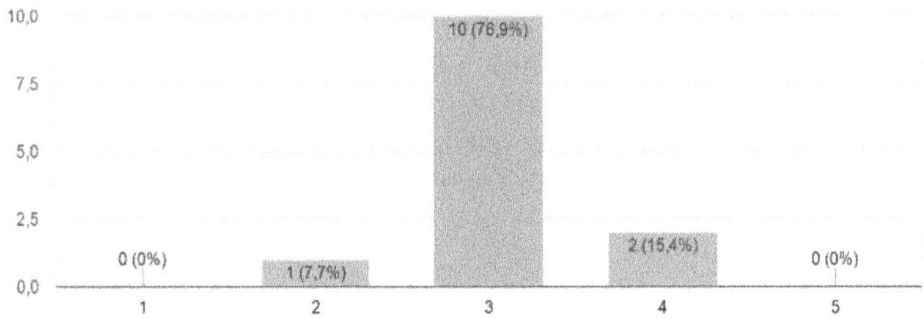

Fig. 6. From a technical point of view, how do you rate the work you had to do to realise the Digital Storytelling? (1: very difficult – 5: very easy)

attitudes (see Fig. 7). On the other hand, students believe that simply watching the digital storytelling video does not generate adequate changes: only one group (23.1%) goes beyond the intermediate level, the others are between the lowest and intermediate level (see Fig. 8). The gap is partly understandable: it is the process of making the video and the activation of the network of relationships that work in changing attitudes rather than simply watching the video.

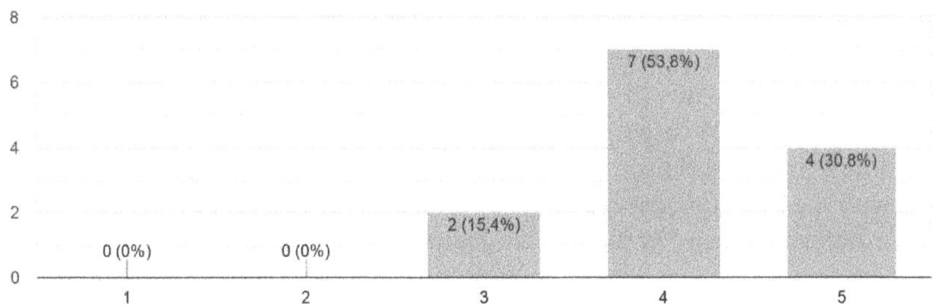

Fig. 7. How effective do you think is the use of digital storytelling in improving people's attitudes? (1: at all – 5: a lot)

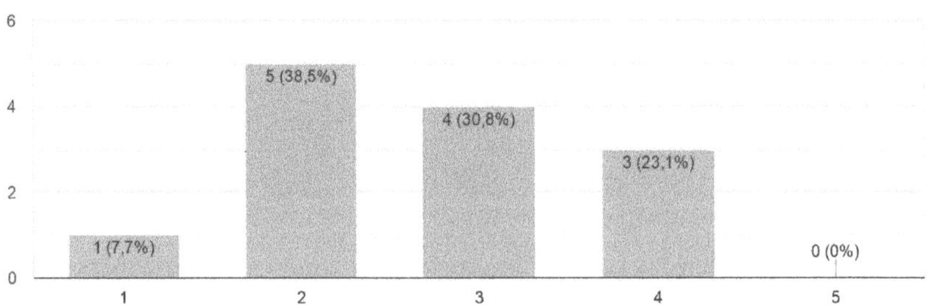

Fig. 8. How much did the project you realized changed the attitude of the people who have seen your digital storytelling? (1: at all – 5: a lot)

Concerning the fifth area, the perception of the effects on the students who participated in the research, we report an overall positive result but with a specific limitation.

In the first place, the project changed students' attitudes: although the main group is at the intermediate level (46.2%) the tendency is toward the higher levels (see Fig. 9). Similarly, the trust in the importance of active citizenship has increased (see Fig. 10). Even considering the increase of participation in social activities in their area, although the majority is positive (69.2%), a minority but substantial share (30.8%) is at an intermediate/low level (see Fig. 11). There is a clear issue about maintaining relations with the people and associations involved in the making of the digital storytelling: the majority declare that they will not maintain contact (61.6%) (see Fig. 12). This point needs additional investigation: although the search for a job is highly likely to take students out of the region, we still need to identify the reasons for this position. Finally, it is worth noting that students feel they have increased their digital skills, although the largest group (46.2%) is only at the intermediate level (see Fig. 13).

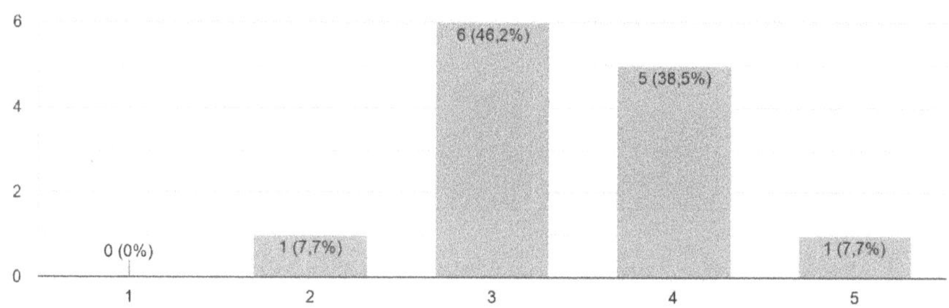

Fig. 9. How much do you think the project changed your attitude in promoting the knowledge of territory, people or associations? (1: at all – 5: a lot)

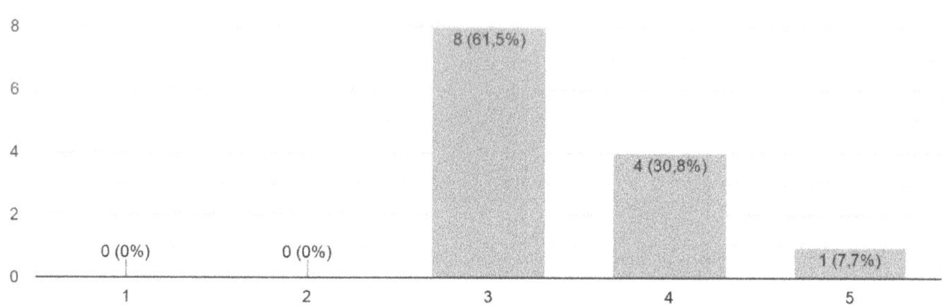

Fig. 10. After your experience, has your perception of the importance of having an active citizenship in the territory increased? (1: at all – 5: a lot)

Concluding, the fourth and fifth areas present oscillating indications regarding the effects on students and the territory: on the one hand, the experience perception is positive, and the method of intervention adequate; on the other, persists perplexity about the effectiveness emerge, and this is a matter for further investigation in the future. Both the characteristics of the area and the career prospects of the students, who often move to other regions, could play a role.

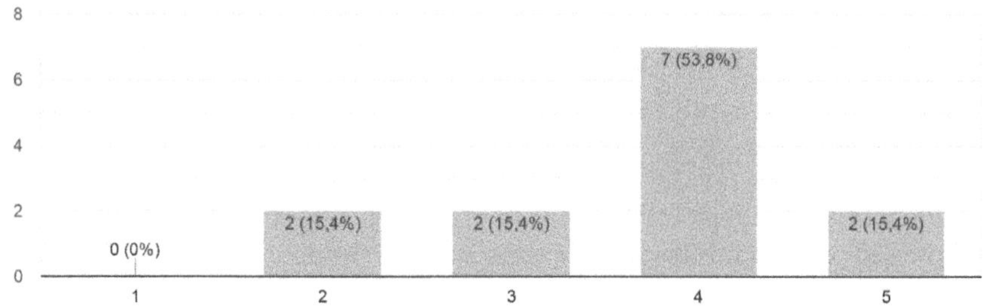

Fig. 11. After this experience, I think I will participate more in social activities in my area. (1: at all – 5: a lot)

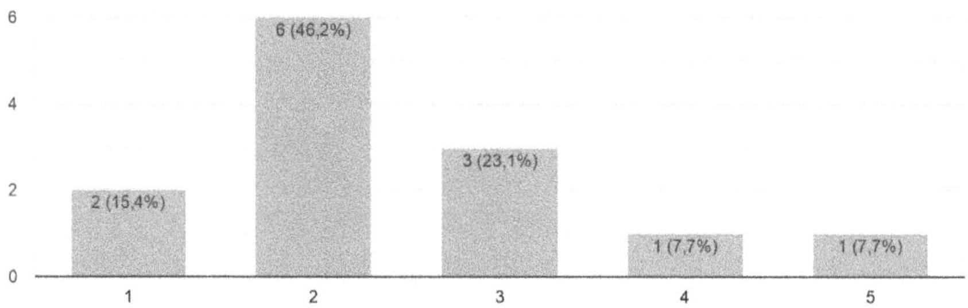

Fig. 12. Do you think you are going to keep contacts with people/associations involved in your digital storytelling? (1: absolutely no– 5: absolutely yes)

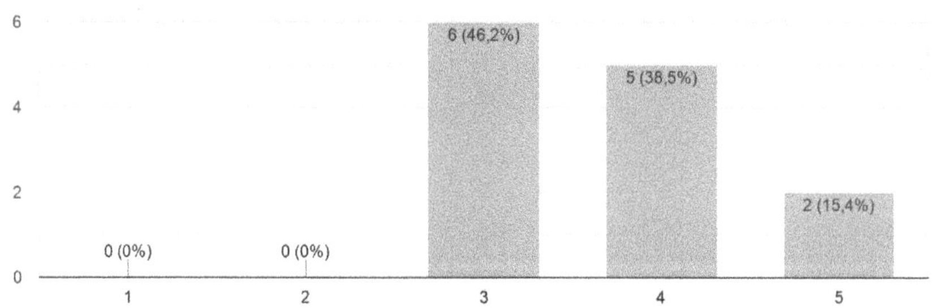

Fig. 13. After this experience, how much do you think your digital skills have improved? (1: at all – 5: a lot)

4 Conclusions

Recalling that the sample taken is not statistically significant and that this is only a preliminary survey to develop the management of a research project in collaboration with other universities, we could highlight the following points concerning the questionnaire and the analysis of the videos produced:

1. Limited difficulties related to video editing with a high variety of software used. Several digital skills, also linked to the specificity of the Communication Sciences course, are already acquired, but there is a lack of some skills.

2. An interest in social issues (immigration, disability, LGTB, youth,...) [18]. A partial but significant picture of the difficulties within the region emerges from the videos. There are also significant interests in the promotion of artistic heritage and craft activities.
3. Difficulties in focus on the social dimension, avoiding the documentary and promotional side. This difficulty probably stems from seeing the enhancement of the artistic heritage and the economic promotion of a specific area as the solution to problems of a social nature.
4. A marked differentiation about personal interaction in making videos: the approaches go from the use of the interview on the field - an indication of a strong involvement with people and associations - to a narrative dimension from a personal point of view. The journalist is one of the prospective careers for these students: this may be one of the elements that weighed in the production of the videos.
5. A high level of engagement and satisfaction among students. The degree course includes laboratory and works placement activities, but a significant part of the course delivers traditional lecture-based teaching: the production of videos, as other digital artifacts, is an innovative approach.

From a future perspective, we can point out two aspects.

The first is the need to build or improve tools that allow measuring the increase of learning levels beyond the emotional involvement of the students. Any activity that presents itself as innovative, especially if linked to the expressive dimension, generates attention, involvement and customer satisfaction. The use of digital technologies brings forms of innovation that are not automatically effective [19–21]. The point is to understand if these aspects last over time and if a better level of learning is achieved by developing specific assessment tools implemented with the students and to be made known before the start of the activities.

The second is the opportunity to develop forms of civic sense in an even more targeted and conscious way: on the one hand, positive aspects emerge, linked, for example, to a high level of knowledge of the local contexts (see Fig. 1) and confidence in the possibility of contributing to change (see Fig. 2); on the other hand, awareness of the limits to the effectiveness of the product realised (see Fig. 8) and the precariousness of the relationships established with people and associations (see Fig. 12). Problems related to immigration and interculturalism, the fight against poverty, gender education, discrimination, and social and economic hardship require new and effective approaches from an educational and didactic point of view, going beyond rhetorical and moralistic approaches. The challenge is to promote the use of media to foster civic engagement: digital culture can effectively support democratic participation [22]. Work linking civic education and media education is a challenging perspective [23]. And, deepening this perspective, it may be useful to use the notion of the third space [24]: between a private and personal space such as the home and the school or university space proper for formal learning, the third space allows, in a logic of continuity and not separation, to connect education to technologies, digital media and the culture of the learner. The third space is thus characterised as a place of negotiation and construction of meanings, bringing together formal and informal learning, university teaching and local contexts.

References

1. Kearney, M., Schuck, S.: Students in the director's seat: teaching and learning with student-generated video. In: Kommers, P., Richards, G. (eds.) Proceedings of Ed-Media 2005 World Conference on Educational Multimedia, Hypermedia and Telecommunications, pp. 2864–2871. Association for the Advancement of Computers in Education, Norfolk (2005)
2. Goldman, R., Pea, R., Barron, B., Derry, S.J. (eds.): Video Research in the Learning Sciences. Laurence Erlbaum, Mahwah (2007)
3. Hakkarainen, P.: Promoting meaningful learning through video production - supported PBL. Interdiscip. J. Probl. -Based Learn. **5**(1), 34–53 (2011)
4. Bruner, J.: Actual Minds, Possible Words. Harvard University Press, Cambridge (Mass.) - London (1986)
5. Longo, G.O.: Il nuovo Golem. Come il computer cambia la nostra cultura. Laterza, Roma – Bari (1998)
6. Lambert, J.: Digital Storytelling: Capture Lives, Creating Community. Digital Diner Press, Berkeley (2004)
7. Schank, R.: Tell Me a Story: A New Look at Real and Artificial Memory. Charles Scribner's Sons, New York (1990)
8. Abrahamson, C.: Storytelling as a pedagogical tool in higher education. Education **118**(3), 440–452 (1998)
9. McDrury, J., Alterio, M.: Learning through Storytelling in Higher Education. Kogan Page, London (2003)
10. Ryan, M.L. (ed.): Narrative Across Media: The Languages of Storytelling. University of Nebraska Press, Lincoln (2004)
11. Ohler, J.: Digital Storytelling in the Classroom. Corvin Press, Thousand Oaks (2008)
12. Kogila, M., Ibrahim, A.B., Zulkifli, C.Z.: A powerful of digital storytelling to support education and key elements from various experts. Int. J. Acad. Res. Progres. Educ. Dev. **9**(2), 408–420 (2020)
13. Demetrio, D.: Raccontarsi. Cortina, Milano (1996)
14. Petrucco, C., De Rossi, M.: Narrare con il Digital Storytelling a scuola e nelle organizzazioni. Carocci, Roma (2009)
15. Astin, A.W., Vogelgesang, L.J., Ikeda, E.K., Yee, J.A.: How Service Learning Affects Students. Higher Education Research Institute UCLA, Los Angeles (2000)
16. Petrucco, C.: Fostering digital literacy between schools and the local community: using service learning and project-based learning as a conceptual framework. Int. J. Digit. Literacy Digit. Competence **4**(3), 10–18 (2013)
17. Petrucco, C.: Narrative digitali come attività di Service Learning nel territorio. In Colazzo, S., Ellerani, P. (eds.) Service learning: tra didattica e terza missione. Ripensare e riprogettare l'organizzazione nelle scuole e nelle università, pp. 127–138. Università del Salento, Lecce (2018)
18. Adams, M., et al. (eds.): Readings for Diversity and Social Justice. Routledge, London (2018)
19. Cuban, L.: Teacher and Machines: The Classroom Use of Technology Since 1920. Teachers College Press, New York (1986)
20. Cuban, L.: Oversold and Underused: Computers in the Classroom. Harvard University Press, Cambridge (2001)
21. Ranieri, M.: Le insidie dell'ovvio. Tecnologie educative e critica della retorica tecnocentrica. ETS, Pisa (2011)
22. Gordon, E., Mihailidis, P. (eds.): Civic Media: Technology, Design, Practice. MIT Press, Cambridge (2016)
23. Buckingham, D.: The Media Education Manifesto. Polity Press, Cambridge (2019)
24. Potter, J., McDougall, J.: Digital Media, Culture and Education: Theorising Third Space Literacies. Macmillan, London (2017)

Engaging with Media Constructs and Power Dimensions in Initial Teacher Education: Enabling Student Teachers to Challenge Stereotypical Representations of Minorities in the Classroom

Maria Campbell[1] (✉) and Peter Stevenson[2]

[1] School of Education, St. Angela's College, College of National University of Ireland Galway, Galway, Republic of Ireland
mcampbell@stangelas.nuigalway.ie

[2] Department of Business Studies, St. Mary's University College Belfast, Belfast, Northern Ireland

Abstract. The past twenty years has seen an increase in new technologies of communication or media. These powerful tools, underpinned by values or moral positionings, have the potential to manipulate, marginalize and promote cultural stereotypical representations of groups in society. Similarly, the culturally diverse nature of societies has increased, a phenomenon not always reflected in the relatively homogenous nature of teaching populations. This research utilizes a critical media literacy intervention with student teachers in Northern Ireland and the Republic of Ireland, to identify synergies between the unique cultural context of each jurisdiction; historical, political, educational, religious, ethnic, racial, economic and social factors and the evolution of culturally sensitive teachers who adapt pedagogies, minimizing stereotypical representations and the exclusion of learners in their classrooms. Utilizing a theoretical framework incorporating the concepts of social justice, teacher identity development and transformational learning, and data from reflective journals and focus groups, the effectiveness of the intervention is discussed. Findings indicate the student teachers moved beyond an initial emotional response, demonstrating heightened awareness of taken for granted norms and beliefs; ability to critique their own privileged positioning and perpetuate cultural imperialism, with indications that transformative learning occurred as evidenced in modified use of media and pedagogies.

Keywords: Social justice · Critical media literacy · Transformative pedagogy · Student teachers · Intervention

1 The Context

The past twenty years has seen a rapid increase in the development of and access to new technologies of communication or media. Much of the development and circulation of

M. Ranieri et al. (Eds.): ATEE 2021, CCIS 1649, pp. 13–29, 2022.
https://doi.org/10.1007/978-3-031-20777-8_2

these powerful media tools relate to power and for-profit organisations and consequently, these powerful tools often employ subliminal pedagogies underpinned by particular value or moral positionings [1]. Consequently, the various media have the potential to "dominate, manipulate, or enlighten" [2], which can result in the marginalising or the promotion of cultural stereotypes and/or deficit representations of individuals or groups in society. In tandem with this growth in new media, the past twenty years has also seen a significant increase in the diverse nature of societies in both Northern Ireland (NI) which is part of the United Kingdom and the Republic of Ireland (ROI), resulting in a rise in the number of children from different geographical, cultural, ethnic, racial and religious backgrounds, in classrooms on the island of Ireland [3, 4]. We maintain that the increased diversity of pupil populations is not reflected in what we describe as the relatively homogenous nature of the teaching population, a phenomenon which prevails in other jurisdictions beyond the island of Ireland [5] and which presents both opportunities and challenges for teachers working in a time of change. For example, in the ROI, the most recent Census figures from 2016 indicate that people born outside Ireland rose from less than 1% in 1996 to 17.3% in 2016; people who identified their religion as 'other than Catholic' rose from 24% in 2011 to 31% in 2016 and people who identified as 'Black or Asian' rose from 3% in 2011 to 8% in 2016 [6]. This diversity is not reflected in the teaching population with 95% of teachers declaring as 'white Irish', 80% as middle class and 79% as female [6]. Recent research carried out by Heinz and Keane [7] indicates that 99% of student teachers (STs) identified as 'White Irish' as compared to 83% of the population and less than 5% of STs indicated that they have a disability compared to 14% of the population. In NI, the most recent official figures from Census 2011 and which reflect the demographics that existed over ten years ago, indicate that 98% of the population identified their ethnicity as 'white'; 90% indicating their place of birth as NI and a total of 17% identifying as 'no religion', 'other religion' or 'religion not stated' [4]. The recent report from the General Teaching Council Northern Ireland (GTCNI) which gathered data in relation to teacher gender and age, indicated that 77% of the teaching population was female [8]. The lack of detailed official statistics in relation to the diverse nature of the teaching populations on the island of Ireland, could be seen as reflecting a discomfort with or a lack of awareness of the importance of acknowledging and addressing diversity in the teaching population at government level, which until recently, has resulted in teacher diversity being identified primarily in terms of gender, religious and language indicators [9]. It could be argued that this potential discomfort with or lack of awareness of the importance of addressing diversity at government level, is reflected in the dearth of education policy development and enactment addressing diversity in both jurisdictions, creating both opportunities and challenges for those who work within and inhabit the wider education community.

As academics who work in teacher education institutions in both NI and the ROI respectively, we were anxious to examine the extent to which our STs were adequately prepared and supported to become critically sensitive teachers, equipped to decode and unpack the subliminal messages contained in all media and to adapt their pedagogies to reflect their understanding of the power dimension of media. We applied for and received funding for our research from the Standing Conference for Teacher Education, North and South (SCoTENS), a network for all institutions and organisations with responsibility for and an interest in teacher education on the island of Ireland. Our research utilised a critical media literacy (CML) intervention to help identify factors which enable or hinder STs to become culturally sensitive teachers, who critique and subsequently adapt their pedagogies to minimise the promotion of stereotypical representations and the potential for exclusion or minoritising of individual learners or groups of learners in their classrooms. By carrying out the same intervention in two different jurisdictions, the research aimed to identify synergies between the unique cultural context of each jurisdiction, namely historical, political, educational, religious, ethnic, racial, economic and social factors and the extent to which STs evolved as culturally sensitive teachers. It was intended that the findings from this research would identify how initial teacher education (ITE) programmes on the island of Ireland and further afield, could take account of local cultural contexts and modify/adapt their programmes accordingly to support the development of culturally sensitive teachers who were enabled to view all media with a critical lens. For the purpose of our research, we define media as all artefacts used in communication, namely spoken language/terminology and text, images, movies, sounds, music for example.

2 Theoretical Framework

Our theoretical framework consists primarily of three related stances or concepts, located within the wider context of social justice, teacher identity development and transformative learning. The first or starting point for this research is based on the premise put forward by Young's [10] concept of 'Cultural Imperialism', which maintains that norms are socially constructed forms of representation and communication involving "the universalisation of a dominant groups experience and culture and its establishment as the norm" [11]. Consequently, these perceived norms may go unquestioned or unchallenged by individuals or groups who represent the majority, dominant or privileged within society. We also draw upon another closely aligned concept, Choules's [12] concept of the 'Circle of Privilege', namely a positioning "of those who occupy the centre of the social, economic and political life" [13]. Choules maintains for those occupying the circle of privilege, the normalised gaze is outwards and consequently, "social problems can conveniently be located with 'the other' and with the presumed deficits found among 'others' (ibid). By enabling our STs to recognise and acknowledge that they occupy the circle of privilege, a position that is "unearned, arbitrary, an accident of birth, the luck of the draw" [14], they may be enabled to critique the presumptions and discourses such as deficit and charity discourses that underpin the subliminal messages contained in media and to act to address these in their role as teacher. From this perspective, our stance is in keeping with the post-modernist approach to injustice where the gaze or critique needs to be inwards, "aimed at the centre, with the suggestion that maybe the problem is located there!" (ibid). We purport that norms left unquestioned, could result in STs engaging in 'othering', namely in viewing other's or those perceived to be outside the circle of privilege and who do not appear to conform, uphold or represent the status quo, as disrupting the habitus [15] and/or from a deficit or charitable perspective, resulting in the potential marginalising or exclusion of pupils and the promotion of stereotypical representations in the classroom. This has particular relevance in the context of the increasingly diverse nature of pupil populations on the island of Ireland which is not reflected in the teacher population in both jurisdictions as indicated earlier.

Our second point of reference is that of teacher identity development. As a teacher's identity develops, they 'use their identity or political belief system to justify the way they choose to engage in their work' [16]. Cabaroglu and Roberts [17] unpack the formation of teacher identity further, maintaining that "belief development is a dimension of the assertion of identity…student teachers' beliefs reflect the ways in which they make sense of an evolving identity; self-as-teacher…and mediate how they interpret information about learning and teaching and how they translate that information into classroom practices" [18]. Consequently, there is a risk that teachers' pedagogical choices which include incorporating various media or means of communication such as language, both spoken and text, images, movies, sounds and music, for example, and which may represent the ideology of the dominant culture, has the potential to marginalise, alienate or subject their learners to deficit ideologies and perpetuate stereotypical representations. Hope-Rowe [19] highlights the importance of such considerations, in particular in the context of teaching populations which do not reflect the diverse nature of their learners, stating that "minimising the importance of students' identities and prior experiences with cultural diversity presumes that past experiences are unimportant or irrelevant to the type of teachers they will become" [19]. She highlights the influence that STs' previous life experiences have on how they perceive their role as teacher and which may result in a lack of openness or willingness to change or modify pedagogical practices. This raises the question as to whether heightened consciousness, awareness and acknowledgement of the particularity of one's own stance/viewpoint and the ability to trace it back to familial, political, religious, regional, and educational influences [20], could constitute what is our third point of reference, namely transformative learning, which could result in modified pedagogical practices by a teacher with enhanced cultural sensitivity?

The concept of transformative learning was originally attributed to Mezirow [21]. Mezirow maintained that people faced with a disorienting dilemma or experience that didn't fit with their beliefs or match their world view, are often forced to reconsider their beliefs as they engage in critical reflection which may result in them becoming more inclusive, reflective, discriminating and emotionally able to change their ways or practices, thus constituting transformative learning [22]. Our interpretation of the concept of transformative learning which has gone through many modifications and has incorporated new constructs, aligns with the concept of critical pedagogy or transformative pedagogy put forward by Robertson and Scheidler-Benns [23] who also maintain that transformative learning occurs "when a person, group, or larger social unit encounters a perspective that is at odds with the prevailing perspective' [24]. They expand this argument further, stating that for transformative learning to occur, teachers need to view schooling within its broader cultural and social contexts and in doing so, utilise critical pedagogical approaches which question whose knowledge is valued in schools, how traditional categories or classifications used in schools construct identities which may constitute barriers to the success of some students and which "may result in assumptions about students' abilities…based on their postal code, country of origin…or attributed to their category of difference" [25]. Therefore, in a space where transformational learning occurs, individuals are encouraged and enabled to "question and challenge the dynamics of power, privilege and disadvantage for segments of society relative to their race, gender, class, sexual orientation, ability, body size, membership in indigenous communities and age, etc." [26]. Based on this argument, we maintain that three elements are necessary to determine if transformative learning has occurred namely, awareness or a heightened consciousness; in-depth critique followed by actions that reflect this heightened consciousness and critique. It is our contention that subjecting STs to a CML intervention, which both challenges and calls for critique of preconceived values and beliefs, could result in transformational learning involving heightened consciousness and actions which reflect this. By enabling and supporting STs to decode, unpack and critique various media, the STs may be enabled to move along a spectrum from a position of culturally aware teachers to that of culturally sensitive teachers who modify their pedagogies accordingly. This would involve the critique and unpacking of subliminal messages contained in images, text, and language for example, identifying the particular value or moral positioning associated with how media is selected and used [27–29], and modifying their pedagogies accordingly to ensure no students is further minoritised, alienated or subjected to stereotypical representations.

Finally, as a key component in the journey of becoming culturally sensitive teachers, we maintain that for transformative learning to occur it is necessary for STs to move beyond the initial emotional response which occurs when taken for granted norms are challenged, as these reflect the internal conversations that occur as individuals make sense of and interpret situations [30]. Nussbaum maintains that "you can't sever emotion from belief…if so then you sever it from identity" [31]. She elaborates further stating "there is something correct in the contention that empathy is psychologically important as a guide, as it underwrites both the judgement of size and the eudaimonistic judgement. Without an attempt at empathy, we would surely be less likely to have appropriate compassion, or to take any actions that might be associated with this emotional response" [32]. Consequently, eliciting an empathetic emotional response constitutes the first step in acknowledging that something is not right, that those presented as different, outside the circle of privilege and/or marginalised are blameless. We acknowledge that this initial emotional response is often a necessary starting point, when faced with questioning one's own positioning, values and beliefs. However, we maintain that if this initial engagement is not supported by the inclusion of continued social analysis and critique, there is a danger that common emotional responses such as denial, resistance, projection, apathy, guilt and paralysis may prevail [33, 34] leading to their subsequent actions being informed by deficit and/or charitable ideologies as opposed to rights ideologies [35]. Consequently, we proffer that engagement with ideology critique is key in ensuring transformative learning occurs; namely analysing the politics of representation [33, 36] and examining the issues of social context, control, and power that pedagogical practices represent in the wider context of social justice for all learners.

3 The Intervention

As indicated previously, the emergence of new technologies and new means of communication or media, provides all and significantly, teachers, with powerful tools underpinned by particular value or moral positionings. The majority of media production and circulation relates to power and for-profit organisations who employ the stratagems of spectacle and sensationalism to provide public entertainment [29]. Kellner and Share [28] argue that spectacle itself has become a main organising principle of society, the economy, polity and everyday life, with spectacle and sensationalism used to attract larger audiences, resulting in increased power and profit for the media industries and organisations. For example, references to terminology and phrases such as 'swarms of migrants' in the popular media and images which ridicule or make fun of groups which have been minoritised by society, sensationalises while dehumanising and promotes stereotypical representations. Karanxha takes this a step further and argues that "Deficit perspectives and stereotypes about subjugated ethnic groups that prevail in mass and social media now constitutes a form of public entertainment" [37], which in turn has led to a new subculture within media culture, namely 'Edutainment' [36], with the public often being unaware that they are being educated by media culture [28].

Consequently, educators need new literacies in order to develop a critical lens to decode the various media they and their pupils engage with on a daily basis, as the messages embedded in media have the potential to promote deficit or charitable perspectives as opposed to rights perspectives or as Young [38] claims, to "promote cultural imperialism…and lead to edutainment". To this end, we choose to implement a CML intervention respectively, with our STs who were in the third year of their four-year full-time ITE programmes, consisting of 32 post-primary STs in NI and 96 post-primary STs in ROI. We chose CML as Robertson and Scheidler-Benns [39] argue that CML not only "builds skills of analysis and critique in the deconstruction and interpretation…of media…it can also give voice to students and empower them to take action to make changes in society". Our CML intervention contained three underpinnings, similar to the model outlined by Alvermann and Hagood [40], including enjoying media; exercising choice in media selections; and producing media. This approach acknowledged the importance of media in everyday life, enabled the STs to develop a critical lens with which to unpack the subliminal messages contained in media and positioned themselves as active agents of change as they selected and created media, as opposed to passive recipients and transmitters of the messages contained in media. We drew heavily upon the CML framework as outlined by Robertson and Scheidler-Benns [23] which includes guiding the students' media critique and reconstruction through the use of a series of messages and questions, accompanied by a selection of developmentally appropriate texts and media in the design of an eight-hour compulsory, assessed intervention.

The eight-hour intervention was delivered within existing modules with the third-year cohort of post-primary STs, by the researchers in their own institutions respectively. STs were introduced to CML [28] as a concept and practice and supported in the critique of popular media, in particular the unpacking of hidden messages and/or subtext contained in the representation of individuals and groups minoritised by society, across various media forms including language, terminology, images, movies, etc. Short inputs from guest speakers representing marginalised groups, critique of movies depicting abuse of power, popular media including advertisements and news streams, group activities including student presentations, discussions and debates which allowed for more emotive responses [41], formed the basis of the intervention. Finally, the STs created resources designed for culturally diverse classrooms which were displayed in a public space in each institution and which were assessed as part of coursework. This approach endeavoured to support the three elements necessary for transformative learning, namely heightened awareness, critique and actions reflecting the learning that has occurred.

4 Methodological Design

Our research question was: Can heightened consciousness, awareness and acknowledgement of the particularity of one's own stance/viewpoint and the ability to critique and trace it back to familial, political, religious, regional and/or educational influences, constitute transformative learning which translates into modified pedagogical practices by a teacher with enhanced cultural sensitivity? By using a CML intervention, we wanted to identify the factors which enable or hinder transformative learning or enable or hinder our STs to become culturally sensitive teachers; namely, to acknowledge and critique their beliefs and values, locate them within the wider social and political landscape they occupied and the extent to which they were willing to or did modify their pedagogies (use of media), to ensure pupils or groups of pupils were not marginalised, alienated or subject to deficit ideologies by the uncritical or insensitive choice, design and use of media. Ethical approval for the research was sought from and approved by the institution in the ROI. As this research focused on 'how people make sense of their everyday world' [42], was specific to temporal, cultural and contextual factors [43], and the intervention attempted to support the co-construction of meaning, knowledge and critical thinking skills, this research aligned with the interpretivist paradigm [44]. Epistemologically, this paradigm perceives knowledge as subjective and unique to individuals as it is based on their beliefs and is co-constructed; constructed by individuals through interactions [45, 46].

Data was gathered initially by the researchers using their own reflective journals [47, 48], which involved logging their immediate thoughts and subsequent reflections, following their viewings of all resources created by the STs that were on display in both institutions. The use of reflective journals in this way, constituted secondary data, namely field notes and reflections. This has many benefits according to Jasper [49] as it allows the participants, in this case the two researchers, to express themselves freely, to pose questions and to return to the data at a later stage and insert further comments and reflections, which contributes to the legitimacy of the knowledge claims and ensures their thoughts, opinions and emotional responses visibly constitute part of the data analysis and interpretation process.

The second source of data was gathered via focus groups, which allow for the development of discussion among participants and enable them to voice opinions [50]. While the thoughts and reflections of the two researchers were gathered in the first data source, utilising focus groups, where the researchers take a more peripheral role, namely facilitator or moderator [51], enables participant discussion, interactions and reactions which could elicit "qualitative data that would not emerge using other methods, i.e., individual interviews [52]. However, for participants to fully engage in group discussion, Krueger [53] suggests that ideally, participants should share some similar characteristics such as age, ethnicity and social backgrounds for example. As our participants were in the third year of their ITE programme and so were familiar with each other, were of similar age and their invitation to participate was issued by a third party and not the researchers, we hoped they would feel comfortable and willing to participate in the group discussion. Using a focus group schedule consisting of an ice-breaker activity and six prompts, data was gathered data via four focus group sessions, two in each institution/jurisdiction, each lasting over one hour, carried out after the intervention and their school placement experience and before the end of semester. Larger numbers of participants volunteered [52 in total] and attended on the days in question, than anticipated or indicated initially by the students. In NI, a total of 24 STs out of a possible 32 [24:32] participated in two focus group sessions, 10 participants, 6 identifying as male and 4 female in focus group 1 (FG1) and 14 participants, 4 male and 10 female in FG2, which were facilitated by the researcher from the ROI. In the same week in the ROI, a total of 28 STs out of a possible 96 [28:96] participated in two focus group sessions, 16, all identified as female and 12, 1 identified as male and 11 female in FG4, which were facilitated by the researcher from NI as opposed to. We acknowledge the large numbers attending the focus groups were not ideal, but were reluctant to turn students away as the institutions had altered timetables to ensure classes were not scheduled for 2 h, to facilitate students wishing to participate in the focus groups.

The sessions were recorded, transcribed and thematic critique [54, 55] involving the division of all data into descriptive categories/themes was employed. A deductive coding approach was utilised, employing a priori themes [56] which included 1) awareness and critique of their positioning, privilege and cultural imperialism; 2) teacher identity development and perceptions of their role as teacher; and 3) evidence of transformative learning. Utilising these three overarching, organising themes enabled patterns and sub-themes to be identified using the data from the reflective journals and focus group sessions and to be assigned to or located within the three main organising themes which is presented and discussed in the next section.

5 Findings and Discussion

Unsurprisingly, the topics that the STs focused on in their discussions in the focus groups related primarily to recent political events in each jurisdiction, such as the referendum in the ROI on same-sex marriage and the collapse of the Northern Ireland Assembly. Consequently, data relating to gender and to a lesser degree race and religion reflected the dominant topics that the STs from the ROI or FG3 and FG4, chose to engage with. The ongoing religious and political tensions in NI, in particular the collapse of the afore mentioned political structures, was of primary concern to the STs from NI and consequently data relating to religion, politics and to a lesser degree disability reflected the dominant topics discussed in FG1 and FG2. The influence of factors outside both jurisdictions and which reflected the potential of various media to permeate jurisdictions and geographical boundaries, such as Trumpism [57], was evident in the data from all four focus groups.

The discussion on the findings from this research is organized under three sub-headings as indicated earlier; 1) STs' awareness and critique of their positioning, privilege and cultural imperialism; 2) STs' identity development and perceptions of their role as teacher; and 3) Evidence of transformative learning. We acknowledge that all data did not fit discretely under each heading and as a result, there is some overlap with findings being referred to under more than one heading. The data from the reflective journals falls mainly under the third heading, evidence of transformative learning, while data from the focus groups [FG1; FG2; FG3 and FG4] falls mainly under the first two headings, with some examples present under the third heading. The STs impressions of the suitability and effectiveness of the CML intervention are noted and discussed throughout.

5.1 STs' Awareness and Critique of Their Positioning, Privilege and Cultural Imperialism

There was evidence that STs from both jurisdictions recognised and demonstrated heightened awareness of their positioning, taken for granted norms and associated values and beliefs and were able, in most instances to trace these to their familial, religious, political and social origins. For example, awareness of the influence and segregated nature of religion and religious beliefs was acknowledged consistently in both FG1 and FG2 with one ST indicating "*I think the young generation has moved on, but the older generation is stuck in the past*" [FG2]. Further evidence of their ability to critique their positioning and locate it within the familial or societal context was indicated by another ST who responded by saying "*It's hard to go against what your parents say or think, even down to buying certain newspapers... Some newspapers reflect one side or viewpoint, and others clearly reflect the other. You might not think it's important which paper you buy but they do" [FG2].* Similarly, the societal norm and legal status of marriage by heterogenous couples was cited frequently when discussing positioning in the ROI, referencing the referendum on same-sex marriage in the ROI with one ST indicating *"It was the norm... I was the norm...anything else was... Was seen as wrong in the past... I mean the Church said so, everyone said so, it was just the way things were"* [FG3].

The data also revealed the strong emotional responses elicited when the STs encountered different viewpoints and challenges to their taken for granted norms and beliefs, indicating the potential for transformative learning to occur. A ST in [FG4] indicated "*you feel bad, guilty, that you hadn't thought of that before. I mean when you look in this room and think everyone is the same because we're all white but when you actually look into it, there are things we don't know about each other that make us very different"*. Across all four focus groups, the STs indicated feelings of guilt relating to their lack of awareness of their privilege and feelings of anger, which they directed primarily at the various media sources, for what was described by one ST as the "*super manipulation of us all*" [FG1]. It was apparent that the exercises on critiquing news streams, newspapers and news items on social platforms elicited initial emotional responses of shock and anger and resulted in animated group discussions which the STs valued as indicated in [FG3]; "*Even the focus on the wording that they use in certain articles. I know in that online thing we did in groups about the 'jungle', it said that the refugees were rioting and then in another news stream and I can't remember which one it was, it was more sympathetic to them and said there was an altercation. The way they word that, 'rioting', makes it sound an awful lot more violent than 'altercation' does"*. In all four focus groups, the activities critiquing newspapers and new streams proved the most popular among the STs: "*I like the bit about the newspaper we did. It shows you the perspectives and viewpoints and that as well and how everybody has an opinion on something. I thought the newspaper bit and news streams was the best"* [FG2].

There were mixed responses on the STs' perception of the effectiveness of the use of videos in the CML intervention. Data from FG3 and FG4 elicited positive responses, indicating that the movies were the second favourite element of the intervention, while data from FG1 and FG2, indicated that the majority didn't find the movies helpful, citing that the subject matter was too removed from their lives or as one ST expressed "*I couldn't empathise, I couldn't connect, I don't know why, I just didn't enjoy them and tuned out*" [FG1]. Whether these feelings were in any way connected with the political turmoil that was evident in NI at the time is unclear, as was the reasons why the subject matter did not 'connect' with the STs, but the distinctive difference in relation to the impact of movies on challenging beliefs in each jurisdiction was noteworthy. On the other hand, data from all four focus groups indicated that the STs found presentations and talks from people representing groups that were minoritised caused them to reflect and critique their own positioning, indicating a heightened awareness of their privileged position and of their role in supporting cultural imperialism, with participants in FG2 indicating they would have liked "*much more of that*". To conclude, there was evidence that all STs demonstrated heightened cultural awareness and the ability to critique the beliefs and values underpinning various media including stereotypical representations of minorities in the print media, text, images and social media as captured by this extract from FG1, "*I think before we did this when I would have thought of diversity, I would have thought of different races and religions and felt they were so different to us, no connections, had nothing to do with me really, I never thought about how they felt"*. The next section discusses the extent to which this heightened awareness and critique, was evident in the development of their identity as teacher.

5.2 STs' Identity Development and Perceptions of Their Role as Teacher

This section discusses the extent to which there was evidence in the data that the STs' identity development and perceptions of their role as teacher had been influenced by their engagement in the CML intervention and against the backdrop of the influences of their local environment and jurisdiction. There was evidence that the STs' perception of their role as teacher in the classroom changed significantly, due to their heightened awareness, critique and acknowledgement that their pedagogies needed to be underpinned by social justice principles. In all four focus groups, the STs indicated that they needed to be "*open minded*", and both accept and embrace other viewpoints in the classroom that were contrary to their own, thus acknowledging the centrality and privilege of their own positioning. These sentiments were captured in the statement consistently used by the STs in FG1 and FG2, when referring to how their pupils should feel in their classrooms; "*it comes down to three words, comfortable, valued and respected*". Similarly, in FG3 one ST maintained: "*I think with open-mindedness, if you come into the classroom, one sided on something or have a view on something, it's just a personal view. You can't gain anything. You can't mature or grow, and your pupils can suffer because of you and your views"*.

When probed further in relation to how they as teachers, could ensure their learners were comfortable, valued and respected, the STs in all four focus groups indicated that it was their role to accommodate and be mindful of the needs and rights of all learners, "*and not just the visible differences, you need to think of things like hearing impairments and visual impairments, their backgrounds, their ethnicity*" [FG2]. These sentiments were reiterated in all focus groups, associating a heightened level of awareness of the diverse needs and rights of their learners as a key aspect of their role as teacher as indicated by the following statement: "*I think it's developed a little bit more in the scope of my knowledge on the different diversity that exists within a classroom. It was definitely maturing. Like it's not just physical. I suppose that's what's obvious to the eye but there is a lot more different diversity…as a teacher I need to be aware of that" [FG3].*

The data from all four focus groups indicated the important role class debates and group work played in their teacher identity development, by providing a relatively safe space and sometimes, the first opportunity to discuss topics they were uncomfortable with. While the STs indicated that the debates in particular generated strong emotional responses, they were valued as a strategy; "*the debates were where we had to talk about stuff that we were really uncomfortable with, sometimes for the first time publicly in class, it was hard, but it worked well, more of that would be good in every year of the degree*" [FG4]. Similarly, another strategy valued by the STs and that appeared key in informing their teacher identity development, was the group task of designing lesson plans underpinned by principles of social justice and reflecting the topics of their debates. These activities enabled them to link theory to practice or to realise heightened awareness and ability to critique in the form of modified pedagogies and with the support of their peers.

The STs accounts indicated that their role as teacher also involved a strong pastoral dimension underpinned by glimpses of rights ideologies. While they struggled with detailing many of the specific actions they needed to take to ensure the rights of their learners were not adversely impacted in the classroom and wider afield, they were very clear that they had a duty as teachers to protect, defend and affirm the rights of all their learners as indicated in FG1; "*13/14 year old's putting up stuff about their weight on FB and Instagram, and it's just crazy. You have to make them feel it's ok to be you. You are ok, regardless of your body size or image, you have to do that as teacher"*. It was also evident that they perceived their role to be underpinned by principles of social justice; *"you can't treat them the same because everybody is different. That would be the bit that I took mostly out of it is that if you're going to try and treat everyone the same, then it's not equal because people don't have the exact same scenario or background or things going on in their life or disabilities or illnesses or things like that. You need to take all that into account to give a fair reflection or a fair crack at it for everyone [FG3].*

At the level of cultural awareness, it was evident that the intervention had enabled heightened awareness of the potential for them as teachers to oppose or support the minoritising of pupils through their use of spoken language and terminology in the classroom; "*before it was just a word, now it has meaning, I never thought about words and terms like that before, how it can make someone feel, dehumanise them, make them seem less worthy than the others in the class, it's not right [FG1].* To this end, the STs expressed their confidence in relation to this specifical pedagogical approach involving the use of media, namely language spoken and text, while struggling with other approaches and strategies, including how best to group students, for fear of accentuating differences in their classroom to the detriment of the learners involved. Similarly, they indicated how they could "normalise" various scenario as outlined in the following extract: "*it all comes together as a teacher. A teacher is sort of like a parent too. You're not just there for the syllabus. You're there for the social media, for your student and there's going to be a child in your class who is possibly gay or whatever and there's going to be bullying and name calling going on. So, you could mention families with two fathers or two mothers, make it normal" [FG4].* It was obvious that all the STs struggled with how best to enact their role as socially just teacher and to enact fair and just practices in their classrooms, citing lack of experience of engaging with people with diverse needs and from diverse backgrounds; "*I think it can be difficult because there can be such a fine line between recognising and providing for diversity and alienating somebody because of it. But making sure that everybody else doesn't see them as different and it's not setting them apart from their peers" [FG2].* These accounts indicate the STs' awareness and acknowledgement of the importance of avoiding identity reductionism (Sen, 2006) in their role as teacher. However, this awareness was not evidenced in all the resources the STs' created and in the samples that 12 STs from NI and 4 STs from ROI, brought to the focus group session. Data from the researchers' reflective diaries indicates that charity ideologies and identity reductionism were evident in approximately one third of the resources created while rights ideologies underpinned the remaining resources. The next section discusses this finding further and examines the extent to which there was evidence that the intervention went beyond heightening awareness, developing and supporting critique and resulted in transformative learning for the STs.

5.3 Evidence of Transformative Learning

This section utilizes data from the focus groups and the researchers' reflective journals to examine whether there was evidence of transformative learning in the STs' accounts of their experiences and pedagogical choices while on school placement and in the extent to which principles of social justice underpinned the teaching resources they created. In both jurisdictions, the most common source of evidence that transformative learning had occurred was the STs' accounts of how they modified their use of language and terminology in the classroom; '*every word had meaning now… I thought before I spoke on placement this year, even little phrases*' [FG1]. These sentiments were reiterated in all four focus group sessions; *It's about thinking before you speak and how one word, just one word can have such a negative effect on someone in your class* [FG4]. Transformation learning was also evident in the STs accounts of their lack of tolerance of name calling, or the use of demeaning language or terminology in their classrooms while on placement. "*You can't let it go, you have to call them out on it and tell them it's not appropriate language, it's not right!*" [FG2].

There was evidence that some of the STs had developed culturally sensitive pedagogies while on placement which involved supplementing or adapting their usual choice and use of media. "*For instance, last year going into the classroom, I would have just used videos. This year there was a girl who couldn't hear so well, and she sat at the back of the classroom. I didn't want to say to her, you need to move up or to obviously bring attention on her so instead of just using a video, I always used subtitles, and for the learners who didn't have English too, I just never thought of it before". [FG3].* However, there was mixed evidence that transformative learning had occurred when it came to STs' choice and use of images, in particular when representing individuals and groups minoritized by society. This was apparent in their accounts, in the resources they created, some of which they brought along to the focus groups. It was clearly evident that rights ideologies informed the resources created by the STs, as demonstrated by their selection of images representing diverse family compositions, depicting non-stereotypical gender roles, and in the portrayal of people of colour, of ethnic backgrounds and women in 'powerful' roles. The most notable observation by the researchers was that rights ideologies were not reflected to the same degree, in the depiction of people with disabilities in their resources and in the discussion of people with disabilities in the focus groups. For example, the majority of resources and images which referenced people with disabilities, depicted people in compromised situations, eliciting sympathy and potentially were underpinned by charitable ideologies. Similarly, in the STs accounts, in particular in FG1, references to learners with disabilities while on school placement, were emotive, reflecting feelings of guilt and pity, and without significant reference to the rights of disabled people and the efforts of the STs' to address and ensure these rights were met. We acknowledge that arriving at this conclusion is down to our interpretation but our observations of and reflections on the resources created by the STs and their accounts, supports this assertion. Overt references to religion were not evident in the resources created, with the STs indicating in all focus groups that they did not feel confident in addressing religious diversity in the classroom, citing fear of causing offence despite having good intentions. To conclude, in relation to the development of culturally sensitive pedagogies, the findings indicated that the students struggled in some instances with the development of cultural sensitivities and competencies when it came to creating and adapting some classroom resources and pedagogies, citing their lack of confidence, knowledge and experience of engaging with people from various cultural backgrounds for their fear/reluctance to modify classroom resources and pedagogical approaches. However, all STs appeared to have undergone some degree of transformative learning which was evidenced by their modification of language, terminology and to some extent, use of images and media.

6 Conclusion

Going forward, we maintain that revision of the ITE curricula in both institutions, incorporating a developmental approach which ensures CML is embedded in all years of the programme, would ensure STs are supported and enabled to become culturally sensitive teachers throughout their ITE journey. We base this recommendation on the evidence that this short CML intervention, appeared to be an effective tool or strategy to support the initial development of culturally sensitive teachers, at least with reference to heightened awareness and ability to critique their positioning and the messages contained in media. However, further reflection on, consideration of and research which explores the selection of strategies and the tailoring or modifications needed to reflect and address the local context/jurisdiction, would seem prudent. This assertion is based on the negative reaction by the majority of STs from NI to the same selection of movies viewed by STs from the ROI, who in turn, responded positively to the movie selection. This discrepancy highlights the need for continued research incorporating collaboration and consultation with various stakeholders, in order to fine tune the content and methods employed in any CML intervention, to ensure the local and jurisdictional context is adequately reflected and sufficient time and supports given to enable transformative learning to be actioned.

The potential for CML interventions to support the development of cultural sensitivity, is not only reflected in the findings from this research, but reflect similar findings by Hameleers [27], who stresses the effectiveness of CML interventions as a means for supporting the critique of and in tacking political misinformation in both the US and the Netherlands. Similarly, findings from research carried out by Bruinenberg et al. [58] in the Netherlands, indicates the need to tailor curricula by co-creating reflexive, culture and context aware educational programmes with teachers. Creating such curricula and interventions is all the more relevant and necessary, in particular in the context of many western societies, where it is well documented that the relatively homogenous nature of the teaching population does not reflect the diverse nature of the societies in which they teach [5]. We maintain the identification of local, contextual factors and the subsequent tailoring of teacher education programmes which acknowledge and address these factors, is essential in enabling STs and teachers to move beyond a heightened emotional response when engaging in a CML intervention and embody transformational learning in becoming active agents for change. In this way, teacher education programmes can enable the development of culturally sensitive teachers who ensure their pedagogical practices are underpinned by social justice ideologies, who do not reinforce stereotypical representations from the dominant culture they represent and whose pedagogies hinder the potential for exclusion or minoritising of individual learners or groups of learners in their classrooms.

References

1. Karanxha, V.: Instructional leaders' impact on the implementation of sheltered instruction observation protocol model. Southern Connecticut State University (2014). https://doi.org/10.5539/eltv14n9p67
2. Kellner, D., Share, J.: Critical media literacy: crucial policy choices for a twenty-first-century democracy. Policy Futures Educ. **5**(1), **62**:59–69 (2007). https://doi.org/10.2304/pfie.2007.5.1.59
3. CSO Central Statistics Office Report. Government of Ireland Stationary Office (2017). https://www.cso.ie/en/releasesandpublications/ep/p-vsar/vitalstatisticsannualreport2017/. Accessed 20 Apr 2022
4. NISRA (Northern Ireland Statistics and Research Agency) 2011 Census (2016). https://www.nisra.gov.uk/publications/2011-census-table-lookups. Accessed 11 May 2022
5. Cochran-Smith, M.: Teacher education for justice and equity: 40 years of advocacy. Action Teach. Educ. **42**(1), 49–59 (2020)
6. CSO Central Statistics Office Report. Government of Ireland Stationary Office (2017)
7. Heinz, M., Keane, E.: Socio-demographic composition of primary initial teacher education entrants in Ireland. Irish Educ. Stud. **37**(4), 523–543 (2018)
8. GTCNI General Teaching Council of Northern Ireland Digest of Statistics (2017). https://gtcni.org.uk/cmsfiles/Resource365/Publications/digest-of-statistics/2017.pdf. Accessed 22 Apr 2022

9. McGinnity, F., Grotti, R., Russell, H., Fahey, E.: Attitudes to Diversity in Ireland. The Economic and Social Research Institute, Dublin (2018)
10. Young, I.M.: Justice and the Politics of Difference. Princeton University Press, Princeton (2011)
11. Young, I.M.: Justice and the Politics of Difference. Princeton University Press, New Jersey 59 (2011)
12. Choules, K.: The shifting sands of social justice discourse: from situating the problem with "them", to situating it with "us." Rev. Educ. Pedagogy Cult. Stud. **29**(5), 461–481 (2007)
13. Choules, K.: The shifting sands of social justice discourse: from situating the problem with "them," to situating it with "us". Rev. Educ. Pedagogy Cult. Stud. **29**(5), **472**:461–481 (2007)
14. Choules, K.: The shifting sands of social justice discourse: from situating the problem with "them," to situating it with "us". Rev. Educ. Pedagogy Cult. Stud. **29**(5), **465**:461–481 (2007)
15. Bourdieu, P.: The Forms of Capital: Handbook of Theory and Research for the Sociology of Education. JG Richardson, New York (1986)
16. O'Connor, K.E.: "You choose to care": teachers, emotions and professional identity. Teach. Teach. Educ. **24**, **119**:117–126 (2008)
17. Cabaroglu, N., Roberts, J.: Development in student teachers' pre-existing beliefs during a 1-year PGCE programme. Teach. Teach. Educ. **28**(3), 387–402 (2000)
18. Cabaroglu, N., Roberts, J.: Development in student teachers' pre-existing beliefs during a 1-year PGCE programme. Teach. Teach. Educ. **28**(3), **390**:387–402 (2000)
19. Hope-Rowe, G.: Student teachers and cultural diversity in an Australian regional university. J. Res. Spec. Educ. Needs **6**, **50**:42–54 (2006)
20. Elphinstone, L.: Cultural competence for teachers and students. In: Culture and Psychology. Culture Across the Curriculum: A Psychology Teacher's Handbook, pp. 46–67 (2018)
21. Mezirow, J.: Perspective transformation. Adult Educ. **28**(2), 100–110 (1978)
22. Mezirow, J.: Transformative learning theory. In: Mezirow, J., Taylor, E.W. (eds.) Transformative Learning in Practice: Insights from Community, Workplace and Higher Education. Wiley, New Jersey (2009)
23. Robertson, L., Scheidler-Benns, J.: Critical media literacy as a transformative pedagogy. Literacy Inf. Comput. Educ. J. **7**(1), 2247–2253 (2016)
24. Robertson, L., Scheidler-Benns, J.: Critical media literacy as a transformative pedagogy. Literacy Inf. Comput. Educ. J. **7**(1), **2250**:2247–2253 (2016)
25. Robertson, L., Scheidler-Benns, J.: Critical media literacy as a transformative pedagogy. Literacy Inf. Comput. Educ. J. **7**(1), **2249**:2247–2253 (2016)
26. Robertson, L., Scheidler-Benns, J.: Critical media literacy as a transformative pedagogy. Literacy Inf. Comput. Educ. J., **7**(1), **2248**:2247–2253 (2016)
27. Hameleers, M.: Separating truth from lies: comparing the effects of news media literacy interventions and fact-checkers in response to political misinformation in the US and Netherlands. Inf. Commun. Soc. **25**, 1–17 (2020)
28. Kellner, D., Share, J.: The critical media literacy guide: engaging media and transforming education. Brill, Boston (2019)
29. Karanxha, V.: Instructional leaders' impact on the implementation of sheltered instruction observation protocol model. Southern Connecticut State University (2014)
30. Nussbaum, M.: Upheavals of Thought: The Intelligence of Emotions. Cambridge University Press, Cambridge (2001)
31. Nussbaum, M.: Upheavals of Thought: The Intelligence of Emotions. Cambridge University Press 30 (2001)
32. Nussbaum, M.: Upheavals of Thought: The Intelligence of Emotions. Cambridge University Press 331–332 (2001)

33. Ward, S.J.A.: Political emotions and global ethics. In: Ward, S.J.A. (ed.) Handbook of Global Media Ethics, pp. 41–57. Springer, Cham (2021). https://doi.org/10.1007/978-3-319-32103-5_3
34. Tisdell, E.J.: Critical media literacy and transformative learning drawing on pop culture and entertainment media in teaching for diversity in adult higher education. J. Transform. Educ. **6**(1), 48–67 (2008)
35. Bajaj, M.: Human rights education: ideology, location, and approaches. Hum. Rights Q. 481–508 (2011)
36. Agosto, V., Dias, L.R., Kaiza, N., McHatton, P.A., Elam, D.: Culture-based leadership and preparation: a qualitative metasynthesis of the literature. In: Tillman, L.C., Scheurich, J.J. (eds.) Handbook of Research on Educational Leadership for Equity and Diversity, 1st edn. Routledge, Oxfordshire (2013)
37. Karanxha, V.: Instructional leaders' impact on the implementation of sheltered instruction observation protocol model. Southern Connecticut State University 54 (2014)
38. Young, I.M.: Justice and the Politics of Difference. Princeton University Press, New Jersey 61 (2011)
39. Robertson, L., Scheidler-Benns, J.: Critical media literacy as a transformative pedagogy. Literacy Inf. Comput. Educ. J. **7**(1), **2247**:2247–2253 (2016)
40. Alvermann, D., Hagood, M.C.: Critical media literacy: research, theory, and practice in "new times." J. Educ. Res. **93**, 193–205 (2000)
41. Karanxha, V.: Instructional leaders' impact on the implementation of sheltered instruction observation protocol model. Southern Connecticut State University 60 (2014)
42. Cohen, L., Manion, L., Morrison, K.: Research Methods in Education, 8th edn. Routledge, Oxfordshire 23 (2018)
43. Schwandt, T.: Three epistemological stances for qualitative inquiry: interpretivism, hermeneutics, and social constructionism. In: Denzin, N., Lincoln, Y. (eds.) The Landscape of Qualitative Research: Theories and Issues. Sage, London (2003)
44. Haverkamp, B., Young, R.: Paradigms, purpose, and the role of the literature: formulating a rationale for qualitative investigations. Couns. Psychol. **35**, 265–294 (2007)
45. Bryman, A., Cramer, D.: Quantitative Data Analysis with IBM SPSS 17, 18 & 19: A Guide for Social Scientists. Routledge, Oxfordshire (2012)
46. Charmaz, K.: Constructing Grounded Theory, 2nd edn. Sage, London (2014)
47. Zulifikar, T., Mujiburrahman.: Understanding own teaching: becoming reflective teachers through reflective journals. Reflective Pract. **19**(1), 1–13 (2018)
48. Ortlipp, M.: Keeping and using reflective journals in the qualitative research process. Qual. Rep. **13**(4), 695–705 (2008)
49. Jasper, M.A.: Using reflective writing within research. J. Res. Nurs. **10**(3), 247–260 (2005)
50. Richards, L., Morse, J.M.: Read Me First for a User's Guide to Qualitative Methods, 3rd edn. Sage, London (2013)
51. O. Nyumba, T., Wilson, K., Derrick, C.J., Mukherjee, N.: The use of focus group discussion methodology: insights from two decades of application in conservation. Methods Ecol. Evol. **9**(1), 20–32 (2018)
52. Flynn, R., Albrecht, L., Scott, S.D.: Two approaches to focus group data collection for qualitative health research: maximizing resources and data quality. Int. J. Qual. Methods **17**(1), 1–9 (2018)
53. Krueger, R.A.: Focus Groups: A Practical Guide for Applied Research. Sage, London (2014)
54. Gelston, L.: Types of Analysis. The Research Competition (2021)
55. Braun, V., Clarke, V.: Using thematic analysis in psychology. Qual. Res. Psychol. **3**(2), 77–101 (2006)
56. Crabtree, B., Miller, W.: Doing Qualitative Research. Sage, London (1999)

57. Kleyman, K.S., Hazel, K.L.: Introduction to the JPIC issue: social inequality: impact on school, youth, and families: social inequalities matter: from the great depression to the rise of trumpism. J. Prev. Interv. Commun. **47**(4), 275–278 (2019)
58. Bruinenberg, H., Sprenger, S., Omerović, E., Leurs, K.: Practicing critical media literacy education with/for young migrants: lessons learned from a participatory action research project. Int. Commun. Gaz. **83**(1), 26–47 (2019)

Immersive Environments in Higher Education: The Digital Well-Being Perspective

Stefano Cuomo(✉), Alice Roffi, Damiana Luzzi, and Maria Ranieri

University of Florence, 50121 Florence, Italy
stefano.cuomo@unifi.it

Abstract. In less than half a century, digital environments have pervaded nearly all aspects of our lives. Presently, the importance of Immersive Environments (IE) in education is rapidly increasing, offering interesting new opportunities for learning in higher education, but at the same time presenting some risks related to their use. In particular, the IE pose some issues to be considered in terms of digital well-being, such as access and inclusion, cognitive overload, and physiological discomfort. Furthermore, it has to be considered that there is a lack of a general methodology and a theoretical grounded approach for the implementation and evaluation of IE for educational purposes. The main aspects to be considered for their impact on the digital well-being have been collected from the current literature and analysed, exploring 4 main dimensions: cognitive, physiological, social and educational. Based upon the findings a first set of guidelines on digital well-being for IE in education have been developed leading to the production of a learning scenario that has been evaluated, by several stakeholders. The results of this evaluation process are positive, underlining the compliance of the learning scenario with the digital well-being requirements for an effective IE integration in the educational context.

Keywords: Immersive environments · Digital well-being · Higher education

1 Introduction

1.1 Immersive Environments

In less than half a century, digital environments have pervaded nearly all aspects of our lives. From "informatics" to "information and communication technologies", to "pervasive computing and IoT" to the "social media" boom in the second half of 2010's, digital is increasingly a key aspect of everyday life. As demonstrated during the COVID-19 lockdown period, digital technologies have become an essential instrument to support work, education, social activities, and also affective interactions. Thus, many people on the right side of the digital divide have a very powerful tool at their disposal, whose evolution, benefits, and potentials are yet to be fully understood, as well its risks and drawbacks such an overuse and lack of physical interaction. In light of these developments, digital well-being, illustrated in the next section, is key to making it possible for everyone to take advantage of something that we may well define as a "cognitive-social

M. Ranieri et al. (Eds.): ATEE 2021, CCIS 1649, pp. 30–41, 2022.
https://doi.org/10.1007/978-3-031-20777-8_3

infrastructure" connecting a large part of us. Presently we are at a time in which Immersive Environments (IE) are at the cusp of a new stage with even further potential but also, posing new challenges.

IE are part of immersive technologies grouped under the umbrella term Extended Reality (XR) that encapsulates the full spectrum of Augmented Reality AR), Mixed Reality (MR), 360° video and Virtual Reality (VR) as distinguished in the well-known "Reality-Virtuality (RV) Continuum" [1, 2].

On one side there is the real world, where everything experienced is part of our shared physical reality. On the other side there are the virtual worlds (also the metaverse, to use a term that came back to the forefront after Mark Zuckerberg) where all perceived content is artificially generated and has no connection to real-world objects or places. Between these two extremes are two conceptualized mixed reality environments: Augmented Reality (AR) where computer-generated content is embedded in users' perceptions of the real-world environment; and Augmented Virtuality (AV), where the perceived world is mostly computer-generated with real-world content mixed or overlaid. The XR can be enjoyed at different degree of immersiveness, according to the display device used: from low immersiveness of planar screen devices (e.g. notebooks, tablets, smartphones) through cardboards to the highest degree of immersiveness with Head Mounted Displays (HMD).

Together with immersiveness, another key concept in IE is the presence, considered as "the subjective experience of being in one place or environment, even when one is physically situated in another" [3]. In the literature [4] linked to the concept of presence or 'being there' is often the concept of immersion. Immersion is an experience where one is intensely absorbed in something, "I am in" where one is inclined to temporarily forget their surroundings [5]. For example, when a person is immersed in music, a work of art, a performance, a scenic view, or even in their thoughts. Delving deeper, a clear distinction between presence and immersion is provided by Slater and Wilburn [6]: "Immersion is a description of a technology and describes the extent to which the computer displays are capable of delivering an inclusive, extensive, surrounding and vivid illusion of reality to the senses of a human participant. […] Immersion can be an objective and quantifiable description of what any particular system does provide. Presence is a state of consciousness, the (psychological) sense of being in the virtual environment. […] The fundamental idea is that participants who are highly present should experience." Thus, immersion is a technological attribute that can be objectively assessed, in contrast there is another position in which immersion is considered a psychological phenomenon, i.e., a subjective and individual belief [3].

The capacity of being immersed in environments, which can be real, virtual and/or augmented, to explore and to interact with them and with other people is presenting new interesting scenarios in several fields, as entertainment and culture, but mainly in education giving also the chance of a full and direct interaction with environments hardly to be visited in person (e.g. an archeological site, an ocean floor, a volcano interior, a surgery room, a dangerous working place as a refinery or an oil plant), with, or without, the guidance of the teacher.

As demonstrated by the growing number of studies in this topic and by some EU initiatives [7, 9] the importance of IE in education is rapidly increasing. At the same time, due to the risks associated with these technologies, it is necessary to understand and thus balance the opportunities with the main drawbacks, particularly in this educational perspective [10].

The present work refers particularly to the use of 360° videos in Higher Education. According to Milgram, the 360° video is placed in between Augmented Reality and Augmented Virtuality being therefore able to exploit the strengths of both while allowing a relatively ease of production and distribution among the students. From a technical point of view, a 360° video (frequently called also "spherical videos" or "immersive videos") are video recordings where a view in multiple directions is recorded simultaneously. They are typically shot using a specialist omnidirectional camera, or a collection of separate, connected cameras mounted as a spherical array. The 360 videos can be non-interactive or interactive. Non-interactive 360 videos are experiences where the viewer cannot influence the viewing experience except pausing the video or moving their head to orient their gaze. Interactive 360 videos are experiences where the viewer can interact with the user interface or other interactable elements using a controller. For example, a 360° video can embed interaction points such as hotspots, hyperlinks, texts, images or 2D videos, quiz with multiple choice questions, true/false, etc., area highlights, teleport in another point of the 360° video.

1.2 Digital Well-Being

The term "digital well-being" refers to the concept of well-being in a society where digital technologies have covered every aspect of our life, just thinking of the last years of the pandemic that forced us behind a screen for work, education and also recreational purposes. Digital well-being is not a new concept and also the European Digital Competence Framework for Citizens [11] associated it to the safe use of technologies. However, since the role of digital technologies is constantly evolving, it is necessary to recontextualize it and expand its meanings.

The well-being and health concepts are strictly related as defined by World Health Organization: "Health is a state of complete physical, mental and social well-being and not merely the absence of disease or infirmity"[1]. This definition underlines the several dimensions included in the health definitions (physical, mental and social) not only related to a concept of disease. Similarly, the aspect of digital well-being requires investigation and understanding in a multidimensional aspect. In fact, the definition of digital well-being in a publication of Burr, Taddeo and Floridi [12] as the "impact of digital technologies on what it means to live a life that is good for a human being in an information society" highlights its multidimensional nature.

Thus, it is necessary to understand the implications in terms of digital well-being when introducing the IE in the educational field, also considering the lack of a general methodology and a theoretical grounded approach for the deployment and evaluation of IE for educational purposes.

[1] https://www.who.int/about/governance/constitution

2 The Dimensions of Digital Well-Being

2.1 The Approach to the Digital Well-Being

In accordance with these premises, the digital well-being in education cannot be approached only with technological or educational considerations but it needs a multidisciplinary approach considering all the different aspects of the well-being. With no pretense of exhaustivity, in this preliminary work, four main dimensions have been identified for investigating the relationships between digital well-being and IE, namely:

- **Cognitive**: about the threats posed by the technology (i.e., cognitive overload or isolation);
- **Physiological**: about effects of the IE on the user (i.e., the motion sickness in wearing helmets);
- **Social**: about possible impact of IE on relationships within working groups (i.e., classrooms);
- **Educational**: about learning opportunities offered by IE.

For each dimension a selection of the current literature has been analysed leading to the following findings.

2.2 Cognitive Dimension

From a cognitive perspective, some interesting aspects that require careful consideration in the educational field emerged from literature. Some studies [13, 14] showed that IE has an impact on memory, being able also to alter it, and this can be exploited in particular for psychological therapy [14]. The possibility to alter memory in a positive way is the basis of the study by Cuperus and van der Ham [13], that altered the memory of soccer players through a manipulation of VR replay to investigate if this manipulation could affect feeling of competence, as well as subsequent sports performance. The results underlined that the replay manipulation positively correlated with feeling of competence without any influence on sport performance.

Besides the effect on memory, the IE can also have a positive impact on the mood, and apathy, recognizing in IE the role of cognitive stimulator for improving well-being as explored by D'Cunha and collaborators [15] in a mini review on the VR/AR use for dementia and cognitive impairments.

2.3 Physiological Dimension

From a physiological point of view some drawbacks have been reported for IE use, such as cybersickness and simulator sickness, that should be carefully considered especially for its extended and prolonged use.

As reported in the study of Davis, Nesbitt & Nalivaiko [16] some individual factors could influence cybersickness, as age, gender, illness and also duration of the IE experience [16, 17]: in particular the susceptibility of cybersickness symptoms is high in children from 2 to 12 years old but decrease in the 12–21 age range. Moreover, a particular attention to the duration of the content and the tasks to be carried out by the user conveyed through immersive technologies must be taken into consideration when designing the contents in the educational field.

2.4 Social Dimension

The social dimension refers in particular to the dynamics of social relations using IE. A demonstration of influencing the interpersonal emotions by IE derived from the study of Schutte & Stilinović [18]. They showed that the higher engagement level, with respect to 2D, can influence the emotions as empathy. Future research should investigate and focus on the impact of IE on empathy and other characteristics as effective interpersonal communication, emotion expression, psychological and physical well-being. Furthermore, Liu and collaborators [19] demonstrated that the use of 360° videos in VR environments positively affect young's emotional well-being with respect to viewing the same videos on smartphones, while for elderly people the contrary happens, having more positive emotions with the smartphone. This implies that the characteristics of the subjects is an important factor for a fruitful immersive experience.

Another interesting aspect is the dynamics of social relations between young and older adults. Hauskneck and collaborators [20] explored the idea of using Alternate Reality Games (ARG) for intergenerational collaborative learning between 9–13-year-old and their parents. Even if positive results have been found in terms of parent-child relations, one challenge encountered was related to the directions and desires of each pair guided by traditional societal roles (e.g., the need of father to be the leader in the game not allowing the son to negotiate the games direction.

The dynamics of social relations in terms of traditional roles in IE should be deeply investigated, especially considering the integration of IE in an educational context and thus the role between students and teachers.

2.5 Educational Dimension

The educational dimension of digital well-being refers to the opportunities offered by IE as vicarious learning experiences and the balance with possible risks derived from their use. As previously explained, the IE represents an opportunity of a full and direct interaction with environments hardly to be visited in person for students. Their use in higher education context offers several benefits for learning process such as motivation, interest in learning, and for improving/acquiring skills [7, 21, 22]. Considering the usefulness HMDs, they offered some advantages for understanding and retaining visual and spatial aspects of a place (cognitive skills), for psychomotor skills acquisition when related to the movement of the head (as visual scanning or observational skills) and for controlling emotional response to stressful or difficult situations (affective skills) [22]. On the other hand, it has to be considered that a widespread use of IE may offer little additional benefits compared to less immersive technologies or traditional instruction, being in some cases counterproductive, because of the physical discomfort and cybersickness derived from their use [22].

Finally, a transversal theme is related to the ethical aspects in IE use. Madary & Metzinger [23] identified some aspects: among those the unknown effect of long-term immersion, especially in young people not yet fully developed from a psychological and neurophysiological point of view and the problem of the type of data collection from during immersive experiences (e.g., eye movements, facial gestures). Ramirez & LaBarge [24] raised the attention on the virtually real experience offered by IE, that resembles real experience, and on the equivalence principle that "if it would be wrong to allow subjects to have a certain experience in reality, then it would be wrong to allow subjects to have that experience in a virtually real setting". These aspects and those will come with the development of technologies and devices must be considered when integrating the IE in the educational setting.

The Fig. 1 summarizes the main pros, cons, and threats of literature findings in each considered dimension.

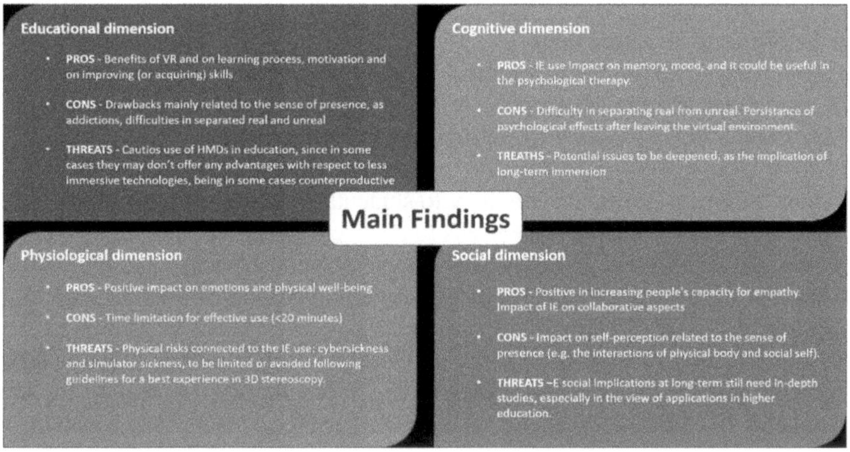

Fig. 1. PROS, CONS and THREATS of main literature findings in each dimension

3 The Design and Evaluation of Learning Scenario in a Well-Being Perspective

3.1 The Digital Well-Being in IE

Although the design of learning scenario is a well-established practice, its creation in an IE poses some specific issues in terms of digital well-being such as access and inclusion, student's engagement, and physiological discomfort mitigation.

According to the literature findings the authors have developed a preliminary set of guidelines for digital well-being using IE, highlighting some aspects that need to be carefully considered for teaching with IE in higher education.

Area 1 - Access and Inclusion

This Area is dedicated to the recommendations for ensuring the IE experience to all students regardless of physical (disability or impairments) or technological (digital divide) aspects.

When planning for IE experience, it is necessary to consider:

- the accessibility to the technologies (PC, smartphone or tablet) for all students both for activities proposed in the classroom and for remote activities, thus avoiding planning learning activities that require specific (and expensive) software and devices;
- the accessibility to the technologies in terms of digital competences of students, providing some training activities to make easier to enjoy the immersive experience;
- the role of teachers during IE activities, as a guide for the students for a more understandable experience;
- some modalities (as, subtitles) and assisting technologies for the inclusion of students with different impairments.

Area 2 - Student's Engagement

This Area is dedicated to the recommendations to foster student's engagement during the IE experience and thus making the learning experience more effective.

In particular, it is necessary to consider the following points:

- Context: tailoring teaching technology to students' needs (personalization);
- Visual aspect of IE: the interface needs to be nicely designed
- Quality: the educational and the training topic must be attractive and the interaction during the learning need to be fluid without any technical drawbacks such as slow response.
- Complexity: repeating the same scenario, directing the learner's attention to different aspects (himself/herself, others, place, tools…). It's an effective way to capture the complexity of certain phenomena. At the same time the possibility to watch the same learning scenario as many times needed allows students to reduce the novelty effect of using immersive environment, thus focusing on learning;
- Control of the difficulty level: to suit the students' level of knowledge and ability;
- Feedback: the possibility to have the guide of teachers that provide feedbacks during the activities in IE;
- Collaborative activities: the possibility to make immersive activities in groups (both in presence and in on-line modalities), thus experiencing teamwork (collaboration) in this particular context.

Area 3 - Physiological Discomfort

This Area is dedicated to the theme of physiological discomfort that may be derived from the use of IE (such as, cybersickness).

Although the most recent technologies seem to be reducing this issue, it is important to underline an important approach for avoiding this unpleasant situation:

- Training and Repetition: the possibility to be trained before the IE experience and to repeat the same scenario several times, to understand the degree of the discomfort and to be more confident with this technology.

3.2 The Tool for the Scenario's Design

According to the context described in Sect. 1 and 2, a learning scenario has been designed and evaluated leveraging IE in higher education while addressing the digital well-being according to the literature findings. A template for the scenario's design has been developed as a tool for designing the activities also in relation to the technologies used as shown in Fig. 2.

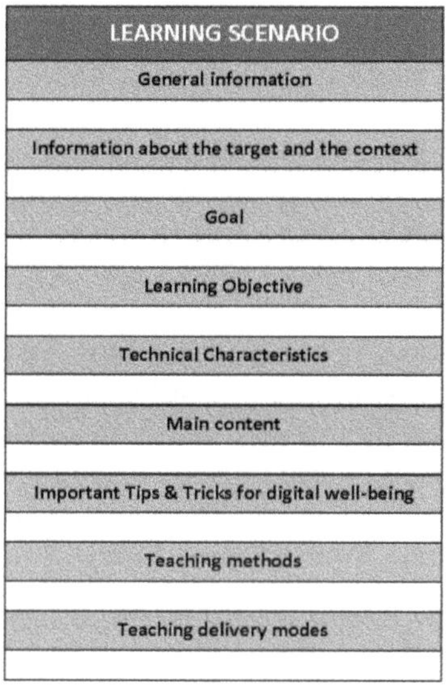

Fig. 2. The template for the design of learning scenario

3.3 Learning Scenario: The Crime Scene Investigation

For evaluating the compliance with the digital well-being, a learning scenario, integrating a 360° video into the didactic path of the lesson has been designed and implemented although the restrictions due to the pandemic unfortunately did not allow to test it until now. Thanks to a 360 camera, the reconstruction of a crime scene was filmed. The lesson has been conceived to be carried out synchronously, in presence with the use of computers and HMD. The duration of 360° video was planned in 10 min and included in a lesson of 120 min (1h = 40 min of lessons with 1 breaks of 20 min). The crime scene is the fundamental part of an investigation, but there are some problems relating to the physical presence on the scene, such as risk of contamination or destruction of evidence that can prevent investigators from staying, visiting and re-visiting the scene. Therefore, it is important to visually capture the crime scene and each evidence to help the investigations. In this sense the 360° video helps the students to acquire the key competencies needed for evidence collection in a crime scene. Furthermore, the 360° video allows the students to review the crime scene as many times as they need to focus on different aspects, compared to the educational visit on the rebuilt crime scene. This learning scenario is developed under the subject “Forensic Biological Investigations. Criminalistics”, aiming at developing competencies for the biological analysis on the crime scene following the international standard: acquisition of analytical procedures for beginners in the forensic field; ability to apply the knowledge in the analysis of a crime scene; ability to critically analysed to use the acquired knowledge in a productive and proper way; ability to work in a multidisciplinary team.

3.4 The Evaluation Process

This scenario has been independently evaluated to understand how much the digital well-being aspects have been correctly addressed for offering a balanced IE experience. This step has been carried out with a specific questionnaire administered, through a Google Modules Form, involving several stakeholders within higher education context (students, professors, and researchers). This questionnaire includes 4 questions where participants report, in their opinion, to what extent (Completely, Above the average, An average, A little bit, Not at all) the scenario meets the aspects of digital wellbeing (Access and Inclusion, Student Engagement, Physical Discomfort, plus a General consideration). A final open-ended question asks for further considerations. The questionnaire has been introduced by an explanation of the digital well-being dimensions considered, in order to make the stakeholders aware of the meanings of digital well-being.

Twenty participants have been enrolled for the evaluation of the Crime Scene scenario, collecting the evaluation forms from 10 Master Students, 4 Researchers, 3 PhD students, 3 Professors and from 4 countries 15 from Italy, 2 from Netherlands and Sweden, 1 from France.

3.5 The Results of Evaluation Process for Learning Scenario

The learning scenario “Crime Scene Investigation” reached positive evaluation: for the 55% of participants it addressed the digital well-being aspects (Access and Inclusion, Student Engagement, Physical Discomfort) “above the average” (“an average” - 25%, “completely” - 15%). In particular, the better addressed aspect was Student’s Engagement with 70% of responders agreeing on “above the average” evaluation. While achieving positive results, the Physiological Discomfort seems to be the aspect with lower score with respect to others (“An average” - 35%), and this has been underlined into one specific comment in the open questions:

> *“It would be helpful to address physiological discomfort mitigation by devising other methods”.*

The other comments suggested to focus on the visual aspect of the IE to favour student’s attention:

> *“It would be good to consider the visual aspects of the IE. Is it complex and fascinating enough to trigger involuntary attention (instead of directed attention) and does it constitute a larger whole? Do all the elements fit together? (balance between complexity and coherence)”*

and on the collaborative aspects that could safeguard the digital well-being that required further considerations:

> *"...If the work were to be in groups this may affect digital well-being as the immersion time is less prolonged and there is no isolation..."*
>
> *"The engagement could be further explained regarding the collaborative part and how it would be tackled when students use HMD".*

Finally, one comments raise attention on a possible strategy for guaranteeing a more inclusive IE experience for students with visual impairments (Fig. 3):

> *"In order to strengthen the inclusion aspect, it would foresee subtitles for students with hearing loss or alternative modality for students with visual impairments".*

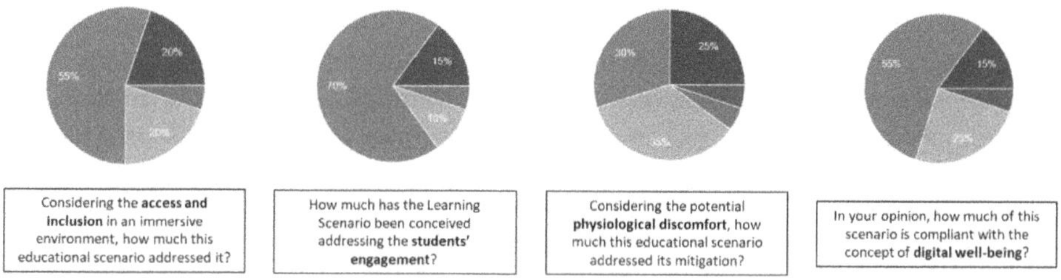

Fig. 3. Synthesis of evaluation for the learning scenario "Crime Scene Investigation". Legend: Blu, *Not at all*; Red, *A little bit*; Yellow, *An average*; Green, *Above average*; Violet, *Completely*. (Color figure online)

4 Conclusions

Presently, the importance of IE in education is rapidly increasing, offering new interesting opportunities for learning in higher education, but at the same time presenting some risks related to their use. In particular, the IE poses some specific issues in terms of digital well-being, such as access and inclusion, cognitive overload, and possible physiological discomfort. Furthermore, it has to be considered that there is a lack of a general methodology and a theoretical grounded approach for the deployment and evaluation of IE for educational purposes. A better understanding of how the digital well-being aspects shall be taken into consideration when designing an educational product requires a multidisciplinary approach considering the different dimension of well-being.

This preliminary work has collected and analysed some up-to-date selected literature identifying and exploring 4 main dimensions: cognitive, physiological, social and educational. Following to the literature findings, a first set of guidelines has been produced and, on their basis, a learning scenario (360° video of a "Crime Scene Investigation") for the use of IE in higher education has been produced.

Although, due to the restrictions posed by the pandemic, this educational tool has not been tested in the classroom yet, the learning scenario has been independently evaluated, by international stakeholders (researchers, teachers, students) for assessing its compliance with the digital well-being in IE.

The results of this evaluation process positive, underlining the compliance of the learning scenario with the digital well-being requirements for an effective IE integration in the educational context, paving the way for future studies of learning scenario testing and refinement.

4.1 Future Perspectives

Several points need to be further deepened. The first is related to the inclusive perspective of IE, since there is a lack of specific guidelines on how to support the learning of students with disabilities in this kind of virtual environment. The second point is linked to the ethical implications that may be derived from the hypothetical adaptation of the IE on the emotional state of the students (confused, bored, frustrated or interested, enthusiastic, stressed…), especially in terms of personal data collection. Finally, it has to be considered the use of interactivity for socialization, exploring the collaborative practices and understanding its possible dynamics, since the virtual collaboration may avoid isolation (especially using HMD) and a long immersion time.

References

1. Milgram, P., Kishimo, F.: A taxonomy of mixed reality visual display. IEICE Transactions on Information System, E77-D(12) (1994)
2. Milgram, P., Colquhoun, H.W.: A framework for relating head mounted display to mixed reality display. In: Proceeding of Human Factor and Ergonomics Society 43rd Annual Meeting, pp. 1177–1181 (1999)
3. Witmer, B.G., Singer, M.J.: Measuring presence in virtual environments: a presence questionnaire. Presence: Teleoper. Virtual Environ. **7**(3), 225–240 (1998)
4. Cummings, J.J., Bailenson, J.N.: How immersive is enough? A meta-analysis of the effect of immersive technology on user presence. Media Psychol. **19**, 272–309 (2012)
5. Yuen, S.C., Yaoyuneyong, G., Johnson, E.: Augmented reality and education: applications and potentials. In: Huang, R., Kinshuk, S.J.M. (eds.) Reshaping Learning. New Frontiers of Educational Research, pp. 385–414. Springer, Heidelberg (2013). https://doi.org/10.1007/978-3-642-32301-0_17
6. Slate, M., Wilbur, S.: A framework for immersive virtual environment (FIVE): speculation on the role of presence in virtual environments. Presence: Teleoper. Virtual Environ. **6**(6), 603–616 (1997)
7. Radianti, J., Majchrzak, T.A., Fromm, J., Wohlgenannt, I.: A systematic review of immersive virtual reality applications for higher education: design elements, lessons learned, and research agenda. Comput. Educ. **147** (2020)
8. Ranieri, M., Bruni, I., Luzzi, D.: Introducing 360 degree video in higher education: an overview of the literature. In: EDEN 2020 Annual Conference, European Distance and E-learning Network, Timisoara, 22–24 June 2020, pp. 345–353 (2020)
9. Scfwaiger, M.: Europe needs to integrate immersive learning quickly at all educational levels - but how? What to learn from 25 EU projects in this field. J. Elem. Educ. **14**(Spec. Iss.) 63–85 (2021)

10. Melo, C., et al. (eds.): Educational technology and addictions. Comput. Educ. **145** (2020)
11. Carretero Gomez, S., Vuorikari, R., Punie, Y.: DigComp 2.1: the digital competence framework for citizens with eight proficiency levels and examples of use, EUR 28558 EN, Publications Office of the European Union, Luxembourg, JRC106281 (2017)
12. Burr, C., Taddeo, M., Floridi, M.: The ethics of digital wellbeing: a thematic review. Sci. Eng. Ethics **26**, 2313–2343 (2020). https://doi.org/10.1007/s11948-020-00175-8
13. Cuperus, A.A., van der Ham, I.J.M.: Virtual reality replays of sports performance: effects on memory, feeling of competence, and performance. Learn. Motiv. **25**, 48–52 (2016)
14. Cuperus, A.A., Disco, R.T., Sligte, I.G., van der Kuil, M.N.A., Vers, A.W.M., van der Ham, I.J.M.: Memory-related perceptual illusions directly affect physical activity in humans. PLoS ONE **14**, e0216988 (2019)
15. D'Cunha, N.M., et al.: A mini-review of virtual reality-based interventions to promote well-being for people living with dementia and mild cognitive impairment. Gerontology **65**(4), 430–440 (2019)
16. Davis, S., Nesbitt, K., Nalivaiko, E.: A Systematic Review of Cybersickness, IE2014, 1–9 December (2014)
17. Kuehn, B.M.: Virtual and augmented reality put a twist on medical education. JAMA **319**(8), 756–758 (2018)
18. Schutte, N.S., Stilinović, E.J.: Facilitating empathy through virtual reality. Motiv. Emot. **41**(6), 708–712 (2017). https://doi.org/10.1007/s11031-017-9641-7
19. Liu, Q., Wang, Y., Yao, M.Z., Tang, Q., Yang, Y.: The effects of viewing an uplifting 360-degree video on emotional well-being among elderly adults and college students under immersive virtual reality and smartphone conditions. Cyberspychol. Behav. Soc. Netw. **3**(3), 157–164 (2020)
20. Hausknecht, S., Neustaedter, C., Kaufman, D.: Blurring the lines of age: intergenerational collaboration in alternate reality games. In: Romero, M., Sawchuk, K., Blat, J., Sayago, S., Ouellet, H. (eds) Game-Based Learning Across the Lifespan, pp. 47–64, Springer, Cham (2017). https://doi.org/10.1007/978-3-319-41797-4_4
21. Chavez, B., Bayona, S.: Virtual reality in the learning process. In: Rocha, Á., Adeli, H., Reis, L., Costanzo, S. (eds.) Trends and advances in information systems and technologies, vol. 746, pp. 1345–1356. Springer, Cham (2018). https://doi.org/10.1007/978-3-319-77712-2_129
22. Jensen, L., Konradsen, F.: A review of the use of virtual reality head-mounted displays in education and training. Educ. Inf. Technol. **23**(4), 1515–1529 (2017). https://doi.org/10.1007/s10639-017-9676-0
23. Madary, M., Metzinger, T.K.: Real virtuality: a code of ethical conduct. recommendations for good scientific practice and the consumers of VR-technology. Front. Robot. AI **3**, 3 (2016)
24. Ramirez, E.J., LaBarge, S.: Real moral problems in the use of virtual reality. Ethics Inf. Technol. **20**(4), 249–263 (2018). https://doi.org/10.1007/s10676-018-9473-5

Cultures, Intersections, Networks. The Role of Algorithms in Defining Power Relations Based on Gender, Race, Class, Disability

Martina De Castro(✉), Umberto Zona, and Fabio Bocci

Roma Tre University, Rome, Italy
martina.decastro@uniroma3.it

Abstract. Technological artifacts represent the historical-cultural products able to mediate our relationship with a world in continuous and rapid transformation. They, therefore, act as intermediaries with the environment around us and especially with the Other with which we are in "connection". Therefore, while technology is affected by the cultural influences of those who produce it, it also directly affects the process of individuation of subjects, social organization and politics, re-proposing and amplifying power relations. In a digitalized capitalist universe, where the dominant paradigms of reference are still white, cisgender, and able-bodied men, the proposal is to adopt an intersectional approach – one that simultaneously takes into account variables of gender, race, class, sexuality, and ability – to reread the bias of cultural choices and responses provided by algorithms.

Keywords: Technological artifacts · Algorithms · Cultural machines · Stereotypes · Intersection

1 Algorithms as Cultural Machines

Our thesis is that, in consideration of the importance acquired by algorithms in orienting people's choices and behaviors both in real life and, especially, in online life, it is appropriate to deepen the definition of algorithm as a *cultural machine*, starting from Vygotskij and his definition of cultural artifact: «All artificial tools [...] serve 'the amplification of our senses' [...] In the evolutionary process, man invented tools and created a civilized productive environment; but this productive environment transformed the man (or the human being) himself, and produced, instead of primitive forms of behavior, complex, cultural forms» [1].

The machine, in the Vygotskian sense, appears to be a hybrid between a social-historical product, transformed and perfected with the passing of time and the changing needs, and an instrument capable of amplifying individual capabilities and potentialities.

The present work is intended as the joint work of the authors. However, for the purposes of attribution of individual parts, it is specified that: Martina De Castro is the author of paragraph 2 and 3.3, Umberto Zona of paragraphs 1 and 3.2, Fabio Bocci of paragraph 3, 3.1 and 4.

M. Ranieri et al. (Eds.): ATEE 2021, CCIS 1649, pp. 42–58, 2022.
https://doi.org/10.1007/978-3-031-20777-8_4

This kind of suggestion is still very powerful in thinkers such as Marshall McLuhan [2, 3], who looks at electronic machines as extensions of the body, or Andy Clark [4, 5], who sees digital devices as artifacts capable of extending the capabilities of the human mind. However, if it is true that the artifact, as a machine, has above all a function of empowering the individual body and mind, we should not underestimate the role it plays in regulating and conditioning the relationships between human beings. In order to effectively carry out their function of "orienting", algorithms need users' data of the Net; the more "sensitive" these data are, the more accurate the profiling of users is. Particularly "hungry" for data are the so-called "predictive" algorithms, whose function, according to the companies that use them, is to predict future behavior, in particular purchasing trends which, let's not forget, are the ultimate goal of any commercial entity operating on the Web. In reality, these algorithms are not able to prophesy anything, but, using machine learning, they continuously monitor the traces that each of us leaves during our surfing, comparing us with other subjects who have made choices and shown preferences similar to ours. It is our behavior as social individuals, therefore, that is kept constantly under control by multinational companies operating on the Net in order to suggest experiences that might be similar, even if not identical, to our preferences. O'Neil's [6] assumption that automated systems tend to further penalize poor people has been investigated in detail by Virginia Eubanks, who has suggested an effective parallelism between the poorhouse system, hospices for the poor established in the United States in the late seventeenth century, and today's automated decision-making systems, which have been transferred the power to decide, through the assignment of scores obtained by abstruse algorithmic calculations, the future of poor people. Eubanks concludes that «High-tech tools have a built-in authority and patina of objectivity that often lead us to believe that their decisions are less discriminatory than those made by humans. But bias is introduced through programming choices, data selection, and performance metrics. The digital poorhouse, in short, does not treat like cases alike» [7]. In fact, when algorithm designers do not have data about the specific behavior to be examined, they use proxy data, vicarious or indirect data, and «establish statistical correlations between a person's zip code or language choices and the likelihood that he or she will pay back a loan or be able to perform a particular job. Such correlations are discriminatory, and some are even illegal» [8]. This is why algorithms can be defined as artifacts that perform social actions and prescribe specific behaviors and we should not be surprised if they were used as tools of mass training, to influence people's conducts and build social consensus around a certain set of values and practices. It is for these same reasons that, in our opinion, algorithms cannot be considered simple mathematical constructs but, rather, real cultural machines that need, on the one hand, the technical knowledge of the designers who instruct them and, on the other, the flows of social knowledge that circulates on the Net, produced by the multitude of people who use it. It is, in essence, a circular process: the answers that the algorithm provides when it is interrogated are conditioned by the cultural criteria adopted in the design and supervision phase and can, in turn, influence (or reinforce) the set of beliefs and the Imaginary of the end users, as in the case of search engines, which we will deal with from now on, focusing our attention in particular on Google. To understand how relevant the role played by the Mountain View giant can be, it is enough to remember that, according to the Digital 2021 report, released annually by *We Are Social* in collaboration with *Hootsuite* [9], Google, in December 2020, was the search engine with the highest web search traffic, with an overwhelming 91.4%. Google is therefore the most widely used search engine in the world – almost a monopoly and, since it was conceived and has its headquarters in the United States, Western culture and values have inevitably influenced the design and implementation process (we will see in a moment how the internal composition of Google's design teams is rather homogeneous and reflects established social hierarchies). Therefore, the fact that Google is also used in countries that have languages, traditions, histories, symbols, beliefs and institutions different from those of the West could represent, at least in some ways, a form of cultural neo-colonialism and constitute a serious risk for the survival of cultures other than the Anglo-American one. In recent years, there has been an increase in research supporting this claim. In 2016, Safiya Umoja Noble and Brendesha M. Tynes, for example, attempted to reinterpret the representations and structure of the Internet itself by having Black feminist Studies and the intersectional critical approach as their reference. They developed a model – the ICRTS (Intersectional Critical Race Technology Studies), defined as «an epistemological approach to researching gendered and racialized identities in digital and information studies» [10] – to denounce that «the blind spots of a model are a reflection of the assessments and priorities of its creators. [...] We need to ask not only who designed the model but also what purpose that person or company set out to achieve» [11]. These pitfalls, on the other hand, have long been highlighted in institutional settings as well: in 2013, the United Nations launched an awareness campaign aimed at bringing out what the public thought about women. To make the message more incisive also on a graphic level, the campaign featured a series of ethnically marked female faces, whose lips were replaced by Google Search suggestions obtained by typing words such as "women cannot", "women should not", "women should", "women need to" (see Fig. 1).

By entering these phrases into the search string, Google provided the following suggestions:

- *Women cannot*: drive, be bishops, be trusted, speak in church;
- *Women should not*: have rights, vote, work, box;
- *Women should*: stay at home, be slaves, be in the kitchen, not speak in church;
- *Women need to*: be put in their places, know their places, be controlled, be disciplined.

As Noble points out, however, the campaign, rather than highlighting the sexism of the world's most powerful search engine, «suggests that search is a mirror of users' beliefs and that society still holds a variety of sexist ideas about women. What I find troubling is that the campaign also reinforces the idea that it is not the search engine that is the problem but, rather, the users of search engines who are. It suggests that what is most popular is simply what rises to the top of the search pile» [12]. But this consideration, as we will try to bring out, does not exhaust the issue since sexist, racist, classist and ableist stereotypes are not only strongly rooted in public opinion but are implemented in the same algorithmic logics. If it is true, in fact, that the search criteria of monopolies like Google reflect the dominant culture and the distortions that it brings with it, it is equally true that, since the Mountain View company, like all others, is primarily aimed at profit, it does

Fig. 1. 2013 UN Women awareness campaign.

not care about the consequences that the proliferation of stereotypes and toxic frames – which it itself increases – can have on people's behavior. The latter is a secondary aspect because, while the opinions of other individuals can be easily questioned or be a reason for comparison, the news and information we find on the Net tend to be uncritically assumed as true, only because a search engine like Google, which is considered *a priori* reliable and objective, has presented them to us and organized them in a hierarchical list. The idea that Google's suggestions or results are hierarchically organized only on the basis of the most popular searches or the most visited sites appears at this point as a false belief, since the information is oriented towards the advertising interests of companies.

Users, in essence, are satisfied by having access to Google and all the services it offers for free (Gmail, Drive, Meet, Maps, YouTube), while Google – as a commercial platform – earns from the data it collects on each user (which, often, are given to other companies). But since it is the data that allow to "personalize" the surfing through advertising suggestions "sewn on" to the Internet user, Google needs continuous interactions to find such data and needs, consequently, the "work" of the users to implement its algorithms. It is illusory, therefore, to believe that the search results we get when we do a search on Google are objective or neutral, since most of the links that are proposed to us, organized according to a hierarchical logic, are advertisements. This is done, as openly stated, because the activities performed on Google services and other websites and apps after logging in are similar to those of people who have told Google that they belong to those demographic categories in which we are then placed as well.

In December 2018, DuckDuckGo – a search engine whose stated philosophy is to improve search relevance by focusing on the privacy of users whose searches and personal information are not stored – released a study titled *Measuring the "Filter*

Bubble": How Google is influencing what you click, the purpose of which was precisely to analyze how Google's filter bubble works: «These editorialized results are informed by the personal information Google has on you (like your search, browsing, and purchase history), and puts you in a *bubble* based on what Google's algorithms think you're most likely to click on. [...] You might think that as long as the same links are shown to users, the ordering of them is relatively unimportant, but that's not the case. A given link gets only about *half as many clicks* as the link before it and *twice as many clicks* as the link after it. In other words, link ordering matters a lot because people click on the first link much more than the second, and so on» [13]. Google, then, seems to organize our search results based on the information it deduces from the profiles it collects in Ads Setting for each of its users, and the personalization of ads – but, by extension, also the hierarchical organization of the links that are proposed to us when we perform a search – occurs based on the information we voluntarily added to our Google Account, the data accumulated by advertisers who collaborate with Google and who, therefore, are interested in mapping our tastes, while our desires are deduced directly by Google through comparison with other users related to us.

For the purposes of our discussion, the social composition of intellectual workers employed at large Silicon Valley companies is of particular relevance, since they are predominantly male and white, as the annual Inclusion and Diversity Reports show. In Apple's technology sector, for example, in 2020 male employees accounted for 76% of the total, whites were 44%, and Asians were 39%. Hispanics/Latinx (8%), Blacks (6%), Indigenous (1%), and multiracial individuals (2%) all together accounted for only 17% of the total [14].

Data from Facebook's Tech sector are updated as of June 30, 2021, and depict a similar situation in terms of differences in the sexual composition of the workforce (males, in fact, represent 75.2% of the total), while, from an ethnic point of view, there is evidence of the overtaking of Asians (54.4% of the total) over whites (35.6) [15]. Let's now delve into the social composition of Google's Tech sector, drawn from the 2021 Diversity Annual Report [16], starting by saying that the report distinguishes between workers in the U.S., those in Asia Pacific (APAC), Europe, Middle East and Africa (EMEA) and the Americas (AMERICAS), and the differences, at least from the perspective of ethnic representation, are notable. In terms of the total number of workers employed at Google, we see that from a racial/ethnic perspective, in 2021 in the U.S., whites account for 50.4% of workers – establishing themselves as the majority group, albeit down from 2020 when they were 51.7% – while Asians are 42.3% of the total, up 0.4 percentage points from 2020. Other ethnic groups, on the other hand, are heavily in the minority: Latinxs represent 6.4%, blacks 4.4% and Native Americans 0.8%. We find it interesting to compare these figures with those of Google workers in the APAC region, where Asians make up 85.8% of the workforce and whites 13.8%, while the representation of groups such as Blacks/Africans, Hispanics/Latinx, Indigenous people, and Middle Easterners and North Africans is just over zero. In EMEA, however, these power ratios appear to be completely reversed, as whites represent 80.4% of the total and Asians only 10.9%, a percentage very similar to that of Middle Eastern and North African workers (7.3%). In the Americas, however, we have a majority of whites and Europeans (48.2%), followed by Hispanics/Latinx (33.3%) and Asians (21.8%). If, on the other hand, we look at gender representation, no particular differences emerge in the various areas mapped by Google, where women always appear to be in the minority: they make up 32.2% of the workforce in the United States, 32.7% in EMEA, 34.6% in APAC and 31% in the Americas.

The U.S. team that monitors Google's Diversity, then, also constructed an intersectional graph that shows that those at the intersection of multiple identity axes are the least represented. If we now look only at those in leadership positions at Google, we can see a significant growth in the percentage of whites in each area under consideration and a concomitant decline in other ethnicities. In the U.S. and EMEA and the Americas, where the white presence was dominant even in the graphs referring to total workers, we see it grow to 65.5% in the U.S. and even reach 87.7% in Europe, the Middle East and Africa, while in the Americas the growth is more limited (the greatest increase is that of Hispanics/Latinx, which reaches 43.8%). In Asia Pacific, however, where total white workers were only 13.8%, they reach 28.8% in leadership positions. On the other hand, if we look at the gender differences in the representation of Google's leadership positions, we can see a general decrease of women in all estimated areas. They decrease to 26.9% in the US and EMEA, 29.2% in APAC and 29.8% in the Americas.

Regarding the intersectional representation of leadership positions in the United States, we can see a growth in the percentage of white women in these roles relative to the intersectional representation of total workers, but a decrease in Asian women, black women, Latinx women, and Native American women. These data seem to us to be further confirmation of what has been stated in the previous pages, namely that there remains an important power imbalance between those who fall into traditionally hegemonic categories – in which masculinity and whiteness dominate – and those who are excluded from them and who, for this reason, suffer a range of discrimination. To hold leadership positions in Google, in fact, means to have the possibility to influence the choices of the company but also, as we have seen, the culture of the Net users themselves.

2 The Intersectional Interpretive Key

As we tried to argue in the previous paragraph, we look at technological artifacts as historical and cultural products that mediate our relationship with a world in continuous and rapid transformation [17]. In this perspective, they would act as intermediaries with the environment around us and, above all, with the Other with whom we are in "connection". Technology, in other words, on the one hand would be marked by the cultural influences of those who produce it and, on the other, is capable of directly affecting the process of identification of subjects, social organization and power dynamics, reproducing and amplifying power relationships. When we talk about culture, referring to the theories of Lev Vygotskij and those developed within the Centre for Contemporary Cultural Studies at the University of Birmingham, in fact, we do not refer to the level of civilization reached by a specific society, as a reading of this type would risk to imply a presumed superiority of Western culture. Culture, on the other hand, is always plural, referring to particular lifestyles and ways of thinking that characterize social beings; consequently, within the same national borders different cultures can coexist. Therefore, culture is not only the one considered high, the academic one, but also the popular and working class one, the female one, the black one, the disabled one, as highlighted by white and black feminist criticism and Disability Studies. Nevertheless, due to the unequal power relations historically determined at global level, the culture that continues to be perceived as preferable and, consequently, as dominant is the white, male, heterosexual and abilist culture, presented as the only one possible. Those who do not fall into this category, therefore, undergo a process of stigmatization and alteration that disempowers them and relegates them to the margins of public debate. Our corporeality is, therefore, read and interpreted on the basis of the power relations that characterize our societies.

Machines are destined to assume an increasingly important role, not only for the sophisticated tasks that are assigned to them (for example, in the field of production of goods and services) but also for the high level of interfacing with the human element, which is already so developed today that we can define them as "transparent technologies" [18]. We no longer perceive them as devices that communicate with our bodies, but rather as a technological "upgrade" of our physical person (in the form of extension and enhancement of our mnemonic capabilities, or as support in the resolution of everyday problems or, in the case of bionics, as a real machinic graft). Our migration towards the cyborg dimension began at the end of the last century [19], when progress in robotics was accompanied by progress in artificial intelligence. The price for the unquestionable help provided by digital technologies, which we would probably no longer be able to give up, is the more or less conscious transfer of an enormous amount of personal data. All our searches on the Net, for example, are tracked and provide essential data to the Giants of the Platforms (Google, Amazon, Facebook, etc.), who use them to set up extremely detailed files on the habits and behaviors of all their users (as in the case of Google Ads Settings). It is for this reason that search engines, social networks, e-commerce and content sharing sites seem to know us so well as to recommend products that are similar to our tastes and, often, perfectly suited to our needs. A regime of permanent surveillance is the *conditio sine qua non* on which to implement increasingly powerful and sophisticated personalization services. The more the mass of data we release on the Net grows, the more it becomes impossible for human capabilities to process it in order to obtain reliable profiling. It is at this level that algorithmic power takes over. The decisions, the questions asked and the goals set by the company and, by extension, by those involved in designing and training the algorithm, directly affect the answers the machine provides. In a digitized capitalist universe, therefore, where the dominant paradigms of reference are still proposed by monopolies such as Google and the teams in charge of designing and training the machines are predominantly made up of white, cisgender and able-bodied men, it is not surprising that the answers provided by the algorithms are often biased, capable of conveying stereotypes and prejudices and of osmotically transferring part of the hegemonic culture. As a result, if the dataset on which the algorithm practices is not diversified by gender, race, class and disability, the machine returns a view of things often marked by biases and stereotypes that can reinforce social asymmetries and injustices [20].

The power of the Internet as an informal educational agency is not comparable to any other mass media or formal educational agency, but this also poses significant problems for democracy: first, the reach of the Net is global but it does not guarantee adequate representativeness to the cultures expressed by the different social groups that populate it, transforming itself, in fact, into a neo-colonial device capable of flattening any deviation from the norm through the supposed neutrality of mathematical language; secondly, since the personalization of results – obtained by placing each user of the Web within a filter bubble along with other subjects who have acted similar digital behaviors – is reflected in the hierarchical organization of search results, it ends up determining what users can or cannot see and, consequently, directly affects their culture, defining on the basis of past choices also their future.

The approach that moves our research is deliberately political, transformative and emancipatory and is aimed at fostering a critical understanding of the illegitimate constraints – based on repression, control and domination – that limit individual autonomy and freedom not only in real societies, but also on the Web.

From the methodological point of view, we started from the screening of national and international literature on the topic and proceeded to trace a series of significant examples of sexist, racist and ableist stereotypes that circulate online. The "cases" examined are in continuous and constant expansion both quantitatively and qualitatively, since the search suggestions, the images proposed by the different browsers and the answers provided by the virtual assistants modify and change very rapidly. Mapping the differences, the oscillations, even if minimal, of meaning contributes significantly, in our opinion, to create a picture of what are the power relations and the ways in which stereotypes and prejudices regarding other bodies are built and socialized. Events of global scope – such as the pandemic phase we are currently going through – not only make social imbalances increasingly evident but are also capable of producing profound changes in behavior and imagination. And the Web is probably the environment that, by its very nature and thanks to the immense amount of information it conveys daily, allows us to take account of these fluctuations.

The key to interpreting these phenomena has been the intersectional one [21, 22], which has allowed us, on the one hand, to contemplate simultaneously the identity variables of gender, race, class, sexual orientation and disability and their recombination on the level of the subject and, on the other, the parallel structuring of related forms of oppression and marginalization: sexism, racism, classism, homophobia and ableism. Considering that power is multidimensional and uses effective offline and online devices to maintain and reinforce social hierarchies, the intersectional approach allows us not only to investigate the persistent power relations existing in the public sphere, but also to make sure that minority cultures are the first to speak and to start transformative processes, without the application of interpretative paradigms derived from the majority ones, the Western ones, going to obscure the complexity of points of view, traditions, lifestyles. The intersectional construct, in fact, aims to mediate the tension between:

- multiplicity, in that the different identity axes recombine in the individual Other in very particular ways, but, depending on the corporeality to which the intersection of these identity lines gives rise, specific systems of oppression are determined;
- globality, since, in order to avoid the risk of an excessive fragmentation of instances and claims and of giving birth to constellations of micro-groups whose voices would be too weak to be heard, it is necessary to adopt a collective political perspective, which can effectively face oppressive systems and propose multiple and new paradigms

of interpretation of complex events. This would also avoid elaborating universal, ahistorical and decontextualized critiques.

In other words, we think that intersectionality should highlight the links between complexity and forms of power and analyze the social and cultural hierarchies formed within it. In other words, in our opinion, intersectionality theory should not be used as a merely descriptive taxonomy of existing differences in identity (if this were the case, it would be a projection of multidisciplinarity rather than transdisciplinarity) but should give voice to subjects and space to their claims, so as to allow us to trace possible points of contact and avoid that they become sclerotized in the form of subcultures, ending up flattened into those processes of marginalization that Creenshaw identifies as one of the causes of the impotence of social movements.

3 The Research

The purpose of this work was to conduct an inter and transdisciplinary research that would attempt to hold together – in an intersectional perspective – different theoretical and methodological approaches: those of Cultural Studies, Postcolonial Studies, Feminist Research, Black Women's Studies, Critical Race Studies, Disability Studies, Feminist Disability Studies, and Disability Studies and Critical Race Theory in Education, all the way to Media Studies and Intersectional Critical Race Technology Studies. This choice was made in an attempt to better understand how the power wielded by a Net mastodon like Google works, to delve into the kind of information and culture it is able to convey, but most importantly to «demonstrate how commercial search engines such us Google not only mediate but are mediated by a series of profit-driven imperatives that are supported by information and economic policies that underwrite the commodification of women's identities» [23], of black people's identities, of poor people's identities, and of disabled people's identities. Typing on Google Images a variety of keywords (for example: black man, nurse, lesbian, schizophrenic) that held together the identity variable of sex with those of race, class, sexual orientation and disability, in fact, we had the opportunity to note that most of the results obtained contributed to reinforce already widespread stereotypes and prejudices. Trends that are already present in our real societies, such as the underrepresentation or stereotyped representation of other subjectivities (women, blacks, poor, disabled, gays, lesbians, transgender, etc..), in fact, seem even increased in virtual contexts. If on the one hand, therefore, algorithmic machines are affected by and reflect the dominant culture, on the other hand they seem to be able to further reinforce and crystallize traditional systems of oppression and their power relations at a global level.

The goals that guided the research, accordingly, were:

- analyze algorithms as cultural constructs;
- track and critically analyze a range of sexist, racist, and ableist stereotypes conveyed in Google image searches;
- map stereotypes and prejudices of teachers and future teachers in training towards the variables of gender, race, class, sexual orientation and disability and detect their trust in the mass media;

- raise awareness among teachers of all levels and future teachers on the need to develop a "culture of the Web" in students in order to introduce them to the potential and hidden pitfalls of the Web.

The basic hypothesis that guided our research, therefore, is to further verify to what extent the Net and the new digital technologies constitute "non-neutral" devices, i.e., complex cultural constructs within which the social system inoculates a certain set of values and behavior patterns. The latter feed and condition the collective imagination by conveying "toxic" frames – such as stereotypes of sex, race and ability – creating consensus towards dynamics and mechanisms that we could define as "neocolonialist". Since, in the technological societies we live in, the boundaries between formal and informal education are becoming increasingly blurred, the risk is that stereotypes and biased and artifactual information will have cultural and social repercussions on the lives and worldviews of Net "surfers", especially the younger ones.

3.1 Sample

The non-probabilistic sample that participated in the research consisted of 304 people. More in detail: 159 teachers of all levels belonging to the "Ambito 15 di Roma" and the IC "Soriano nel Cimino" engaged in training courses on the new discipline of civic education, 102 support teachers enrolled in the TFA (Tirocinio Formativo Attivo) Sostegno 2020 and 43 students of the Degree Course (CdL) in Primary Education Sciences (SFP) of the Roma Tre University who participated in the Laboratory of Didattica Inclusiva (Channel 3) (Table 1).

Table 1. Sample characteristics.

Group	Gender	Frequency
Training courses teachers	Male	7
	Female	152
	Non binary/other	0
TFA 2020 teachers	Male	13
	Female	89
	Non binary/other	0
Future teachers	Male	2
	Female	40
	Non binary/other	1

The choice of conducting the research with a sample of teachers and future teachers was motivated by the fact that their culture and their beliefs, deriving at least in part from the media content they prefer and enjoy, could have direct effects on the students with whom they are/will be interacting in formal educational contexts, but also by the belief that the development of a critical awareness by the new generations about the potential and risks associated with digital media and environments inevitably passes through them.

3.2 Methodology

In order to be coherent with the objectives and hypotheses, it seemed to us that the most appropriate methodology for conducting the research was the multiparadigmatic one, which allowed us to keep together the qualitative, quantitative and critical-participatory dimensions [24]. Consequently, through the technique of case analysis applied to the digital context, we used the qualitative conceptual framework to trace and critically analyze a series of sexist, racist and ableist stereotypes conveyed through Google image searches. By means of the theoretical-critical study and the research-intervention – which was carried out within the Laboratory of Didattica Inclusiva Channel 3 academic year 2020–2021 with the students of Primary Education of the Department of Education at Roma Tre, in training courses with teachers of all levels and during the TFA course 2020 activated at Roma Tre University – instead, we analyzed the algorithms as cultural constructs and tried to raise the awareness of teachers and future teachers on the need to develop a "culture of the Web" in students, in order to let them discern the potential and hidden pitfalls of the Web. Finally, we used quantitative techniques mapping stereotypes and prejudices of teachers and future teachers in training against the variables of gender, race, class, sexual orientation and disability and detecting the trust they place in the media through the administration of the Intersectional Questionnaire (QuIn). The decision to use mixed methods of investigation, therefore, resulted from the need to hold together the qualitative vision, «which tends to see reality from the subjective point of view (internal) of those who live it, with the eyes of those who live the reality under investigation» [25], the quantitative one, aimed at objectifying reality and the methods of investigation, and the critical-participatory one, «which theorizes an inevitable and necessary interdependence between who carries out the research and the object studied, between who investigates and the subjects of investigation. [...] Participatory research therefore aims to critique the ideologies, the organizational and institutional forms that determine power relationships, to improve individual as well as groups, communities and societies conditions [...] and contrast to the inequalities» [26].

The research-intervention, in fact, was conducted in the form of a training course with teachers already in service and with those involved in the TFA [27], while with the "future teachers", still enrolled in the SFP, a more laboratory form was chosen.

The latter were then randomly divided into two groups:

- Group A – divided into four subgroups that participated in the focus groups – commented on some Google Images screenshots identified by the researchers, reported below, and referring to specific social categories.
- Group B searched Google Images for five keywords, cross-referencing the variables of: sex and social role (e.g., work or family role declined to male or female); sex and race (e.g., Italian woman, black man, etc.); sex and (dis)ability (e.g., man with syndrome..., autistic woman, etc.); sex and sexual orientation (e.g., lesbian, gay, heterosexual, etc.).

3.3 Results

Below are some of the most significant screenshots tracked on Google Images conducting the research in italian. For this reason the keywords are in Italian, because as the language changes, so do the visual representations of the subjects. The term "infermiera" is obtained from the intersection of the sex variable with the social class variable. We conducted the search for this term a first time on December 3, 2018 and the results provided by the search can be seen in Fig. 2.

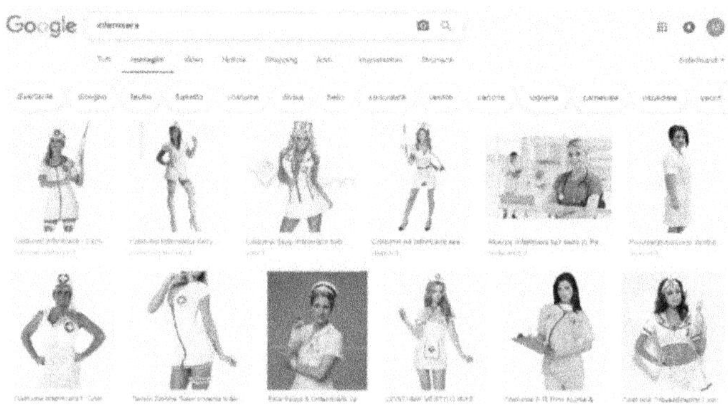

Fig. 2. Google Images result for "infermiera" on 3 December 2018.

Of the 12 images that appear, only one – the fifth in the first line – depicts a professional in scrubs, smiling at the camera with her arms crossed and the stethoscope around her neck. The sixth image in the first row and the fifth in the second one depict a woman in white scrubs and a woman in a pink uniform and refer to sites for purchasing nurses' uniforms. The third image in the bottom row depicts actress Edie Falco dressed as a nurse in the television series Nurse Jackie. The remaining eight images depict women in skimpy outfits and seem to derive from Italian sexy comedies of the 1980s and appear to be the product of male erotic imagery, which very often attributed a strong sexual charge to 'helping professions'.

Searching on Google Images for the term "infermiera" in two different historical phases – pre-pandemic and post-pandemic – we can see how the representation of the profession has changed. If in the previous case, in fact, the image of the nurse returned by the search engine was sexy, following the global spread of the Covid-19 virus, the type of narrative about the nurse's professionalism has transformed. The image returned on June 7, 2020 (see Fig. 3) was that of an angelic woman – sometimes even depicted with wings – exhausted by grueling shifts, falling asleep at her desk at the end of the shift and dressed in scrubs and masks that transfigure her silhouette.

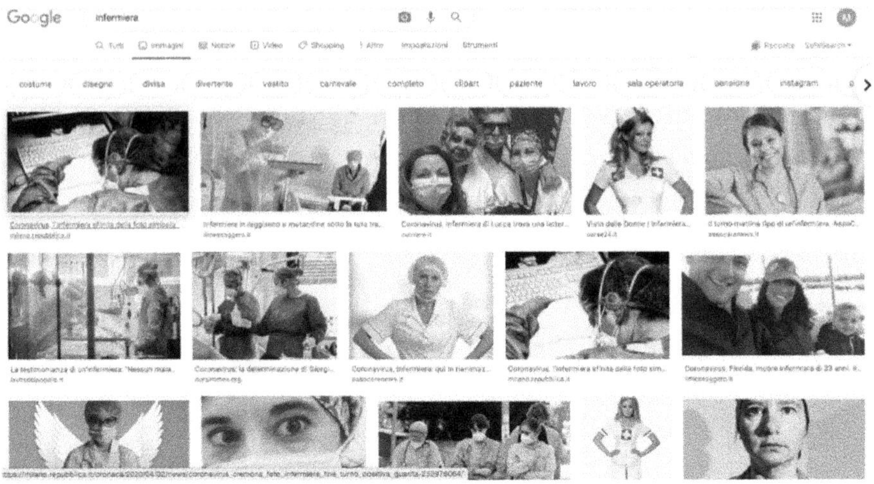

Fig. 3. Google Images result for "infermiera" on 7 June 2020.

The difference in imagery associated with the "uomo nero" in Italian –represented as a monstrous being from fairy tales (see Fig. 4) – has no counterpart in English, where most of the photos proposed for the search 'black man' refer to the struggles for black self-determination. The fact that a search engine like Google accepts that the first images you get by typing 'uomo nero' are scary beings rather than black men seems to us to perpetrate another unacceptable racial prejudice.

Fig. 4. Google Images result for "uomo nero" on 7 October 2021.

The following screenshots (Fig. 5) were obtained using the keywords 'Rumene'. In Italian, the representation that emerges seems to oscillate between the sexy woman available to the Italian male – hence the reference to dating sites – and, on the other hand, the wanted woman stopped by the police and portrayed through a mug shot or accused of prostitution.

Fig. 5. Google Images result for "rumene" on 7 October 2021.

Of the 48 images (and related links) that Google Images proposes as search results for "Rumeni" (see Fig. 6), 36 represent them as criminals. A stereotype already widely spread in society would therefore be confirmed through simplifications and conventional representations, homologating and dangerous even on the web.

Fig. 6. Google Images result for "rumeni" on 7 October 2021.

The comments that emerged from the focus groups (group A) and the Google Image searches conducted by the students in group B are also coherent with the results obtained by the researchers, but for a more comprehensive overview, please refer to future publications on the topic.

By analyzing the responses provided by teachers and future teachers to the Intersectional Questionnaire (consisting of 62 questions: 10 on the sex/gender variable, 12 on race, 11 on sexual orientation, 10 on ability/disability, 10 on the pandemic crisis and its possibility of modifying or maintaining traditional social hierarchies, and 9 on the media), it was possible to detect the most recurrent respondents' stereotypes and prejudices about gender, race, sexual orientation and ability/disability variables. Below are some of the responses that induced us to reflect most.

In response to the question *In your opinion, are there immigrants who create problems of law and order*, a considerable percentage – 33.3% of teachers in training, 28.4% of teachers enrolled in the TFA and 25.6% of future teachers – believe that there are immigrants who create problems of law and order (question 18) and identify Romanians and Albanians as the ethnic groups most likely to commit crimes, while the African continent is the one most cited in this regard (question 19).

When asked whether *issues involving gender differences and the problems of the LGBTQI community should be addressed in school*, 85.3% of TFA teachers, 79% of future teachers and 64.1% of teachers in training courses (28.9% of the latter group shows uncertainty) agree that it is necessary to activate training courses that address gender differences and the LGBTQI community (question 32).

The concept of normalcy is echoed in the statement *Children with disabilities can achieve higher levels of normalcy through therapy* (question 40): 64.2% of training teachers (26.4% neither agree nor disagree), 45.1% of TFA teachers (35.3% neither agree nor disagree), and 51.2% of prospective teachers (20.9% neither agree nor disagree) agree and completely agree.

It is probably because of a system of thinking that is oriented toward integration rather than inclusion that the majority of the sample (71.7% of TFA teachers, 64.7% of TFA teachers, and 62.8% of prospective teachers) support the establishment of a Ministry of disability (question 42), an institution built ad hoc to deal with "special" people. In the section on the pandemic crisis, when asked about a hypothetical strategy of preferring males over females (question 46), implemented by employers to overcome the crisis, over 80% of respondents in the three groups disagreed and completely disagreed (specifically, 80.6% of TFA teachers, 84.3% of TFA teachers and 93.1% of future teachers), while with reference to the equally possible strategy of preferring Italians to foreigners (question 49), the percentage of those who disagree drops to 50.3% for the group of teachers in training courses, to 52% for TFA teachers and 67.4% for future teachers. It would seem, then, that the choice to favor a certain race over a certain gender is more accepted.

The mass media, on the other hand, are perceived by the majority of members of the three groups as having a positive function in overcoming stereotypes and prejudices about the female figure (question 55), differences in sexual orientation (57), multiple ethnicities (59), and different forms of ability and disability (61) present in our societies.

4 Conclusions

In conclusion, referring to our research objectives, we can highlight how even educational figures, such as teachers in service or in training, suffer from some stereotypes and prejudices in dealing with the variables of gender, race, sexual orientation and ability/disability. This is a fact, in our opinion, on which to reason and that would deserve further investigation, since teachers have the power to influence learning and beliefs of the students with whom they are in daily contact. If, therefore, teachers become spokesmen, directly or indirectly, of the dominant culture – whose contents can also be found on the Net by conducting a Google image search – the risk is that the new generations will passively absorb it. At the same time, treasuring the trust that these educational figures seem to place in the media as vectors of conscientization, the socio-cultural relevance of these themes and the centrality of training not only for children and young people, but also for the trainers themselves, emerges clearly from the experience of the workshop with future teachers [28].

References

1. Vygotskij, L.S., Lurija, A.R.: La scimmia, l'uomo primitivo, il bambino. Studi sulla storia del comportamento, pp. 166–167. Giunti Barbera, Firenze (1987)
2. McLuhan, M.: Gli strumenti del comunicare. Il Saggiatore, Milano (1964)
3. McLuhan, M.: Il medium è il massaggio. Feltrinelli, Milano (1981)
4. Clark, A.: Natural Born Cyborgs: Minds, Technologies, and the Future of Human Intelligence. Oxford University Press, Oxford (2003)
5. Clark, A.: Supersizing the Mind: Embodiment, Action, and Cognitive Extension. Oxford University Press, Oxford (2011)
6. O'Neil, C.: Armi di distruzione matematica. Come i big data aumentano la disuguaglianza e minacciano la democrazia. Bompiani, Milano (2017)
7. Eubanks, V.: Automating Inequality: How High-Tech Tools Profile, Police, and Punish the Poor, pp. 194–195. St Martin's Press, New York (2018)
8. O'Neil, C.: Armi di distruzione matematica. Come i big data aumentano la disuguaglianza e minacciano la democrazia, p. 28. Bompiani, Milano (2017)
9. We Are Social, Digital 2021. https://wearesocial.com/digital-2021. Accessed 21 Nov 2021
10. Noble, S.U., Tynes, B.M.: The Intersectional Internet: Race, Sex, Class and Culture Online, p. 4. Peter Lang Publishing, New York (2016)
11. O'Neil, C.: Armi di distruzione matematica. Come i big data aumentano la disuguaglianza e minacciano la democrazia, pp. 33–34. Bompiani, Milano (2017)
12. Noble, S.U.: Algorithms of Oppression: How Search Engines Reinforce Racism, pp. 15–16. New York University press, New York (2018)
13. DuckDuckGo, Measuring the "Filter Bubble": How Google is influencing what you click. https://spreadprivacy.com/google-filter-bubble-study/. Accessed 21 Nov 2021
14. Apple, Inclusion & Diversity (2020). https://www.apple.com/diversity/. Accessed 21 Nov 2021
15. Williams, M.: Facebook Diversity Update: Increasing Representation in Our Workforce and Supporting Minority-Owned Businesses. https://about.fb.com/news/2021/07/facebook-diversity-report-2021/. Accessed 21 Nov 2021
16. Google, 2021 Diversity Annual Report. https://diversity.google/annual-report/. Accessed 21 Nov 2021
17. Vygotskij, L.S.: Pensiero e linguaggio. Laterza, Bari (2008)
18. Clark, A.: Natural Born Cyborgs: Minds, Technologies, and the Future of Human Intelligence. Oxford University Press, Oxford (2003)
19. Haraway, D.: Manifesto Cyborg. Donne, tecnologie e biopolitiche del corpo. Feltrinelli, Milano (1995)

20. On this topic see: Noble, S.U., Tynes, B.M.: The Intersectional Internet. Race, Sex, Class and Culture Online. Peter Lang Publishing, New York (2016); Wachter-Boettcher, S.: Technically Wrong. Sexist Apps, Biased Algorithms, and Other Threats of Toxic Tech. W.W. Norton & Company, New York (2017); Noble, S.U.: Algorithms of Oppression. How Search Engines Reinforce Racism. New York University press, New York (2018); Eubanks, V: Automating Inequality. How High-Tech Tools Profile, Police, and Punish the Poor. St Martin's Press, New York (2018); Buolamwini, J., Gebru, T.: Gender Shades: Intersectional Accuracy Disparities in Commercial Gender Classification. Proceedings of Machine Learning Research 81, 1–15 (2018); Benjamin, R.: Race After Technology. Abolitionist Tools for the New Jim Code. Polity Press, Medford (MA) (2019); Zona, U., De Castro, M.: Edusfera. Processi di apprendimento e macchine culturali nell'era social. Pensa Multimedia, Lecce (2020)
21. Crenshaw, K.: Demarginalizing the Intersection of Race and Sex: A Black Feminist Critique of Antidiscrimination Doctrine, Feminist Theory and Antiracist Politics. University of Chicago Legal Forum, Issue 1, pp. 139–167 (1989)
22. Crenshaw, K.: Mapping the margins: intersectionality, identity politics, and violence against women of Color. Stanford Law Rev. **43**(6), 1241–1299 (1991)
23. Noble, S.U.: Algorithms of Oppression: How Search Engines Reinforce Racism, p. 33. New York University Press, New York (2018)
24. Cohen, L., Manion, L., Morrison, K.: Research Methods in Education, 6th edn. Routledge, London (2007)
25. Benvenuto, G.: Stili e metodi della ricerca educativa, p. 42. Carocci editore, Roma (2015)
26. Benvenuto, G.: Stili e metodi della ricerca educativa, pp. 42–44. Carocci editore, Roma (2015)
27. For more on the subject of teacher training, see: Muscarà, M.: Scuola inclusiva e insegnante di sostegno. La specializzazione come componente essenziale della formazione iniziale dei docenti. Pensa Multimedia, Lecce (2018); Bocci, F.: Pedagogia speciale come pedagogia inclusiva. Itinerari istituenti di un modo di essere della scienza dell'educazione. Guerini Scientifica, Milano (2021)
28. The connections between the participants' stereotypes could also be discussed by referring to the research strand on intercultural education, which has been developed in Italy for several decades. In particular see: Fiorucci, M., Stillo, L.: Intercultural Teacher Training: Experiences, Knowledge and Field Research. Educazione interculturale, vol. 17, issue 1, pp. 7–21 (2019); Bolognesi, I., Lorenzini, S.: Pedagogia interculturale. Pregiudizi, razzismi, impegno educativo. Bononia University Press, Bologna (2017); Colussi, E.: La formazione interculturale dei docenti: professionalità, risorse e sfide globali. Fondazione ISMU, Milano (2021)

Integration of LifeComp and DigComp 2.2 as a Theoretical Framework for Media Education

Andrea Garavaglia[1](✉), Livia Petti[2], and Serena Triacca[3]

[1] Department of Philosophy, University of Milan, Via Festa del Perdono, 7, 20122 Milan, Italy
andrea.garavaglia@unimi.it

[2] Department of Humanities, Social Sciences and Education, University of Molise, Via Francesco De Sanctis, 86100 Campobasso, Italy

[3] Department of Education, Catholic University of Sacred Heart of Milan, Largo A. Gemelli, 1, 20123 Milan, Italy

Abstract. This essay critically discusses the ways in which DigComp 2.2 can be used as a theoretical framework to support media education programs in schools. Since 2006, digital competence has been one of the eight key competencies that were defined by the European Union for lifelong learning. As reported in the recommendations, these competencies are considered to be fundamental for each individual in a knowledge-based society.

DigComp focuses specifically on the acquiring of knowledge, recollection, comprehension, application, evaluation, and creation, without explaining the fundamental activities of critical analysis and reflection directly and extensively. The latter two dimensions form an integral part of the fundamental objectives of media education, which could enable students to make a truly conscious and responsible use of the new media.

The application of the DigComp 2.2 framework for cases of media education projects has highlighted some gaps related to well-being, self-regulation, awareness, responsibiliy and critical thinking.

In order to solve these gaps without abandoning the use of the Digcomp framework, it is proposed that it be integrated with the LifeComp framework.

Keywords: Media education · Digcomp · Digital competence · Media literacy

1 DigComp as a Theoretical Framework for Media Education? – Issues and Implications

This essay critically discusses the ways in which DigComp 2.2 (Digital Competence Framework for Citizens) can be used as a theoretical framework to support media education programs in schools[1]. Since 2006, digital competence has been one of the eight key

[1] This contribution has been developed jointly by the authors. Andrea Garavaglia wrote paragraphs 1 and 3 while Livia Petti and Serena Triacca wrote paragraph 2. Paragraph 4 was jointly written by the authors.

M. Ranieri et al. (Eds.): ATEE 2021, CCIS 1649, pp. 59–70, 2022.
https://doi.org/10.1007/978-3-031-20777-8_5

competencies that were defined by the European Union for lifelong learning. As reported in the 2018 recommendations, these competencies are considered to be fundamental for each individual in a knowledge-based society.

DigComp is one the most important frameworks used in various projects to help students achieve digital competence [1, 2]. It was released by the Joint Research Center and is mainly meant for use by government agencies, educational institutions, and enterprises.

The evolution and diffusion of new media have led to the emergence of a series of risks as well as opportunities [3] which substantially confirm the need to activate critical analytical skills and a profound reflection on the use of devices in students [4–6]. Such aspects concerning the principles of media education have already been elaborated in a previous research [7]. The spread and prevalence of digital media in the recent years make it seem like DigComp and media education can converge towards a singular aim of training responsible and aware citizens. However, an accurate analysis of the DigComp 2.2 framework indicates that the program does not allow the recognition of all the dimensions of media education [8, 9]. DigComp focuses specifically on the acquiring of knowledge, recollection, comprehension, application, evaluation, and creation, without explaining the fundamental activities of critical analysis and reflection directly and extensively. The latter two dimensions form an integral part of the fundamental objectives of media education which could enable students to make a truly conscious and responsible use of the new media.

This discrepancy is probably due to the fact that critical and reflective dimensions are included in three of the other seven key competencies (functional, alphabetical, citizenship, height, cultural, awareness, and expression) for the European lifelong learning framework of 2018 and require educational systems to propose the use of system-structured program-paths across several key competencies.

On the other hand, analyzing DigCompEdu could help identify the inherent competences that assist educators in facilitating the achievement of the learners' digital competence dimensions. This is a competence that was not sufficiently developed in DigComp, and is, hence, reinserted here, in place of safety dimension; it is a dimension that we could consider as an outcome of responsible use.

With a view to use DigComp in media education, the goal of this paper is to suggest solutions to avoid the reductionism of the development of media education skills to the dimensions of DigComp. On the downside, however, an extensive adoption of DigComp by educational programs could increase the risk of the disappearance of the reflexive critical dimension. These dimensions are fundamental elements that form the foundations of media education [10] and are included in the LifeComp Framework.

2 Application of DigComp as a Framework in Media Education Projects

In order to understand how the DigComp framework can be applied, two projects are analyzed below.

In recent years, many schools and academic projects in the Italian context that were aimed at developing digital competence explicitly refer to the DigComp framework, considered the goal standard for digital training in the European context [11, 12]. We present below two media education projects: in one case the choice of adopting this framework was made by the research group and in the second, it was as requested by the Ministry. Projects refer to the most recent version of DigComp (2.1) at the time of implementation. The minor differences between versions 2.1 and 2.2 of DigComp do not affect the reflections and analysis described in this contribution.

2.1 The Project Digital Well-Being - Schools

The three-year project "Digital Well-being – Schools" was funded by a public-private agreement: on the one hand, the project won an Innovation Grant from the University of Milan-Bicocca and on the other Fastweb S.p.a. co-financed the project as part of its social responsibility activities.

The project has been carried out since the scholastic year 2016–17 with the purpose of offering media education training activities for upper secondary school students in Lombardy.

The first year was dedicated to the design of the project. The research group, formed by an inter-departmental team of the University of Milan Bicocca, created a teacher training course structured in four modules. These modules were designed to incorporate media education activities among students.

The training course aims to introduce the participating teachers to the main themes of citizenship, the use of new media by young people, and prompt "media awareness experiences" to be applied in the classroom. Specifically, 171 s classes from 18 schools were selected from the Milano and Monza-Brianza areas, according to Clustered Randomized Controlled Trial – CRCT [13].

In Table 1 are the training modules based on the main themes of DigComp.

Table 1. Description of the training course modules

Module	Topics	DigComp area (2.1 and 2.2)
Managing time and attention	Awareness of the time spent with digital devices (video games, social networks, smartphones…)	Safety (+ Problem solving)
Using online communication	Conflict simulation and management in social networks, digital identity, online reputation, and online collaboration	Communication and collaboration (+ Problem solving)
Finding and evaluating information online	Search for information, evaluation of the validity of sources, and knowledge management	Information and data literacy (+ Problem solving)
Creating online content responsibly	Making and sharing of content, authorship, copyright	Digital Content Creation (+ Problem solving)

The articulation of the format of the training course required an accurate analysis of the theoretical framework and of the recent innovations in the didactic field [14] which was necessary to outline the method, called HaDIMB, an acronym of the essential components on which it is based: Habit, Debriefing, Inverted Classroom, Microlearning and Blended learning. In Table 2 is the articulation of the training proposal.

Each module is divided into a theoretical part and an application part that contains the indications on the activities to be carried out in the classroom and on the specific media awareness to be developed. At the end of each module, teachers and students are invited to share a good practice and blend in with the classroom life (habit) to establish the achievement of digital competence.

Table 2. The HaDIMB method

Phase	Description
Online preparatory study	The use of online resources in self-training is foreseen for sensitizing participants to the main contents of the course
Face-to-face training	After the online moment in the classroom, the basic elements of the preparatory study are resumed and the lesson plan to be carried out with the students is explained. The moment is also fundamental for a comparison between participants and between trainers and participants
Online insight (optional)	Subsequently, teachers are invited to use some in-depth materials
Online design	Teachers can re-design the proposed lesson plan considering the specificities of their school context. This moment takes place online thanks to the support of an expert
Application of the lesson plan	It consists of the moment dedicated to the implementation of the lesson plan in the classroom with the students whose structure provides a first approach of the students to the dimension of competence through a presentation of the theme. Following this, it moves on to the performance of an activity that allows to understand the characteristics and the functioning of the specific aspect of the media that is addressed and finally at the time of debriefing, which is essential to achieve the awareness desired
Habit consolidation	The ultimate goal of the teaching experience is to establish virtuous habits (good habits), important elements for developing any competence. Since the training intervention has a limited duration (3 h), it becomes important to recall the established habits throughout the school year and promote reflection and awareness so that they become virtuous behaviors for students to be adopted not only at school but wherever they go in life

2.2 The Project Cogito Ergo Sum

Action #15 Innovative scenarios for the development of digital skills of the Italian National Plan for the Digital School (PNSD) aims to create, experiment, and make available 25 new innovative, structured, open curricula that are able to involve the extended school community.

On 23rd September 2016 the Italian Ministry of Education issued a call for the selection of digital curriculum projects on a specific thematic area conceived by state schools and educational institutions of all types and levels established in a network, with a minimum of three institutions including the leader (see Table 3)[2]. As already anticipated, the government specifically requested that the projects refer to the DigComp framework.

Table 3. N. of projects eligible for funding for each thematic area

Thematic area	N.
Internet rights	2
Media (and social) education	3
Information literacy	3
STEM (digital skills for educational robotics, making, 3D printing, Internet of Things)	4
Big and open data	2
Coding	2
Digital art and culture	4
Education in reading and writing in digital environments	2
Digital economy	2
Digital entrepreneurship	1

"Cogito Ergo Sum" is the name of the proposal funded in 2020 at the Liceo Statale "Duca degli Abruzzi" (Treviso, Veneto region), engaged with state upper secondary education institutes "Giuseppe Verdi" (Valdobbiadene) and "Marco Casagrande" (Pieve di Soligo), which focuses on the topic of media education.

CREMIT (Research Center about Media Education, Innovation and Technology) of Catholic University of Milan is a partner of the project and is involved as an expert for the consultancy and validation of the curriculum model—articulated over the five-year period—and the didactic materials produced.

ESL (EAS in Italian)—Episodes of Situated Learning [15]—is the qualifying and distinctive methodological framework adopted here. It is based on three steps, i.e., anticipating, producing and reflecting. Anticipating is the step for activating the first appropriation of contents, producing is for working on constructs, and reflecting is for fixing the key-elements, favoring metacognitive processes and the development of awareness about what has been experienced and learned. In this sense, digital becomes a vehicle

[2] In Internet, URL: https://www.istruzione.it/scuola_digitale/curricoli_digitali.shtml.

to produce meanings, a specific object of reflection and an arena for activation in every phase of the lessons.

The curriculum—accompanied by a vademecum which illustrates its structure and topics (see Table 4)—consists of 90 h of lessons articulated in 30 ELS. The 30 lesson plans are equipped with resources, a glossary, and cards for the use of the suggested apps. Finally, 20 podcasts with a listening guide are proposed as transversal stimuli to several ESL to encourage reflection and discussion, starting from listening to some emblematic and current cases.

Table 4. Description of the digital curriculum

Target	Topic	DigComp area (2.1 and 2.2)
I–II class	1_1 Know and use the main communication and information sharing tools to interact and encourage inclusion as well	Information and data literacy Communication and collaboration
I–II class	1_2 Participate and inhabit the Net and communication environments	Communication and collaboration
I–II class	1_3 Awareness of own actions	Digital content creation
III–IV class	2_1 Digital ethics	Information and data literacy Digital content creation
III–IV class	2_2 Scripta manent: Raise awareness of the risks of computer traces in relation to privacy	Safety Digital content creation Problem solving
III–IV class	2_3 Consumer rights and duties	Communication and collaboration Safety Problem solving
V class	3_1 National and European law, transnationality of the Network	Communication and collaboration
V class	3_2 Digital culture and innovation	Communication and collaboration Digital content creation Problem solving

At the end of the first year dedicated to outlining the curriculum and the design of activities (SY 2020/21), the teachers of the leader school were trained in the ESL methodology; in turn, the Digital Team of the leader school took care of training the teachers of the two schools that are part of the network. An offer of online coaching guarantees teachers support in the experimenting phase of the curriculum (SY 2021/22). The coach is an expert of the research group whose function is halfway between that of the tutor and that of the consultant able to offer an external point of view and orientation.

2.3 Application of DigComp as a Framework for Media Education

The analysis of the two projects presented above focuses on identifying:

- the application of critical analysis to artifacts and media communication;
- the promotion of responsible acting on the network;
- the recognition of awareness dimension;
- the development of reflection.

In this contribution, we take into account two examples of activities, one for each project.

The first didactic proposal analyzed within the "Digital Well-being – School" project, "Create online content responsibly" (in Module 4 of the training course) concerns the third area of DigComp, i.e., "Creation of digital content". Specific competences taken into consideration are the following:

3.1 Developing digital content
3.2 Integrating and re-elaborating digital content
3.3 Copyright and licences
5.2 Identifying needs and technological responses.

In fact, the module concerns the aspects of authorship of the Web, specifically the responsible production and publication, the promotion and sharing of contents considering objectives, and targets and problems related to copyright and privacy. To carry out this didactic proposal, a check-list created collaboratively in the classroom is used, paying particular attention to metacognitive and self-reflective processes related to the meaning of the content to be created and disseminated.

With reference to the description of the specific competence "3.1 Developing digital content" (create and edit digital content in different formats to express yourself through digital means) and "3.3 Copyright and licences" (understand how copyright and licensing apply to data, information and digital content), it emerges that DigComp was overly oriented towards avoiding legal problems and acquiring technical skills.

The second didactic proposal analyzed within the "Cogito Ergo Sum" project, "Netiquette for responsible prosumers" (proposed to students of the first and second grades), touches the second area of DigComp 2.1/2.2, i.e., "Communication and collaboration". The specific competences taken into consideration are the following:

- 2.3 Engaging in citizenship through digital technologies
- 2.5 Netiquette.

The proposal focuses on the communicative and critical competence of the digital citizen as a prosumer. Students are invited to collect at least one netiquette of their social networks and online groups, producing a reflection on the motivations of netiquette by analyzing them. Then they produce a useful netiquette for different environments by leveraging the possibility of expressing one's opinion in online spaces and promoting interventions capable of making the web more hospitable. Finally, the central aspects will be commented on to activate a more active way of experiencing communication, with an a posteriori lesson on prosumers, dimensions of citizenship, network communication.

Referring to the description of the specific competence "2.5 Netiquette" (to be aware of behavioral norms and know-how while using digital technologies and interacting in digital environments. To adapt communication strategies to the specific audience and to be aware of cultural and generational diversity in digital environments) we can notice that DigComp was overly oriented to selecting the right digital service to participate in society and solving problems in netiquette management.

Analyzing the two projects, it emerges clearly that if the goal is to promote media education activities, DigComp is not a sufficient framework to guide the development of media skills.

The dimension of critical analysis is limited to the first area "Information and data literacy" and does not concern, for example, the online communication. The awareness dimension is flattened on the cognitive aspects regarding the know-how and the norms; it doesn't dwell on the implications about the consequences of one's own online behavior. The DigComp does not aim at promoting reflection; the term "reflection" does not appear in either DigComp 2.1 or 2.2.

In DigComp 2.2 there is little attention to the development of responsibility, especially in the examples of knowledge, skills and attitudes of the dimensions 2.3 "Collaborating through digital technologies" and 2.4 "Netiquette".

The choice of methods adopted in the two projects (HaDIMB and ESL, as previously seen) is also significant and in line with the importance attributed to the dimensions of critical analysis which finds space within the preparatory phase of ESL. This is through problem solving, awareness and responsibility on which the final phase in HaDIMB invests with habit consolidation and reflection, stimulated through dedicated debriefing moments, as evident in both the projects.

3 A Proposal: Integration of LifeComp and DigComp as a Theoretical Framework for Media Education

The proposed solution emerges as an answer to cover the shortcomings left by the DigComp. The outcome highlighted that information literacy seems to be well-covered by the DigComp framework, while the dimensions of critical analysis, awareness and responsibility, as they are defined, do not allow for extensive and complete application.

This proposal was born with the intention of not abandoning the DigComp and trying to use the other frameworks proposed by the European Union. The framework that can be used for this aim is the recent LifeComp, published in 2020.

LifeComp is the European framework for Personal, Social and Learning-to-Learn key competence and is one of the eight European lifelong learning frameworks. An initial brief analysis of LifeComp enables us to understand the transversality of media education in relation to the eight European lifelong learning frameworks of competences:

- In the first area (Personal) of the LifeComp Framework, the dimensions of *wellbeing* and *self-regulation* are relevant for media education. These competencies integrate and complete the dimensions of DigComp [16].
- In the second area (Social), *communication* and *collaboration* are presented with a strong emphasis on *awareness, understanding* and *responsibility*, which are key elements of media education that are not included in DigComp.
- In the third area (Learning-to-Learn), *critical thinking* and *reflecting* are presented as key dimensions of the analysis and creative production of digital artefacts.

3.1 Wellbeing and Self-regulation

In various contributions, the well-being is considered one of the priority objectives of media education. One of the main ones is the dossier "Mapping Media Education Policies in the World" created by the United Nations, Alliance of Civilizations, UNESCO, European Commission and Grupo Comunicar [17]. The dossier analyzes the key elements for building up civic engagement, identity and media literacy and promotes a call through new media to rewrite the corporate responsibility to contribute to the wellbeing of society.

Another important contribution was produced by the Education Department of the Council of Europe in 2016 [18]: The Digital Citizenship Education (DCE) was a project aimed to set guidelines for the ministry committee of education of the member states to implement strategies to develop a democratic culture that respects human rights and cultural diversities. The wellbeing online was identified as a main domain in order to guarantee ethical behavior and empathy for positive online interaction based on positive online images of themselves and online interactions that are coherent and consistent.

In the LifeComp framework, one of the wellbeing descriptors is "Understanding potential risks for wellbeing and using reliable information and services for health and social protection" [19]. This is a relevant point of attention since the new media makes us responsible for actions concerning the dissemination of information that can harm social protection.

Many authors have stressed the importance of developing self-regulation processes. Among them Gonsalves emphasizes the importance of educating young people through slow process of self-regulation [4].

In the DigCompEdu, self-regulation appears as an activity among those considered for the collaboration dimension, specifically among peers [20]. With regard to this dimension, Salomon's contribution emerges with importance, arguing that over time, the processes of media education and media literacy will be a part of the regulation and self-regulation process, both by the producers and by consumers of media productions [21].

Finally, Tisseron's contribution is very relevant where self-regulation is one of the cornerstones of media education for children [6].

In the LifeComp framework, one of the self-regulation descriptors is "Understanding and regulating personal emotions, thoughts, and behaviors, including stress responses" [19]. A point of contact with many media education projects is the cyclical process of self-regulation, carried out through three main steps: establishing a desired state, comparing the current state with the desired one and applying a solution to modify the current state if it is not consistent with the desired one [22].

3.2 Awareness, Understanding and Responsibility in Communication

This is the dimension that the DigComp covers better than the others but in the transition from versions 2.0 to 2.1 [1], confirmed in version 2.2, we would probably have expected a greater depth with respect to the levels of competence concerning awareness and responsibility in communication. In the highly specialized level of proficiency of communication competence in DigComp is not explained how to express a full awareness and responsibility.

On the other hand, in the LifeComp framework, the communication is a key competence of the social area. It is defined as "the use of relevant communication strategies, domain-specific codes and tools, depending on the context and content" [19] and the descriptors completely cover the awareness and understanding of interactions in different languages and socio-cultural contexts, with the aim of ensuring listening to others with confidence, assertiveness, clarity, and reciprocity.

3.3 Critical Thinking and Reflecting as Key Dimensions of Analysis and Creative Production of Digital Artefacts

Critical thinking is crucial in media education [23]. It looks at how we analyze, synthesize, and evaluate information and involves considering alternative ways of looking at a problem [24].

Different from our initial expectations, critical thinking in DigComp is present in a very limited way. It is identified in the information and data literacy competence, in the second point dedicated to evaluation data, information and digital content. Proficiency level 5–6 is defined as "critically assess the credibility and reliability of sources of data, information and digital content" [2].

The processes of analysis and critical thinking are therefore focused on the use of information while no equal attention is paid to the production of digital artefacts. In the dimension of DigComp "3. Digital content creation", reflexive and critical thinking are not proposed in favor of the development of solutions to complex problems.

In the LifeComp framework, the L2.1 descriptor develops the awareness of potential biases in the data and one's personal limitations while collecting valid and reliable information and ideas from a diverse and reputable source. On the other hand, the L.2.2 descriptor is concerned with comparing, analyzing, assessing, and synthesizing data, information, ideas, and media messages in order to draw logical conclusions.

4 Conclusions

This work suggests how to integrate DigComp and LifeComp in order to establish a more complete and enhanced framework for media education projects. One way to achieve integration is to consider the areas dedicated to communication and collaboration, then extend the key elements of the LifeComp in full to the other areas of the DigComp (Fig. 1).

In our opinion, this integration is necessary in cases where the grant calls establish the necessary use of the DigComp framework in the media education proposal, but it does not solve the problem of defining a definitive framework for media education.

An interconnection between the two frameworks is suggested in a note in the DigComp 2.2 report [24], referring to some examples of dimension 4 (knowledge, skills, attitudes).

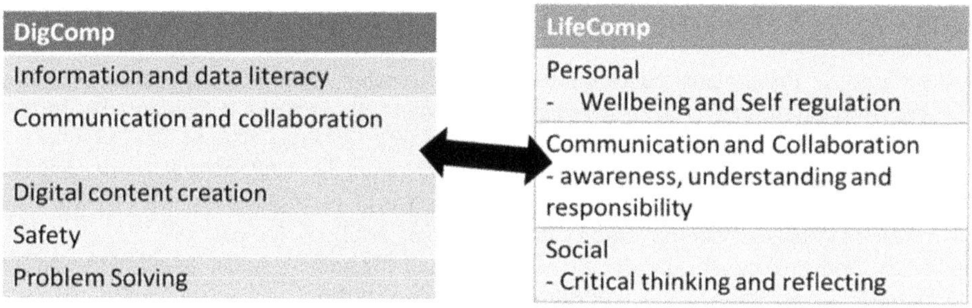

Fig. 1. Integration of DigComp and LifeComp for media education project

Acknowledgements. This research was funded by the Department of Philosophy "Piero Martinetti" of the University of Milan under the Project "Departments of Excellence 2018–2022" awarded by the Ministry of Education, University and Research (MIUR), the Department of Education of the Catholic University of Sacred Heart of Milan and the Department of Humanities, Social Sciences and Education of the University of Molise.

References

1. Carretero, S., Vuorikari, R., Punie, Y.: DigComp 2.1: the digital competence framework for citizens with eight proficiency levels and examples of use. Publications Office of the European Union (2017)
2. Vuorikari, R., Kluzer, S., Punie, Y.: DigComp 2.2, the digital competence framework for citizens: with new examples of knowledge, skills and attitudes. European Commission, Joint Research Centre (2022). https://data.europa.eu/doi/10.2760/115376
3. Rivoltella, P.C.: Media education. Idea, metodo, ricerca. La Scuola, Brescia (2017)
4. Gonsalves, P.: Exercises in media education. Don Bosco Communications. Matunga, Mumbai (1995)
5. Hobbs, R.: Create to Learn: Introduction to Digital Literacy. Wiley-Blackwell, Hoboken (2017)
6. Tisseron, S.: 3-6-9-12. Apprivoiser les écrans et grandir. ERES, Tolouse (2014)
7. Masterman, L.: Teaching the Media. Commedia, London (1985)
8. Kačinová, V.: From a reductionist to a holistic model of digital competence and media education. Commun. Today **10**(2), 16–27 (2019)
9. Swertz, C.: DigComp 2.2 AT. Hintergründe und Kontexte. Medienimpulse **57**(1), 1–35 (2019)
10. UNESCO: Grunwald Declaration on Media Education (1982). http://www.unesco.org/education/information/nfsunesco/pdf/MEDIA_E.PDF
11. Menichetti, L.: La competenza digitale: dalla definizione a un framework per la scuola. Media Educ. **8**(2), 175–195 (2017)
12. Soriani, A., Trisolini, G.: Using blog and other on line tools for improving educators' digital competences and professional development. Media Educ. **8**(1), 1–18 (2017)
13. Gerosa, T.: Il disegno sperimentale dell'intervento. In: Gui, M. (ed.) Benessere Digitale a scuola e a casa. Un percorso di educazione ai media nella connessione permanente, pp. 99–131. Mondadori Università, Milano (2019)
14. Garavaglia, A., Petti, L.: Sviluppo della proposta formativa "Benessere Digitale - scuole". In: Gui, M. (ed.). Benessere Digitale a scuola e a casa. Un percorso di educazione ai media nella connessione permanente, pp. 73–98. Mondadori Università, Milano (2019)

15. Rivoltella, P.C.: Fare didattica con gli EAS. Episodi di Apprendimento Situato. La Scuola, Brescia (2013)
16. Soriani, A.: From media education to digital citizenship. Origins, perspectives and policy implementations in the school systems across Europe*. Ricerche Di Pedagogia e Didattica-J. Theories Res. Educ. **13**(3), 3 (2018). https://doi.org/10.6092/issn.1970-2221/8557
17. United Nations, Alliance of Civilizations, Grupo Comunicar, UNESCO, & European Commission: Mapping Media Education Policies in the World. In *Challenges* (2009). https://www.unaoc.org/images/mapping_media_education_book_final_version.pdf
18. COE: Competences for democratic culture. Living together as equals in culturally diverse democratica societies. Council of Europe Publishing (1991)
19. Sala, A., Punie, Y., Garkov, V., Giraldez, C.M.: LifeComp: the European framework for personal, social and learning to learn key competence. EUR 30246 EN, Publications Office of the European Union, Luxembourg (2020). https://doi.org/10.2760/302967. JRC120911
20. Redecker, C., Punie, Y., European Commission: Joint Research Centre: European framework for the digital competence of educators: DigCompEdu. Publications Office of the European Union (2017). https://ec.europa.eu/jrc/en/publication/eur-scientific-and-technical-research-reports/european-framework-digital-competence-educators-digcompedu
21. Salomon, E.: The role of broadcasting regulation in media literacy. In: United Nations et al (eds). Mapping Media Education Policies in the World, pp. 197–209 (2009)
22. Baumeister, R.F., Heatherton, T.F.: Self-regulation failure: an overview. Psychol. Inq. **7**(1), 1–15 (1996). https://doi.org/10.1207/s15327965pli0701_128
23. Rivoltella, P.C.: Nuovi alfabeti. Educazione e culture nella società post-mediale. Scholè Morcelliana, Brescia (2020)
24. Buckingham, D.: The Media Education Manifesto. Polity Press, Cambridge (1999)

Digital Citizenship Education Curriculum. Results of a National Investigation and Didactic Proposals

Loredana Perla[1](✉), Laura Agrati[2], Viviana Vinci[3], Alessia Scarinci[1], and Rosa Palermo[1]

[1] University of Bari Aldo Moro, Bari, Italy
{loredana.perla,alessia.scarinci,rosa.palermo}@uniba.it
[2] University of Bergamo, Bergamo, Italy
laurasara.agrati@unibg.it
[3] Mediterranea University of Reggio Calabria, Reggio Calabria, Italy
viviana.vinci@unirc.it

Abstract. Citizenship education is now a priority at European and national level. The continuous historical, political, social and cultural changes entail new definitions of the construct of citizenship which becomes multidimensional, since the dimensions that compose and define it are different. Among these emerges the digital dimension which involves new ways of involving citizens in an active and participatory way. The development of ICT has led to an increase in new social media also in civic participation. Although evidences have shown effects on the civic engagement of young people, the use of social media and digital resources is still marginal in the 'every day' school context. The results of a national research on citizenship education are described - the few digital components in the design of civic education teachers - and the proposals for a digital citizenship education curriculum are shared.

Keywords: Social media · Civic education · Critical thinking · Curriculum · Teacher training

1 Theoretical Framework

When we talk about citizenship, we refer to rights, freedom, equality, solidarity, etc., we describe our-selves, our history, the world we inhabit, we refer to the relationship that the individual has and builds with society [1]. The development of civil, political and social rights, the historical-political transformations of society have led to an evolution of this concept: if historically, as UNESCO highlights in the document "Education for Global Citizenship" [2], citizenship was a the exclusive right of a few, today, growing globalization has expanded its borders beyond the terms of the nation-state indicating a "sense of belonging to a larger community and a shared humanity, political, economic, social and cultural interdependence and a intertwining between the local, the national

M. Ranieri et al. (Eds.): ATEE 2021, CCIS 1649, pp. 71–87, 2022.
https://doi.org/10.1007/978-3-031-20777-8_6

and the global" [2]. Citizenship is a multidimensional concept, characterized by a plurality of meanings, of contents, qualified by different adjectives that define its meaning: multicultural, active, democratic, inclusive, participatory, digital, global. Citizenship expresses the status, the position that the citizen has towards the state and determines his belonging to it with his rights and duties towards the community. But it is also an activity linked to active participation and commitment to public life, characterized by action and the exercise of skills [3]. The 2018 European Recommendations underline the need to promote the development of skills to ensure active citizenship and "strengthen awareness of common values" [4], recognizing among the key competences those in the field of citizenship: "citizenship refers to the ability to act as responsible citizens and to participate fully in civic and social life, based on an understanding of social, economic, legal and political structures and concepts as well as global evolution and sustainability" [4]. The attention placed at European level on the need to acquire these skills highlights the role that education and instruction must play in the process of developing active, conscious and responsible citizenship [1, 3]. Educational and training institutions, as a place for meeting, comparison, dialogue with others and for the development of critical thinking and autonomy, must allow students to "learn through participation to enter the great horizon of human culture" [1] to become *cives*. Education is the tool that allows students to build a "human future" [1], to build future citizens of the world. Citizenship education presupposes an educational project that takes into account the multidimensional and interdisciplinary nature of this concept, capable of developing a dynamic set of knowledge, attitudes, attitudes and values [5]. In this regard, the UNESCO 2018 Global Citizenship Education: Topics and Learning Objectives, offers a list of Global Citizenship Education (GCED) topics, learning objectives, and themes organized under three GCED learning areas - the socio-emotional, cognitive, and behavioral. It also identifies, in relation to the learning areas, three characteristics of the students that global citizenship education aims to develop [2]: be informed and have a critical spirit; be socially involved and respectful of otherness; be ethically responsible and committed. Responsibility, critical thinking and participation are the categories that must guide the redefinition of teaching that has as its objective the development of the citizen of tomorrow.

2 Research Topic

The digital ecosystem in recent years has undergone an evolution such as to transform the way and places of communicating, learning and relating, leading to an increase in new social media also in civic participation [6–8].

Digital technologies and the web have created a new social space to inhabit in which to build one's identity and knowledge without being tied to a form of "learned learning", as reported by Rivoltella [9]. Castells in 2004 spoke of the "space revolution", a revolution that took place with the "internet revolution" which expanded the global connection, amplified the dimension of flows and places, reproducing and reorganizing the structure and morphology of society in company networks [10]. "We are facing an extremely pervasive change, full of implications due to the exponential growth of connections and interactions, which cannot be ignored" as reported in the syllabus for digital civic education promoted by MIUR [11]. Technologies are changing the nature of the democratic processes of society and creating new forms of participation in social and public life, leading to an evolution of the concept of citizenship into digital citizenship [12]. Navigating and inhabiting this digital ecosystem requires the development of a full digital citizenship that sees the development of critical thinking and responsibility as the key aspects for its implementation. Technologies, digital and social media also define an informal space within which to share a new culture characterized by a horizontal socialization, capable of generating informal learning communities, in which to mediate knowledge, relationships and representations of history [9, 13, 14].

These informal learning communities are defined by Gee as "spaces of affinity" within which people learn and actively participate, according to their skills and interests [15]. These are spaces that differ from formal educational contexts as they present provisional, innovative structures capable of responding to short-term needs and temporary interests [15]. It is the way we inhabit this space of the network which, as Carenzio [16] argues, defines the way in which we are citizens both on and off the screen. According to Meyrowitz [17], the revolutionary significance of the media lies in the fact that the medium and the representations of reality it conveys transform the social environment and that such changes can affect the behavior of individuals. For a "full and active participation in public life and in the community and in economic life" [18] it is necessary to provide for media education interventions to develop young people the digital citizenship skills necessary to become critical consumers, responsible digital content producers and aware surfers, as stated in the document on digital civic education, skills that allow us to face the challenges of the 21st century. Bertram and Bruce said that "Teens need to learn to integrate knowledge from multiple sources, including music, videos, online databases, and other media. They need to think critically about information that can be found almost instantly around the world. They need to participate. to the types of collaboration that the new communication and information technologies allow, and which require more and more" [15]. The school, therefore, as a place for the transmission of knowledge and for the expression of citizenship, for personal, social and cultural development and growth, must act as a mediator in the use and interpretation of the culture that young people produce through digital media [9]. The teacher is called to develop a critical awareness of the implications of the use of technologies in the new generations and it is no coincidence that digital competence implies critical thinking and ethical-social skills [19–21]. The promotion of global citizenship passes from actions aimed at promoting key competences related to critical thinking, active citizenship, holistic approach and complexity, collaborative practices, transformative learning and awareness and responsibility [2]. Computer and Information Literacy refers to the individual ability to use technologies in order to investigate, create contents, communicate and participate in the community [7]. Critical thinking and responsibility are the essential objectives to enable students to "identify, access, manage, integrate, evaluate, analyze and synthesize digital resources, build new knowledge, create media expressions and communicate with others in the context of life situations specific in order to allow constructive social actions and reflect on the process" [13]. Policies and research offer conceptual models - Web Literacy [22], MediaSmarts [23], DigComp [24] - useful for reflecting on the possibility of developing content based on *responsibility, security, freedom of expression* criteria [25].

As the DigCompEdu document [26] highlights, children and young people are born and grow up in a world characterized by a technological ubiquity that does not necessarily involve the possession of the skills necessary for the correct use of tools. The objective of national and European policies is to develop digital skills in order to make citizens active, critical and responsible users and producers in the use of technologies [4, 15].

3 Methodological Design

The promotion of an active and responsible citizen, of a global citizen, inevitably also passes through digital citizenship for which it is necessary to start digital civic education paths and schools are faced with the task of redesigning this teaching. With a view to starting the new teaching, a specific collaborative research-training project was created, funded by the Ministry of Education "National Plan for the promotion of the culture of legality", pursuant to art. 15 of the Ministerial Decree 851/2017, "At the school of citizenship. Vertical curriculum and evaluation of citizenship skills" in which it was possible to explore the forms of transposition of the knowledge included in this area of knowledge and hypothesize a conceptual matrix from which to derive specific curricular designs for the teaching of civic education, differentiated by grade of school.

The project carried out by the University of Bari (Italy), in cooperation with the CREMIT research group (University of Milan), UCIIM teachers' professional association and a national network of schools (N = 10; target: 72 teachers, 10 Headmasters). The project falls within the framework of professional teaching through the 'analysis of practice' devices and the collaborative research [27–30]. This Project aimed at design and realize a vertical curriculum of citizenship education and, alongside, to train teachers for its development also by constructing of scoring rubrics of citizenship competences. In order to explore the representations of teachers struggling with a transversal teaching that requires specific assessment, they were asked to respond to three assignments online with other teachers or individually:

1. the identification of a topic within the teaching of citizenship or civic education considered by teachers to be "indispensable" in a curriculum of this type and potentially developable in a vertical diachronic sense;
2. the proposal of one or more AU relating to the chosen theme;
3. the reasoned presentation of one or more citizenship or civic education projects already carried out in the last three years in the schools involved in the network.

84 text corpora were collected: No. 27 for the first assignment, No. 30 for the second and 27 for the third respectively. Professional writings [31] were analyzed with the Qualitative Data Analysis (QDA) procedure based on an inductive process rooted in the 'principle of fidelity of analysis' [32, 33] which led to the emergence Grounded Theory [32, 34–37]. The QDA analysis process was marked by the following phases: a) open coding - first open conceptualization of textual data in meaningful text units with identification of labels; b) axial coding - identification of frequent macro-categories, emerging from text strings; c) selective coding - analytical hierarchy among the identified macro-categories and emergence of the core categories. The validity of the analysis was ensured by triangulating the viewpoints of the researchers involved.

4 Results

Below we describe the results relating to an initial analysis of the documentary products of the teachers involved in the project. The first assignment - *Identify a theme within the scope of Civic Education that it considers useful to develop vertically, justifying the answer* - attempted to investigate what were the themes considered to be 'founding' in the teaching of civics with respect to the grade of the teachers' school. From Table 1 emerges a variety of themes attributable to the three pillars of teaching identified in the Guidelines (Annex A of MD 35 of 22 June 2020) [11]. There is little attention paid to education for digital citizenship, a useful topic identified in only one case. Popular topics are awareness of the diversity of reality related to respect and acceptance of the other (Table 2).

Table 1. Axial coding of the first delivery

I cycle of education	II cycle of education
Knowledge of the Constitution for the promotion of active citizenship Digital citizenship Human rights and promotion of the convention on the rights of the child Creative writing Educate on the importance of rules Human rights Reading education Environmental sustainability Sport Citizenship Importance of culture	History of the Constitution Electoral system and Democracy Respect for shared rules Educating for differences The State and International Relations Citizenship Supply-demand, market laws Addiction prevention Territory Work

Table 2. Axial coding of the first delivery (excerpts from textual analysis)

I cycle of education: themes	Excerpts from textual analysis
Knowledge of the constitution for the promotion of active citizenship	Education for the Constitution envisages the acquisition of knowledge and skills also through the educational contribution of the various fields of experience as far as pre-school is concerned, as well as of all the other areas and disciplines envisaged in the curricula of schools of all levels

(*continued*)

Table 2. (*continued*)

I cycle of education: themes	Excerpts from textual analysis
Digital citizenship	In the area of Constitution and Citizenship/Civic Education, we have chosen to develop the theme of 'digital citizenship', as it fits in with the planning of our Institute (PTOF 2019–22) aimed at promoting the development of transversal social and civic competences in the perspective of a vertical curriculum, which are part of the broader concept of promoting global citizenship, in order to form aware and responsible citizens in a modern, connected and interdependent society
Human rights and promotion of the convention on the rights of the child	The project stems from the implementation of a national action entitled promotion and diffusion of the Convention on Children's Rights, promoted by the Childhood and Adolescence Authority; whose main objective is to make more children aware, through playful-animative methods, of what is a right and a duty, starting with themselves and the performance of their daily lives
Creative writing	Playing with words lightens the heaviness of everyday school life and teaches how to turn limitations into strengths, difficulties into opportunities Starting from the assumption that the ordinary functioning of our language is a game we play using our memory to search for words and combine them with each other to produce sentences and utterances of various kinds, the CREATIVE WRITING PROJECT aims to use the game route to recover, consolidate and improve language learning
Educate on the importance of rules	Life at school is a great educational gymnasium from an ethical and social point of view: spaces, games, materials, time… Are and must be shared by all with equal opportunities. To respect this conviction and the pupils' need to feel good about themselves and others while avoiding conflict, a desire to share common rules was born in the third classes

(*continued*)

Table 2. (*continued*)

I cycle of education: themes	Excerpts from textual analysis
Human rights	"HUMAN RIGHTS" is the theme that was developed in the context of Constitution and Citizenship in the fifth classes of our school. The objective is to activate, stimulate and consciously exercise active citizenship in children and to develop the centrality and participation of pupils in the social context of their environment, to acquire a sense of identity and belonging to their community and to prepare for responsible growth and solidarity as 'citizens of the world'
Reading education	The second macro-area (Appointment in the library, Books are wings that teach you to fly, Invitation to reading) where the focus is on reading education as the construction of maps of sensations and emotions
Environmental sustainability	Under the guidance of the teachers of each class council, through the development of a specially drafted UdA, a path was followed with the pupils of the entire school community to explore the issues and problems related to the theme of environmental sustainability. In particular, an attempt was made to grasp the value of acquiring a style oriented towards energy saving, waste reduction and separate waste collection, also by reading specific texts, watching films and using resources available on the Internet. Experts from the sector were also invited to strengthen the school-territory-institutions link
Sport	Approaching the values that sport promotes awareness and acceptance of one's own and others' limits, ability to work as a team, education in mutual tolerance. These objectives are further amplified in the experience, for secondary school pupils, of the Student Championships: the confrontation with pupils from other institutions enables the students to exercise active citizenship skills by practicing fair play in sport
Citizenship	It is necessary to promote in young citizens (pre-school, primary school and secondary school pupils) the awareness of belonging to a social and institutional body that grows and changes over time and space and that guards the culture of respect and legality

(*continued*)

Table 2. (*continued*)

I cycle of education: themes	Excerpts from textual analysis
Importance of culture	"What is culture good for? It serves to improve people's souls, to make them reflect, to make them more tolerant of those who are different from them, thus to discover the value of democracy and solidarity, to drive out the impulses of violence. Therefore, democracy, i.e. the democratic state, has a primary interest in promoting culture, in expanding its roots and branches
II cycle of education: themes	Excerpts from textual analysis
History of the Constitution	Starting from the awareness of the high value that knowledge of the Constitution assumes today, it is deemed necessary to acquaint young people with the historical, institutional and ideological events that led to the ratification of the Italian Constitution as a document of democracy and a reference model for the construction of their personal, local and national identity
Electoral system and Democracy	Also interesting as an authentic task to train a student capable of critical thinking is the proposal by Prof. Ernesto Galli della Loggia to acquaint students with the history of the Constitution, because in order to talk about things one needs to know their history and illustrate the problems of democracy, asking a number of questions such as: 1) Does the idea that the majority must win seem right to you? 2) Democracy is caught between two poles, between formal equality and substantial freedom; 3) What is it that does not work in the mechanism of representation?
Respect for shared rules	A theme in the area of the Constitution and Civic Education that it is useful to develop vertically is RESPECT FOR SELF AND OTHERS, RESPECT FOR THE SHARED RULES. In fact, from an early age, with age-appropriate means, it is a duty, in a society where many families are separated, to make them understand the importance of respecting themselves and therefore others for peaceful and collaborative coexistence in order to build a humane society

(*continued*)

Table 2. (*continued*)

I cycle of education: themes	Excerpts from textual analysis
Educating for differences	The time in which we live is characterized by an increase in racism and violence between individuals and especially this can be seen among adolescents through social media. The school's task is to educate to respect differences and above all to grow up applying in everyday life the principle of equality recognized by Article 3 of the Constitution
The state and international relations	It is essential, in a multi-ethnic and composite society, that the child understands that, in addition to his or her own country, there is a supranational reality, both in the European sense and in a broader sense, which is the international scenario. After having acquired the concepts of: State, people, territory, nation, it is necessary to be able to understand that we are European citizens and citizens of the world and that we have rights and duties that derive from such 'citizenships' and that rights, in fact, are often found in universal Declarations and regulations dictated by several states
Citizenship	Citizenship education is a transversal and interdisciplinary task that cannot be 'confined' only within a single discipline or school cycle Citizenship education is still a major challenge for schools today and that is why we have chosen to raise awareness and raise awareness of the fundamental rules for proper civil coexistence and personal well-being
Supply-demand, market laws	The start of your business! You have an idea about a product or service for which you feel there is a market. The first thing you will have to do is to assess whether the basics of your idea will hold. Briefly sketch the product, outline the potential market, define the business concept and estimate the initial funding. The end product of Step I will be a "blueprint" of your product, market and business

(*continued*)

Table 2. *(continued)*

I cycle of education: themes	Excerpts from textual analysis
Addiction prevention	It seems to me that it is a theme relevant to Citizenship and Health and that it lends itself well to being dealt with vertically because it is good to get used to taking care of oneself from an early age; the theme can be tackled in a simple way in primary school and enriched as the students grow up with considerations of a legal/mathematical/historical nature. Unfortunately, the addictions we hear about in the news are varied, so the theme is more topical than ever and can be interpreted in various ways (prevention of addictions to drugs, alcohol, smoking, food, gambling, the web, etc.))
Territory	The theme I have chosen is Territory. Recent migratory dynamics to and from Italy end up too trivially in preconceived slogans, bans and broad discussions and divisions on who can or cannot, forgetting the human, sociological, cultural, environmental aspect of the territory Citizenship is linked to the territory, think of the diatribes on ius soli
Work	Work is a fundamental element in the life of every individual and therefore protected by the Constitution of our country; Article 4 emphasises its importance (…). Not only: work can be understood and understood as a tool for inclusion. However, work is not only synonymous with dignity, but often, on the contrary, can itself be a reason for human rights violations

For the second delivery it was decided to share an accompanying device for the design [28] and it was asked to decline the chosen theme in units of competence. Here (see Table 3 are some representative examples of the coding passage from labeling in the first phase, to the identification of text strings in the second and third and last phase, to the definition of the core categories (Table 4).

The third delivery involved the uploading to the platform of projects already carried out at school with the aim of photographing the state of the art of civic education teaching and bringing out the didactic action [38] underlying the practice of design.

Among the characterizing elements of the projects presented, in most of the documentary products analyzed, the choice of heuristic didactic strategies is highlighted. Both second cycle and first-cycle teachers prefer the following teaching strategies: cooperative learning, role playing, laboratory activities, guided debates.

In terms of skills, the teachers agree with the importance of making the student aware of "different points of view, of enhancing their own and others' abilities, managing

Table 3. Examples of steps from open coding to selective coding

Text unit	Open coding	Axial coding	Selective coding
The student participates in communicative exchanges (conversations, class or group discussions) with classmates and teachers and respecting the turn and formulating clear and relevant messages, in a register that is as appropriate as possible to the situation You listen and understand oral texts "direct" or "transmitted" by the media, capturing their meaning, main information and purpose	Development of communication skills Lexical relevance Understanding skills	Comprehension and proper use of the vocabulary Professional communication	Understanding and appropriate use of the professional vocabulary
Acquire the basics of professional communication and understand the importance of coordination between colleagues;	Professional communication		
It is aware that the human community is an expression of individual and cultural diversity to be known and appreciated from a perspective of mutual respect	Awareness of diversity Respect	Citizen aware of diversity and respectful Behavior appropriate to the circumstances	Conscious citizen and respectful of diversity even in work contexts
The pupil knows his rights and duties as a student and citizen	Conscious citizen		

(*continued*)

Table 3. (*continued*)

Text unit	Open coding	Axial coding	Selective coding
The pupil recognizes and appreciates cultural diversity with a view to dialogue and mutual respect	Awareness and respect for diversity		
The student identifies the rules and responsibilities of each	Rules and responsibilities		
Behave in a correct manner and be able to fit into a work group respecting its rules and hierarchy	Behavior appropriate to work circumstances		
Respect shared rules collaborate with others	Respect for the rules		
Assume your responsibilities, ask for help when you are in difficulty and know how to provide help to those who ask for it	Ask for help		

Table 4. Participating schools and core categories.

Partner schools	Core category
I.C. Don Lorenzo Milani Bari (Lead School) I.S. Michelangelo Bari	Constitution
I.C. Volterra (PI)	Territory
14 °C.D. Re David Bari	Market
I.I.S. Pacinotti Bagnone (MS)	Human Rights
I.C. Capozzi-Galilei Valenzano (BA)	Sustainability
I.T.T. Panetti-Pitagora (BA)	Affectivity
Alberotanza Institute Bari	Digital citizenship
I.T.E. E. Tosi – Busto Arstizio (VA)	Sports
I.C. G. Ungaretti, Melzo (MI)	Work

conflicts, contributing to common learning and the realization of collective activities, in recognition of the fundamental rights of others". Therefore, there is a need for planning in a situation that creates the conditions for developing reflective capacities.

Three cultural axes emerged from the analysis as a whole for the development of a conceptual matrix of civic education teaching:

1. a juridical-socio-political axis (aimed at developing skills aimed at making people learn the universal and substantial nature of the rights and duties of citizenship);
2. an affective-moral axis (aimed at eco-sustainable education and strengthening of feeling of cosmopolitan solidarity which is the foundation of a theory of education for citizenship);
3. a historical-geographical-technological/scientific axis (aimed at making people learn that only by knowing and recognizing one's own identity - historical, anthropological, religious, technological-scientific, in short: cultural in the full sense - is it possible to understand identity of the other and become companions in the common protection of the terrestrial identity) (Table 5).

Table 5. Conceptual matrix of civic education teaching: cultural axes

Juridical-socio-political axes	Affective-moral axis for eco-sustainability	Historical-geographical-technological/scientific axis
1. The fundamental principles of the Constitution	1. The 2030 Agenda for Sustainable Development	1. Digital citizenship: what it is, what its potential is, what skills is requires
2. Elements of the history of the Constitution (how it was born, who wrote it)	2. Renewable and non-renewable energy resources: basic principles of economics circular	2. Digital identity
3. Basic concepts concerning the institutions of the Italian State, the European Union and international organizations	3. Education to legality and contrast to the mafias	3. Technologies and digital environments for civic participation
4. Fundamental elements of law, with particular regard to labor law	4. Acceptance of the role of the law	4. The history of the Italian flag and the anthem national

(continued)

Table 5. (*continued*)

Juridical-socio-political axes	Affective-moral axis for eco-sustainability	Historical-geographical-technological/scientific axis
5. Basic elements of training in civil protection	5. The protection of personal and public health: principles of hygiene and of prevention	5. The productions and the territorial excellence and Italian agri-food
6. Volunteer work and civil service	6. Education to respect in all its forms (of the dignity of all minorities, of woman, of rights, duties, cultural assets, etc.)	6. Cultural and territorial differences in relation to the micro (local), meso (national) and macro level (global)
7. The "generations" of human rights		

5 Expected Conclusions/Findings

The analysis of the didactic documentation produced by the schools involved shows:

- the lack of themes that are now considered central within the citizenship education policy: 'digital citizenship' and the responsible use of ICT [11, 12, 16, 24, 26, 41], 'protection' of cultural heritage' [39], affective education [1], the evaluation of civic competences [1, 5];
- the main difficulties of teachers in designing a vertical citizenship curriculum (tendency towards solitary planning, poor approach to interdisciplinarity etc.) as useful indicators to direct the training intervention.
- the need for in-depth training on soft skills (moreover strongly embedded in the discourse of civic education teaching) and on teaching methodologies of an active type on the methodological side.

Digital citizenship is defined in Article 5 of Law no. 92 of 20 August 2019 as "the ability of an individual to participate in the social, political and economic life of the country using technological tools". The promotion of an active and responsible citizen, of a global citizen, inevitably also passes through digital citizenship for which it is necessary to start digital civic education paths. The task of educators is to prepare students for the future by promoting digital literacy processes. To set up a media literacy path that starts from kindergarten and that is transversal to all disciplines; who is able to create a space in which to be able to produce meaning, elaborate meanings, collaborate and participate in order to appropriate digital in a correct way, it is necessary to start from the system of skills that students must develop so that they can relate to and face the complexities of today's information society and be able to "make conscious and responsible use of virtual media" as can be seen from the guidelines of civic education. Furthermore, in order to overcome the difficulties of teachers, it is necessary to rethink the design and construction of the digital citizenship curriculum starting from conditions of collegiality. The curricula of civic and digital education, in fact, are characterized by a disciplinary transversality that requires the integration and contribution of different professional skills [1]. The data collected feeds the debate on citizenship education policy and teacher training, in particular on how to integrate digital citizenship education into the interdisciplinary curriculum.

Promoting critical thinking, ethical-social skills and awareness of the implications of their use of technology through digital citizenship education represents one of the main objectives of the current European Policy Cooperation.

Promoting an active and responsible citizen through digital citizenship requires:

- the creation of a space in which to produce meaning, elaborate meanings, collaborate and participate in appropriating digital in a correct way;
- starting from the system of competences that students must develop in order to relate to and face the complexities of the information society;
- the rethinking of the design and construction of the citizenship and digital citizenship curriculum starting from the conditions of collegiality;

The curricular construction of this teaching must be a didactic construction and leverage on some principles such as:

- decision-making in knowing how to organize and set up active learning environments [1], i.e. experiences, projects, case studies aimed at soliciting student participation. The civic mindset is based, in fact, on participatory, cooperative and active didactic routines;
- selectivity: a curriculum of E.C. it does not presuppose the "transfer" of the entire civic and constitutional culture to the student but only a reasoned selection of contents that must be made a means of experiences aimed at the goals of competences.
- multimodal didactic mediation: a curriculum of E.C. it is the result of the transposing "intelligence" of the teacher who organizes all the contingencies for student, or to motivate, delight, persuade students' willingness to learn this;
- educational mediation: a curriculum of E.C. can achieve the effective achievement of its objectives only through an "educational action" of the teacher [40];
- collegiality: a curriculum of E.C. it has the meaning of its approach in disciplinary transversality [1].

Educating in citizenship and responsibility is possible through reflective paths of the person that lead back to the subject himself [41]. And the school must rethink its actions, readjust the contents and forms of teaching, not by putting in place a restrictive mediation towards the media (imparting rules of use) and demonization but by implementing an active mediation of online safety (advice on how to use the internet safely, help to manage problematic situations) and above all it must integrate technology into teaching to teach the media through the media, in order to develop critical and responsible thinking that allows them to become active and participating citizens.

References

1. Perla, L.: L'insegnamento dell'educazione civica: prodromi educativo-didattici e "prove tecniche di curriculo". Nuova Second. **10**(XXXVII), 222–238 (2020)
2. UNESCO: Educazione alla cittadinanza globale. Temi e obiettivi di apprendimento. Organizzazione delle Nazioni Unite per l'Educazione, la Scienza e la Cultura (2018)
3. Sicurello, R.: Educazione alla cittadinanza: significati, linee di ricerca, finalità e pratiche didattiche. Foro Educ. **14**(20), 71–103 (2016)
4. Raccomandazione 2018/C 189/01 del Consiglio Europeo, 22 maggio 2018. Competenze chiave per l'apprendimento permanente. https://eur-lex.europa.eu/legal-content/IT/TXT/PDF/?uri=CELEX:32018H0604(01)
5. Perla, L., Agrati, L.S., Vinci, V.: Vertical curriculum design and evaluation of citizenship skills. In: Andron, D., et al. (eds.) Education Beyond the Crisis. New Skills, Children's Right and Teaching Context. Sense/Brill, London (2020)
6. Schulz, W., Ainley, J., Fraillon, J., Losito, B., Agrus, G.: IEA International Civic and Citizenship Education Study 2016: Assessment framework. Springer, Cham (2016). https://www.springer.com/gb/book/9783319393568. Accessed 05 Dec 2021
7. Fraillon, J., Ainley, J., Schulz, W., Duckworth, D., Friedman, T.: IEA International Computer and Information Literacy Study 2018 Assessment Framework. Springer, Cham (2019). https://doi.org/10.1007/978-3-030-19389-8
8. Kahne, J., Middaugh, E., Allen, D.: Youth, new media and the rise of participatory politics. YPP Research Network Working Paper #1. Youth and Participatory Politics Research Network, Oakland, CA, USA (2014)
9. Rivoltella, P.C.: Digital Education Day – le dieci tesi di Rivoltella (2015). https://medium.com/il-digitale-e-la-scuola/il-digital-education-day-e-le-dieci-tesi-di-rivoltella-su-scuola-e-tecnologie-6f21e4daaf71
10. Castells, M.: La città delle reti. Marsilio, Venezia (2004)
11. MIUR. Ministero dell'Istruzione, dell'Università e della Ricerca. Linee guida per l'insegnamento dell'educazione civica (2020). https://www.miur.gov.it/documents/20182/0/m_pi.AOOGABMI.Registro+Decreti%28R%29.0000035.22-06-2020.pdf/8e785f33-2898-95b1-7326-dcc368228f98?t=1592916355595
12. Ricciardi, M.: Cittadini nell'era digitale. In: Limone, P. (ed.) Media, tecnologie e scuola. Per una nuova Cittadinanza Digitale. Progedit, Bari (2016)
13. Bonaiuti, G., Calvani, A., Menichetti, L., Vivanet, G.: Le tecnologie educative. Carocci Editore, Roma (2017)
14. Rivoltella, P.C., Ardizzone, P.: La media education, fra tradizione e sfida del presente. New Media Educ. anno **LII**(15), 50–52 (2007)
15. Jenkins, H.: Convergence Culture: Where Old and New Media Collide. New York University Press, New York (2006)
16. Carenzio, A.: Cittadinanza digitale. Un modello di ricerca-intervento nella scuola. In: Limone, P. (ed.) Media, Tecnologie e Scuola. Per una nuova Cittadinanza Digitale. Progedit, Bari (2012)
17. Meyrowitz, J.: Oltre il senso del luogo. Baskerville (1995)
18. New London Group: A Pedagogy of Multiliteracies: designing social futures. Harv. Educ. Rev. **66**, 60–92 (1996

19. Ala-Mutka, K.: Mapping digital competence: towards a conceptual understanding. JRC-IPTS, Seville (2011). http://ipts.jrc.ec.europa.eu/publications/pub.cfm?id=4699. Accessed 05 Dec 2021
20. Janssen, J., Stoyanov, S.: Online consultation on experts' views on digital competence. JRC-IPTS, Seville (2012)
21. Calvani, A.: Le TIC nella scuola: dieci raccomandazioni per i policy maker. Form@re - Open J. Formazione Rete **13**(4), 30–46 (2013)
22. Mozilla Foundation Web Literacy, in learning.mozilla.org/en-US/web-literacy (2013). Accessed 05 Dec 2021
23. Hoechsmann, M., Dewaard, H.: Mapping digital literacy policy and practice in the canadian education landscape, MediaSmarts (2015). https://mediasmarts.ca/teacher-resources/digital-literacy-framework/mapping-digital-literacy-policy-practice-canadian-education-landscape. Accessed 05 Dec 2021
24. Ferrari, A.: Digital competence in practice: an analysis of frameworks. Institute for Prospective Technological Studies, Seville (2012). http://ftp.jrc.es/EURdoc/JRC68116.pdf. (Ver. 01 Apr 2013). Accessed 05 Dec 2021
25. Perla, L., Agrati, L.S., Vinci, V.: The 'supply chain' of teachers' digital skills training. The TPACK traceability in the teachers' trainers. In: GRIAL Research Group (ed.) Proceedings TEEM'18 Sixth International Conference on Technological Ecosystems for Enhancing Multiculturality, Salamanca, Spain, 24–26 October 2018, pp. 604–612 (2018)
26. Redecker, C., Punie, Y.: European framework for the digital competence of educators: DigCompEdu. Joint Research Centre (JRC) Science for Policy report (2017)
27. Vinatier, I., Altet, M.: Analyser et comprendre la pratique enseignante. PUR, Rennes (2008)
28. Perla, L. (ed.): I Nuovi Licei alla prova delle competenze. Per una progettazione nel biennio. Pensa MultiMedia, Lecce (2014)
29. Perla, L. (ed.): Valutare per valorizzare. La documentazione per il miglioramento di scuola, insegnanti, studenti. Morcelliana, Brescia (2019)
30. Maubant, P., Martineau, S. (eds.): Fondements des pratiques professionnelles des enseignants. Presses de l'Université d'Ottawa, Ottawa (2011)
31. Perla, L.: Scritture professionali. Metodi per la formazione. Progedit, Bari (2012)
32. Mortari, L.: Cultura della ricerca e pedagogia. Prospettive epistemologiche. Carocci, Roma (2007)
33. Perla, L.: Didattica dell'implicito. Ciò che l'insegnante non sa. La Scuola, Brescia (2010)
34. Strauss, A.L., Corbin, J.M.: Basics of Qualitative Research: Grounded Theory Procedures and Techniques. Sage Publications, London (1990)
35. Charmaz, K.: Grounded theory in the 21° century. In: Denzin, N.K., Lincoln, Y.S. (eds) Handbook of Qualitative Research. Sage, Thousand Oaks (2005)
36. Tarozzi, M.: Che cos'è la grounded theory? Carocci, Roma (2008)
37. Mortari, L.: Cercare il rigore metodologico per una ricerca pedagogica scientificamente fondata. Educ. Sci. Soc. **1**(1), 143–156 (2010)
38. Rivoltella, P.C., Rossi, P.G.: L'agire didattico. Manuale per l'insegnante. La Scuola, Brescia (2017)
39. CE: Recommendation of the Committee of Ministers to member States on the European Cultural Heritage Strategy for the 21st century. Council of Europe Publishing, Strasbourg (2018). https://rm.coe.int/16806f6a03
40. Perla, L., Riva, M.G. (eds.): L'agire educativo: manuale per educatori e operatori socio-assistenziali. La Scuola, Brescia (2016)
41. Perfetti, S.: Nuovi Media e Cittadinanza Digitale. La scuola del ventunesimo secolo come luogo per la democrazia. Ricerche di Pedagogia e Didattica. J. Theories Res. Educ. **10**(2), 131–142 (2015)

Study and Analysis on the Student Response System Adoption: Experimentation in a Programming Course

Fabio Sorrentino[1(✉)] and Giovanni Bonaiuti[2]

[1] Department of Mathematics and Computer Science, University of Cagliari, Cagliari, Italy
fabio.sorrentino@unica.it

[2] Department of Literature, Languages and Cultural Heritage, University of Cagliari, Cagliari, Italy

Abstract. Understanding the impact of different types of questions on learning is still an open problem in the literature. Many tools allow teachers to ask different kinds of questions, such as closed (multiple-choice, true/false, associations, etc.) and open (tag clouds, short notes). Our work aims to compare the effect of open and closed questions on student learning. To analyse the differences in learning results between the two types of question approaches, we carried an experiment in a Programming course (Programming 1 - Italian academic course in a Bachelor of Computer Science degree), dividing the students into two groups. During the first half of the course, we asked multiple-choice questions to the students in the first group, whereas we used an open-ended approach for the students of the second one. In the second part of the course, we inverted the modalities. For this work, carried out in the 2018/19 academic year, we used Mentimeter as Student Response System (SRS). We believe that identifying the right balance between explanation and verification and understanding the effects of the different evaluation types represent a significant contribution to the debate on formative evaluation in complex contexts. This contribution could be helpful in university classrooms where the high number of students does not allow easy interaction. Thanks to the data analysis and relative charts presented in this work, the authors share the learned lesson and offer several discussion points raising new questions that have to be addressed yet.

Keywords: Learner response systems · Student-centered lecture · Questioning · Feedback

1 Introduction

This paper aims to compare the effect of open and closed questions on student learning.

To analyze the differences in learning results between the two types of question approaches, we carried an experiment in a computer science course ("Programming course") held at the University of Cagliari. Thanks to the data analysis and relative charts presented in this work, the authors share the learned lesson and offer several discussion points raising new questions that have to be addressed yet.

M. Ranieri et al. (Eds.): ATEE 2021, CCIS 1649, pp. 88–99, 2022.
https://doi.org/10.1007/978-3-031-20777-8_7

In detail, in Sect. 2, readers will find the theoretical framework where the scientific question finds its foundation. Previous and related works that inspired the experimentation are listed and highlighted. In Sect. 3, the author discusses the method and the learning environment, giving more details on the tools, the different kinds of questions, and the course where the experiment took place. In Sect. 4, the measurement methodology is presented, while in Sect. 5, the data analysis is deeply discussed. Finally, in Sect. 6, the lesson learned and future work are given to the reader.

2 Literature Review and Theoretical Framework

Higher education classrooms are still dominated by teacher talk. However, research indicates that the most important task for teachers is to listen [1], understanding which prior knowledge students are using and the nature and extent of the gap between where they are and where they need to be [2]. Student Response Systems (SRS), now in the form of mobile applications, could represent an exciting opportunity to increase student involvement and cognitive activation [3–5]. SRS improves teachers' conduct of formative assessments, identifies misconceptions, and fosters students to respond without peer pressure, exceptionally when their anonymity is preserved [6].

There has been a considerable amount of research work on the use of SRSs. These tools underline the importance of questions [7], teacher feedback management, and formative evaluation [1]. Mayer and colleagues [8] conducted a series of studies on the effect of immediate response to feedback and promoting active participation, detecting errors and misunderstandings, supporting knowledge organization of the selected material, and facilitating memorization and integration of the material with prior knowledge. Their work shows positive effects from asking students to answer questions during the lecture ($ES = 0.40$), probably due to students paying more attention to be able to answer questions as well as being constantly stimulated to be active.

Mobile-based SRSs are an evolution of clickers. Clickers only allowed closed answers, such as true-false or multiple choice. Today, applications such as Mentimeter allow teachers to also collect open answers in various formats (short texts and word lists). It is, therefore, a problem of how to choose between the different types of questions.

What are the differences in terms of involvement and learning? It is already known that answering closed-ended questions through a device improves student participation and performance. Conversely, few studies have been done on the use of SRS with open questions.

A survey design study [9] was conducted to investigate students' engagement when using open-ended SRS during class time; findings of this study suggest that the use of open-ended questions positively impacts students' engagement, motivation, and learning in an undergraduate-level course. This study also found interesting shifts in students' perceptions about their role as learners and their instructor's role in the classroom, but many questions still remain open.

We suppose that it comes from the fact that students are more focused on concepts and definitions to deal with pending verification. We believe that open-ended questions will increase the ability to rework the concepts [8], but, at the same time, it could increase the risk of cognitive load [10].

Several literature studies investigating the benefits of the SRS indicated that they improve students' academic performance, at least in some limited areas [11, 12]. Students' performance can easily be measured by learning achievement in specific topics, which is more related to mastery-based learning goals [13]. Moreover, students' academic performance may be affected positively by their active engagement during the lecture [14].

Engagement consists of a strong connection between different school players: students, teachers, families, and schools. Student engagement is a crucial element of creating a positive learning environment, and it can take benefits from active learning. Felder and Brent [15] describe active learning as "anything course-related that all students in a classroom are called upon to do other than simply watching, listening, and taking notes". Active learning can improve student engagement and can positively impact student learning.

Active learning focuses on how students learn, not just on what they learn. As discussed in [16], active learning is "generally defined as any instructional method that engages students in the learning process. In short, active learning requires students to do meaningful learning activities and think about what they are doing". It is possible to put the active learning principles into action with the help of technology and, in particular, through student response systems (SRS).

The current consensus is that tools like SRS positively impact students' cognition, attitudes, and behaviors in learning activities [17]. These aspects lead to better learning achievement, higher motivation to learn, higher self-efficacy, and more participation.

3 Method and Learning Environment

As discussed in Sect. 2, student involvement plays the main role in learning activities. To improve this, teachers can use several tools and techniques. One of the tools at their disposal is a student response system.

These tools are now available on web platforms, smartphones, and dedicated devices, thanks to software development. Their adoption could represent an exciting opportunity to increase student involvement and cognitive activation.

3.1 Mentimeter

Among many alternatives, we adopted for the entire experiment the presentation tool Mentimeter [18]. It includes this feature and grants large portability and anonymity. This proposed work started from three specific questions: i) "how can we improve the involvement of students during classes?", ii) "Can we facilitate their learning experience?" and iii) "are questions at the end of the lesson enough?".

We decided to set up an environment adopting a student response system as a support tool. Since understanding the impact of different questions on learning is still an open problem in the literature, we decided to use both open and closed questions.

3.2 Open and Closed Questions

Open questions allow participants to answer in their own words; closed questions require students to select a response from a specific set of options. One practical advantage of closed questions is that the answers are automatically stored as numeric or alphabetic values.

On the other side, they can be problematic from a measurement perspective if the predetermined categories are not exhaustive or influence students. On the contrary, the open ones do need to be coded into categories after the test. Our work aims to compare the effect of open and closed questions on student learning.

3.3 The Course

The experiment was carried out during the "Programming Language 1" course at the University of Cagliari within the Computer Science degree. Teachers have never used such tools during lectures.

Two modules make up the course: the first focuses on the theory of programming languages, while the second part comprises 24 lectures, 3 h each, focusing on laboratory activities. Fourteen of these twenty-four lectures concern the practical part of the laboratory (mainly coding activities).

These lectures are where the experiment took place, and it was a two-month length experiment. Course objectives are related to 1) reading C programs of small complexity and understanding why they are based on the code itself and the associated comments, 2) designing small C applications starting from the guidelines or building over existing code, 3) developing independently, for the design and implementation choices, the final project from the specifications provided, and 4) present the project at the end of the course by discussing the design and implementation choices.

The content of the course is relatively standard for a programming course. We discussed every aspect of the language, from the algorithm to the design of the program. Step by step, from the declaration of variables to the use of pointers, students learn to write and execute medium-complexity projects in the C language.

Every year, 150 students are enrolled in the Computer Sciences degree, a course of the first semester of the first year. For the experiment, and due to the available places in the laboratory, we decided to split the list of students into two groups using their student id: even ids have formed group A, and the others formed the B group. In the end, we made two groups with a total of one hundred and forty-five students. They had different backgrounds, only 10% of them were females, and the average age was 20. The two groups, having been formed by random extraction, are therefore to be considered equivalent.

Each group had a different teacher. We adopted the same program, same order of contents, same pace: two lessons every week. From the 1st lesson to the 7th one, the first group answered open questions; in the meantime, group B answered closed questions. We switched the modality after these seven lessons, so group A answered closed questions while group B opened ones. Changing the answer modality but not teachers allowed us to ensure that the teachers' skills and behaviors were not influent during the entire experiment. This switch also allowed us to investigate the effect of changing the modality from one day to the other and see students' reactions (some effects are discussed in Sect. 5.1).

It's important to say that the same questions were provided; the only difference was the answer modality. For each lesson, we submitted three different questions concerning the explained topics. In total, we proposed and analysed 42 questions.

I.e., during lesson number six, we asked students what the aim of the "return" statement was. Group A answered without any proposed alternative, while students in group B selected one of the given alternatives: A) ends the execution of the function; B) it represents the type of the return value; C) Ends the execution of a function, and returns a value/the control to the calling function; D) Ends the executions of a void procedure and return the value to the main function;

To have a standard approach, we agreed on the following points before starting the experiment: i) have the Q/A section only at the end of the lesson, reserving 15 min: 1 min to give the answer and four minutes to discuss it; ii) propose three questions per lesson on the most complex topics; iii) keep code-related questions as simple as possible due to the constraint of 1 min; iv) let students answer anonymously.

4 Measurement and Methodology

One of the first critical points to prepare a valuable dataset for data analysis was to adopt an excellent way to compare such different modalities. Closed questions can be easily categorised, but open questions cannot. Given answers to open questions need to be coded into categories. For each collection of open question answers, the author labeled each answer as correct or wrong (Fig. 1).

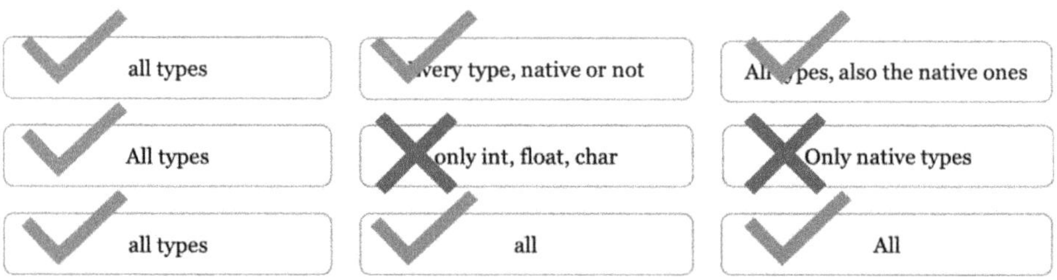

Fig. 1. An example of labelling of the answers given to the question: "**Which types are allowed in a new declared Struct?**".

This part was one of the most time-consuming of the experiment, but this approach allowed authors to determine the number of correct answers regarding the students' responses. Having such data allowed authors to analyse students' engagement, the correctness of answers, solutions trends correlated with the grades given during their courses' examinations.

5 Data Analysis

At the end of the experiment and data collection, a pre-processing phase allows authors to create a unique spreadsheet with all the raw data. Thanks to this spreadsheet, it has been possible to create several charts.

5.1 Students' Participation

The first one Fig. 2 is related to the percentage of participants who answered the proposed questions—data represents the number of correct and wrong answers given by attendees. Answering was not mandatory; we left the decision to students. No pressure, only voluntary answers. In this chart, in light purple, you'll see the second group, B. The light green is the first group.

After seven lessons, as we said before, we switched the modality. As you can see, the main difference is that group B, which started with closed questions and then switched to open questions, shows a negative trend. It started with 100%, which means that all students present in the laboratory answered the first question of the first lesson, then it reached its bottom during lesson number twelve. That lesson was quite complex, and only 25% of students answered the first question—the same behavior in the second and third. After that lesson, the trend continued pretty similarly to the other group.

On the contrary, group A maintains almost the same trend during the entire experiment.

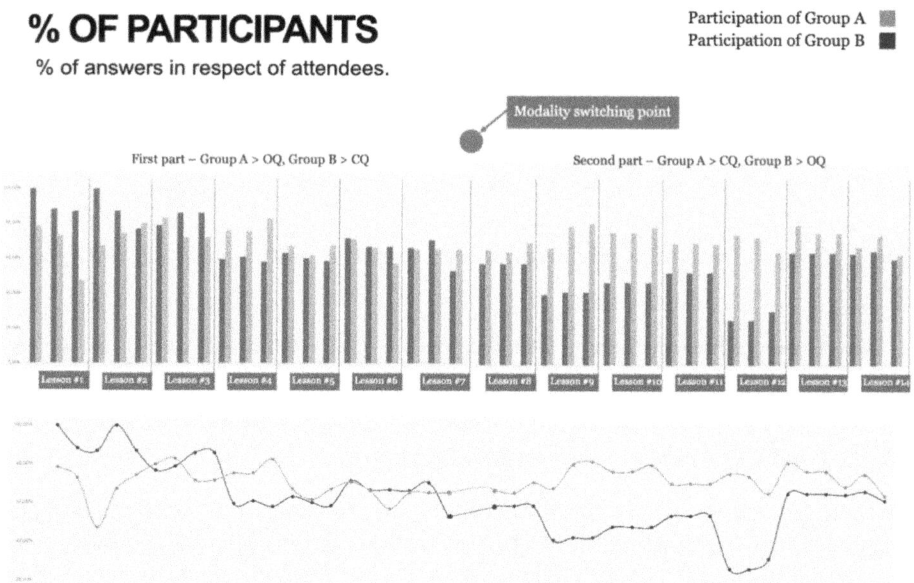

Fig. 2. Percentage of participant, number of answers in respect of attendees. (Color figure online)

This trend could be explained due to cognitive effort. Given that open questions require a higher effort from the students, they can be perceived as more demanding than closed ones. Passing from accessible to difficult questions will probably cause a sense of frustration in students; it leads them to not answer at all.

No changes seem to affect the first group that passed from difficult to easy ones. In general, we noted that closed questions guarantee higher participation of students. We can also state that open questions show a higher percentage of correct answers.

5.2 Correct Answers Comparisons

Comparing the correctness of the answers Fig. 3, we can see that there are no fundamental differences between the total score of the first and second groups. But if we look at the comparison of the two modalities, we'll see that there is a significant difference between open and closed questions in both groups.

It's worth noting that group B moved from 70% of correct answers to 40% after the switching point, dropping 30%. The drop is heavier than the one shown in group A, which is lower than 10%.

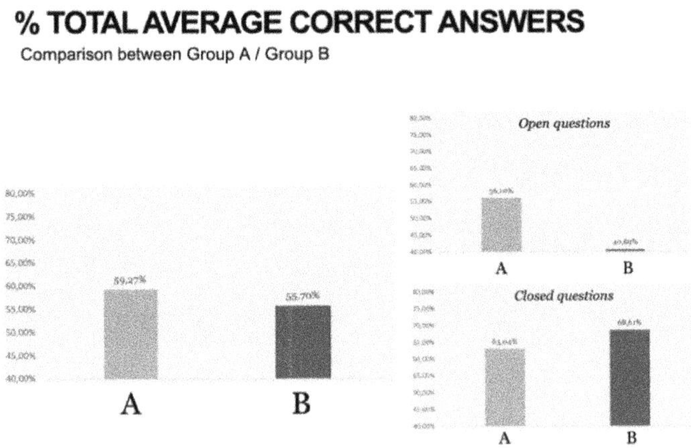

Fig. 3. Comparison between general correct answers ratio and different modalities (OQ, CQ).

This trend could be correlated with the previous chart: with open questions, we have a low percentage of answers and, at the same time, a lower percentage of correct answers.

5.3 OQ and CQ Answers' Correctness Trends

We then decided to analyse the trend of the two modalities Fig. 4. In orange, open questions; in blue the closed ones. As you can see, the majority of questions shows better result in closed questions. Only four times, out of 42 questions, the chart shows better results for open questions. In 15 of them, we see a significant difference between the two modalities.

The result is more evident in next chart Fig. 5. We received 65% of correct answers in closed ones, while around 50% in open questions.

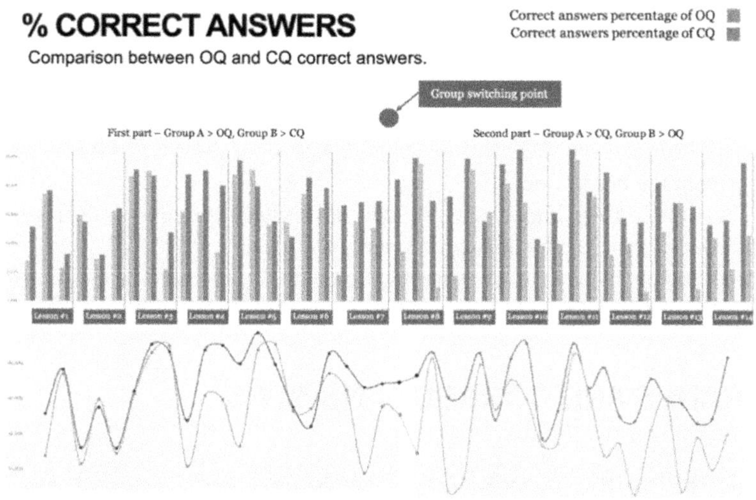

Fig. 4. Comparison between closed and open questions.

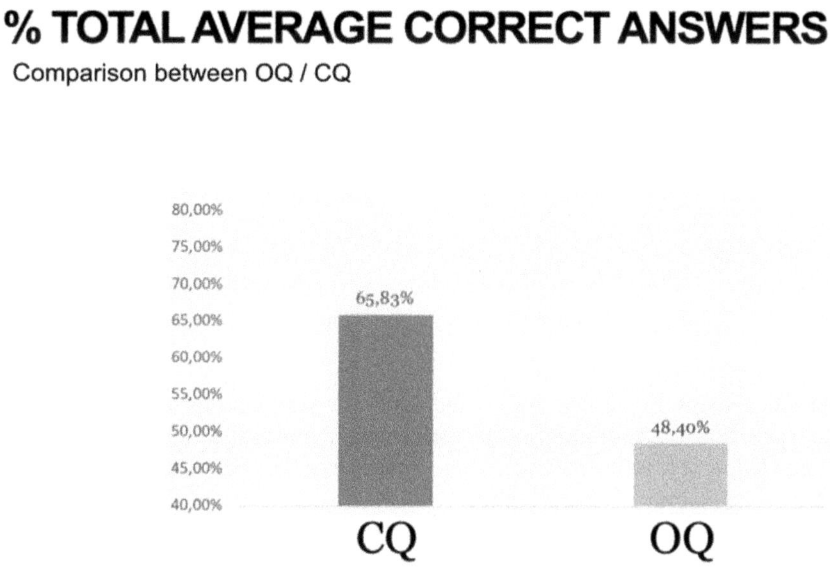

Fig. 5. Comparison between closed and open questions (total average).

5.4 OQ and CQ Answers' Correctness Trends

We then decided to compare the correctness of answers with the grades obtained by the students during the course Fig. 6.

It is essential to say that mid-term evaluation is a coding exercise, not a written test nor a quiz.

As you can see, we have group A on the left, on the right, group B. During the first part of the course, students in group A, which started with open questions, got higher grades regarding the correct answers given during the classes. There is a fundamental gap between these values.

This gap is almost invisible for the second section of the chart. Grades and correct answers percentage are in line.

This phenomenon also happens in group B; the higher gap occurred during the second part of the course, where they answered open questions.

Due to this analysis, we can say that both open or closed could be a tool to anticipate the learning evaluation phase, but they do not appear to differ in boosting the results.

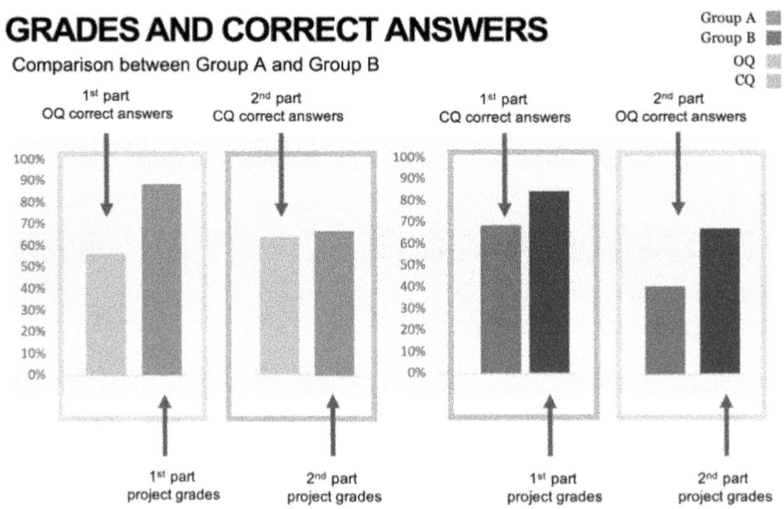

Fig. 6. Comparison between grades and correct answers.

We can also see Fig. 7 that grades and correct answers are pretty similar during the entire experiment for both groups. Data shows no significant differences. It means that their knowledge, at least the average, is the same even if they adopted different modalities regarding the two parts of the program.

5.5 OQ and CQ Answers' Correctness Trends

We also compared the results obtained using the student response system and the one we got the year before where we didn't use them Fig. 8. In grey, you have the previous academic year; in yellow, the one of the experiments.

It's visible that results improved massively during the first part, Q1, and Q2 exam, while in the second part, Q3 and Q4 exam, the result seems better without adopting such kind of systems.

It is clear that during the first parts of the course, we discussed more accessible topics, more based on the fundamentals of programming languages.

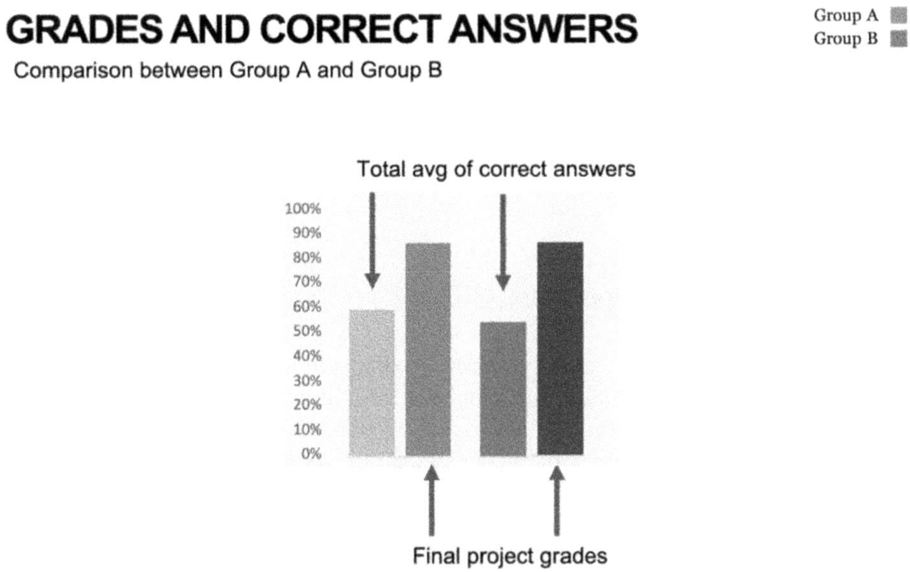

Fig. 7. Comparison between grades and correct answers (total average).

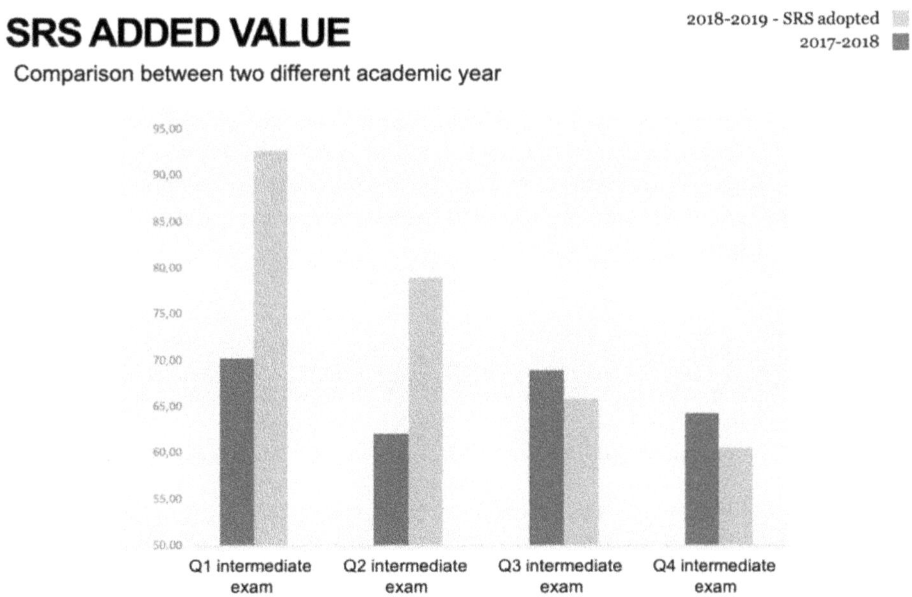

Fig. 8. Comparison between grades of two different academic years.

For these topics, Mentimeter gives us an excellent hand for keeping students motivated and on track.

Thanks to its anonymity, students tend to actively participate and give honest answers which are always helpful for teachers to adjust in real time how they are approaching and providing information.

But the tool seems useless when the subject starts to be complex and requires more aspects related to problem-solving and coding by using complex approaches and skills.

It's worth noting that we adopted the same program, content, examination approach, and difficulty of exams.

6 Conclusion and Future Work

After this experiment, we also can give several considerations. In general, if the answers are shown in real-time, the flock effect should affect students, and if the answers to open questions are shown in real-time, students tend to write comments or responses out of topic. Concerning the complexity of the question, if the question is complex, the number of replies drops more heavily in open questions. Student response systems help students avoid frustration at the beginning and engage them by giving them a chance to voice their knowledge and actively participate in the lecture.

Several discussions were raised during the Q/A sessions, and it was significant for the teacher to get real-time feedback. SRS increase knowledge retention, at least during the less complex part of the program. Last but not least, it requires more effort on the teacher's side, so teachers have to be prepared for it.

This work could be used as a touchstone for further research and, at the same time, as a starting point to deepen the study of understanding the adoption of open and closed questions. It could also be used to facilitate learning and knowledge retention in the programming language teachings and more. A follow-up of this study was planned before the pandemic situation related to C19, but data have been discarded due to extremely different and intermittent setup (online and blended). A new experiment will take place during the next academic year.

References

1. Hattie, J.: Visible Learning: A Synthesis of over 800 Meta-analyses Relating to Achievement. Routledge, London (2008)
2. Hattie, J.: Visible Learning for Teachers: Maximizing Impact on Learning. Routledge, London (2012)
3. Caldwell, J.: Clickers in the large classroom: current research and best-practice tips. CBE—Life Sci. Educ. **6**(1), 9–20 (2007)
4. Fies, C., Marshall, J.: Classroom response systems: a review of the literature. J. Sci. Educ. Technol. **15**(1), 101–109 (2006)
5. Judson, E., Daiyo, S.: Learning from past and present: electronic response systems in college lecture halls. J. Comput. Math. Sci. Teach. **21**(2), 167–181 (2002)
6. Freeman, M., Blayney, P., Ginns, P.: Anonymity and in class learning: the case for electronic response systems. Australas. J. Educ. Technol. **22**(4), 568–580 (2006)
7. Campbell, J., Mayer, R.E.: Questioning as an instructional method: does it affect learning from lectures? Appl. Cogn. Psychol.: Off. J. Soc. Appl. Res. Mem. Cogn. **23**(6), 747–759 (2009)

8. Mayer, R.E.: Clickers in college classrooms: fostering learning with questioning methods in large lecture classes. Contemp. Educ. Psychol. **34**(1), 51–57 (2009)
9. Kietzig, A.M., Orjuela-Laverde, M.C.: Increasing student engagement in class using an open-ended student response system. In: Proceedings of the Canadian Engineering Education Association, pp. 4–5 (2015)
10. Kirschner, P.A.: Cognitive load theory: implications of cognitive load theory on the design of learning, pp. 1–10 (2002)
11. Hung, H.: Clickers in the flipped classroom: bring your own device (BYOD) to promote student learning. Interact. Learn. Environ. **25**(8), 983–995 (2017)
12. Sun, J.C.: Influence of polling technologies on student engagement: an analysis of student motivation, academic performance, and brainwave data. Comput. Educ. **72**, 983–995 (2014)
13. Nicholls, J.G.: Achievement motivation: conceptions of ability, subjective experience, task choice, and performance. Psychol. Rev. **91**(3), 328 (1984)
14. Johnson, G.M.: Student alienation, academic achievement, and WebCT use. J. Educ. Technol. Soc. **8**(2), 179–189 (2005)
15. Felder, R.M., Brent, R.: Active learning: an introduction. ASQ High. Educ. Brief **2**(4), 983–995 (2009)
16. Prince, M.: Does active learning work? A review of the research. J. Eng. Educ. **93**(3), 223–231 (2004)
17. Hunsu, N.J., Adesope, O., Bayly, D.J.: A meta-analysis of the effects of audience response systems (clicker-based technologies) on cognition and affect. Comput. Educ. **94**, 102–119 (2016)
18. Iona, J.: Mentimeter. School Libr. **66**(3), 153 (2018)

Decommodifying Teacher (Digital) Education

Learning Analytics to Foster Quality Culture in Education and Training Organizations

Giovanna Del Gobbo[1(✉)] and Glenda Galeotti[2,2]

[1] University of Florence, Via Laura 48, 50121 Florence, Italy
giovanna.delgobb@unifi.it
[2] University of Florence, Via Laura 48, 50121 Florence, Italy

Abstract. Learning analytics have shown great potential in improving teaching quality, learning experience and administrative efficiency, although several major challenges remain and lie in the intrinsic tensions between innovation and functioning (Tsai Y-S. et al., 2019). The research hypothesis starts from the possibility of exploit LAs into the Quality Assurance (QA) framework and considering the quality assessment devices as a reference for collecting and organizing the data. QA devices can be used to "read" the complexity, define "simplified" processes and arrive at the identification and understanding of the system components, the relationships between them, and their functioning and their effectiveness, also thanks to indicators for measurement of results. On the basis of these reflections, a practice-driven research experience has been implemented within the master course "New digital skills: Open Education, Social and Mobile Learning" of the University of Florence, with the aim of producing new insights and exploring opportunities to exploit LAs into the practice of QA, starting from training of teachers and educators.

Keywords: Knowledge management · Quality assessment · Teachers training

1 Fostering Quality Culture with Learning Analytics

Quality assurance and quality management are key elements in the implementation and development of the educational system, and they are increasingly central challenges in the governance of institutions characterized by growing organizational autonomy [1]. The need to evaluate the provided services has unquestionably become more significant following the process through which the education system is organized in a decentralized and autonomous way. Learning analytics (LAs) have shown great potential in improving teaching quality, learning experience and administrative efficiency, although several major challenges associated with the implementation of Learning Analytics remain and lie in the intrinsic tensions between innovation and functioning [2].

The factors that can hinder this potential, if read in the light of the theories of the diffusion of innovation, can find some criteria of analysis: incompatibility with existing evaluation practices by teachers and institutions, lack of perception of the relative advantage expressed by an evaluation based on dynamic data, complexity in collecting

M. Ranieri et al. (Eds.): ATEE 2021, CCIS 1649, pp. 103–115, 2022.
https://doi.org/10.1007/978-3-031-20777-8_8

and structuring data for their usability, and limited immediate visibility of the results determined by the application of the LAs device [3].

How to enhance LAs and the richness of evidence produced by the use of new technologies, for the purpose of fostering quality culture in educational and training organizations? The research hypothesis starts from the possibility of exploiting LAs into the Quality Assurance (QA) process framework and considering the quality assessment devices deriving from the TQM (Total Quality Management) model, such as the CAF Education (Common Assessment Framework), as a reference for collecting and organizing the data. QA devices can be used to "read" the complexity, defining "simplified" processes and arriving at the identification and understanding of the system components, the relationships between them, their functioning and their effectiveness, also thanks to indicators for measuring results.

In this context, "quality" was considered related to the organizational and managerial skills of integrating complex processes - such as programming, design, delivery and monitoring of services - through management set in a systemic perspective [4]. Quality becomes the expression of an organizational system competence generated and fed by a continuous learning process that requires to be constantly regenerated through an embedded self-directed learning process [5, 6] and which can be determined by the context conditions and by the inter-feedback of the subjects involved with the available resources: to this end, the LAs represent a significant resource.

This holistic perspective of quality can be interpreted, in agreement with Ehlers (2009), as strongly characterized by an educational/transformative connotation, which requires forms of accompaniment of the individual actors in the process of continuous improvement of their educational/didactic practice. To train and support teachers and educators in the conscious use of quality assessment devices using data on teaching/learning processes can foster the development of a culture of quality capable of sense-making to LAs at the system level.

On the basis of these reflections, research was implemented within the master course "New digital skills: Open Education, Social and Mobile Learning" of the University of Florence, in which a learning unit was dedicated to the development of skills for implementing quality of e-learning courses and digital training systems.

It is a practice-driven research experience with the aim of producing new insights and explore opportunities to exploit LAs into the practice of QA, starting from training of operators (teachers, educators, ...). Such research includes practice as an integral part of its method [8, 9].

2 Theoretical Framework

Methods of self-assessment and external evaluation have been consolidated to allow the production of data, which is potentially synergistic, aimed at allowing the verification of the results achieved in terms of effectiveness and impact: self-review is at the core of the quality assurance and improvement process [10, 11]. In this context, as we have introduced it, "quality" is considered to be related to the organizational and managerial capabilities of integrating complex processes (eg EFQM model or CAF model), but also to the sharing of values and practices within an institutional community, cultivated on multiple levels and in various forms. A managerial and organizational vision of education and training services inspired by quality control emerges as a response to the need to guarantee a "production" of knowledge, skills and professionalism capable of guaranteeing cultural growth and the development of the organization, optimizing resources and exploiting the available potential [12].

Faced with the recognition of large spaces of autonomy, self-assessment systems are indispensable governance tools as devices at the basis of internal decision-making processes, while external evaluation systems can balance the wide margins of freedom within a national system, through the identification of standards [13]: both forms of evaluation (internal and external) must make it possible to verify the existence of elements of strength and excellence (for their enhancement) and elements of weakness (to activate support measures). The evaluation processes also contribute to promoting the development of a culture of evidence that represents one of the challenges for educational policies at the international level [14].

Already in 2012, the UNESCO Policy Brief recognized LAs as a potential tool capable of transforming educational research into a data-driven science and educational institutions into organizations that make decisions based on evidence [15]. The implementation of learning analytics for education and training was considered relevant in order to better understand their implications and opportunities for European education policy [16]. LAs seem to be able to go beyond the concept of "evidence" for the purposes of evaluating teaching/learning processes, "validating" procedures or "reporting training results" [17]. According to Becker (2013) LA techniques applied to educational systems stimulate the definition of new frameworks for the analysis of educational processes, both in terms of assessment and the overall quality of interactions, shifting the focus from the measurement of outcomes (learning outcome) towards monitoring and evaluation "in-process", making use of data that are "current and contextual". This approach requires, in Becker's vision, new parameters for the collection of data and their visualization, which are oriented to inform teachers and other figures responsible for the educational context with the aim of stimulating reflections on active processes (living processes). To this end, LAs can help educators to better plan and reflect on their activities by becoming aware of their actions and teaching/learning processes [19]. Being aware of all the factors that enable or hinder a situation is a condition for making decisions and effectively performing objectives: the perception of these factors, while the event occurs, allow for a better comprehension which then leads to the projection of the future implementation and improvement [20]. This is consistent with the implementation of a culture of quality.

On the other hand, culture of quality can be sustained by favouring processes of sense-making and understanding of the overall teaching/learning system, favouring critical access and the interpretation of the artefacts, norms and procedures with which the specific social and cultural community carries out its practices and solves problems, with reference to processes relating to quality assessment and assurance. Quality has offered a perspective to give meaning [21] to actions to improve teaching/learning activities and, at the same time, a perspective of deconstruction and reconstruction of the system. Recently, the culture of quality has been interpreted as a culture that emphasizes continuous improvement processes [22] and allows educational institutions to improve the quality of learning [23]. It should also be noted that quality is understood, from an organizational point of view, as the capacity to integrate the complex processes of programming, design, delivery and monitoring of the service, through a management set from a system perspective [24]. Quality can therefore be interpreted as the competence of the organizational system and as such is generated by a learning process and requires to be constantly regenerated through a process of self-regulation determined by the context conditions and by the inter-feedback of the subjects involved. The e-learning environment is providing an unprecedented opportunity to collect and analyse data to support quality improvement efforts: "With the use of technology, an operator should be able to capitalise on the learning analytics to gain insight into different aspects of a student's learning for continuous improvement. As such, an operator will have to provide evidence that it uses learning analytics to evaluate the effectiveness of the online learning programme, including the extent to which the learning goals are achieved, and uses the results of its evaluations to enhance the attainment of the learning outcomes" [25].

Data analytics can be used to support quality assurance by providing data-driven information for improvements at the course, program, and student-support levels. To this end, data analytics enable institutions to drive quality improvements through valid data, not merely on the basis of anecdotal information or intuition [26].

In this context, our research starts from a question: is it possible to develop quality management skills able to exploit potential of LAs?

3 QA System for Managing Complexity of LAs: A Proposal for Teachers' and Educators' Training

3.1 QA Models as a Hypothesis to Deal with Las

This paragraph presents the results of a practice-driven research experience during a teachers and educators training event. Introducing a research perspective on a teaching/learning event [16, 27, 28] has offered an opportunity to:

- understand how to foster sense-making about quality management processes and devices and a conscious use of LA as a provider of data-driven information
- identify the challenges associated with the implementation of Learning Analytics, which reside in the intrinsic tensions between innovation and operation [29] and generate resistance to use.

The context is the Master course on "New digital skills: Open Education, Social and Mobile Learning" of the University of Florence, during academic years 2017–2018 and 2019–2020 (15 students, all professionals in school, education services or vocational and continuing training sectors).

The hypothesis to connect QA model and LAs took shape from Becker's consideration, for which new parameters are necessary for the collection of the multiplicity of data and for their organization and visualization that enables an effective use for the analysis of teaching/learning processes while they are happening. In this perspective, a model such as the CAF and the connected quality assessment devices have been considered as tools to deal with the complexity of an educational event and the plurality of data that the event itself produces. Quality devices are considered as organized and structured forms of data layout to promote knowledge of the system components, of the relationships between them, and of their functioning and effectiveness.

The CAF is a European model for the self-assessment of public administrations interested in the continuous improvement of their performance results. It is a total quality management (TQM) tool, inspired by the model of the European Foundation for Quality Management (EFQM) [31, 32]. The holistic approach to organisation performance analysis of TQM and CAF only requires that every aspect of organization functioning is carefully evaluated, but also that all the elements of the model have a reciprocal impact on each other (ibidem). CAF helps public administrations (with a specific attention to educational system) to:

- bring all activities back to an overall and systemic vision,
- identify the weaknesses of the organizational performance,
- implement processes of involvement and delegation of responsibilities that motivate personnel and strengthen existing skills pursue, through planned and evidence-based actions empirical, continuous improvement of management.

The CAF aims to be a catalyst for a full improvement process within the organization and it provides support to: "1. Introduce the culture of excellence; 2. Progressively implement the PDCA (PLAN, DO, CHECK, ACT) logic; 3. Carry out the self-assessment process in order to obtain a comprehensive organisation check; 4. Come up with a diagnosis that shows the strengths and improvement areas helping the definition of improvement actions" [33] Other benefits are recognized, consistent with the connections with the use of LAs: 1. as common language, because it allows staff and managers to discuss organisational issues together in a constructive way, promoting dialogue and benchlearning; 2. as self-assessment process which is the basis for the systematic involvement of people in the improvement of the organization; 3. as evidence-based improvement, because it stimulates public sector organisations to gather and effectively use information and data (Ibidem).

The Common Assessment Framework specific to the Education system [30] has been selected to help teachers to develop the ability to identify, organize and use the learning analytics produced by a training activity delivered on a digital platform. The CAF model was developed for the evaluation of the public education system (public administration). However, in the training activities it was used as a reference to try to organize the learning analytics produced in any educational context.

3.2 The E-tivity: Implementation and Results

A specific learning unit (LU) of the Master was dedicated to the introduction of the concepts of QA and LA for the organizational improvement of training and education organizations, in a perspective that considers both data on learning processes and evaluation data. This LU included an e-tivity aimed to help master students (teachers and e-learning educators) to identify Learning Analytics, produced by training courses, delivered through the e-learning platform, consistent with criteria and sub-criteria of the CAF model (Fig. 1).

The specific task was divided into two points:

- identifying the elements of analysis for at least two factors (CAF enabling factors and/or CAF results)
- hypothesizing the use of LA available in the e-learning system, in order to set up actions for the improvement of the delivery process, the learning results, the learning environment and the technologies used.

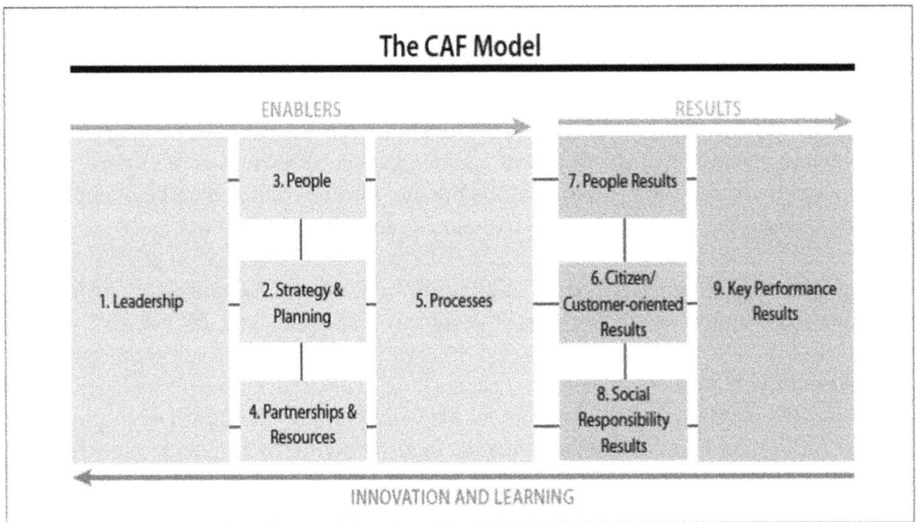

Fig. 1. Common assessment framework model based on EFQM (EIPA, 2013).

Students have been solicited to use quality tools to organize data in a logic functional to their interpretation in order to define areas for definition of improvement plans that could always be verified through the use of LAs.

The work conducted by the Master course students was applied to some experiences related to their work in the blended or online training course, e.g.:

- "Tutor for learning" by the Institute of Military Aeronautical Sciences of Florence.
- Mandatory health and safety training in a Public Company.
- "Course for digital facilitators" realized by Public Libraries.

In other cases, the analysis relates to an generic online training experience. All investigated experiences adopted the MOODLE e-learning platform, so the data collected refer to it.

The analysis of the products delivered to the students allows us to pursue two types of outcomes:

1. to define an overall representation of how the connection between the CAF model with the LAs is possible,
2. to detect which assessment skills of teaching staff are strengthened and the learning achieved by the students through the performed work.

About the first point, the following tables highlight the results emerging from an analytical and interpretative work conducted on the products delivered by the master students and related to the identification of LAs for the CAF criterions of results. Some CAF criteria and indicators have been pre-selected (see tables), identifying those areas most considered in the assessment of an educational service, regardless of the application of quality models, thus assuming a greater familiarity of students with these areas of evaluation.

The master's students were asked to identify all the possible LAs obtainable from the e-learning platforms of which they had direct experience, which could offer evidence for the evaluation of each criterion. Subsequently, the learners compared their selection of evidence with the proposed indicators present in the CAF, stimulating their reflection.

In the first table, the CAF criterion is about the beneficiaries of the training activity and the specific sub criterion "Performance assessment is related to the quality of services delivered to citizens and customer". This criterion is related to the direct measurement of performance in terms of the quality of services delivered to citizens and customers and measured by internal indicators [30]. Specifically, it concerns the user involvement in training or education activities and services and the service quality as a whole.

The Learning analytics about the "Results regarding the Users involvement" in the training cases analysed are 14, while those about "Results regarding the quality of delivery of products or services" that in our case is a training service are 11 (see Table 1).

About the CAF Criterion "People Results", it provides the indicators to measure the results achieved in terms of performance assessment used by the organisation. The LAs identified for this evaluation sub-criterion are 15 in total (see Table 2).

Finally, the CAF Criterion "Key Performance Results" is related to measurable achievements for the success of the training through the sub-criterion "External results: outputs and outcomes to goals", and the other sub-criterion "Internal results" that considers the level of efficiency of the training course being analysed. The LAs identified about these sub-criterions are seven (see Table 3).

It is evident that some of the identified LAs are able to offer data for more than one criterion considered and that therefore their selection and use must be consistent with the type of analysis of the results to be carried out. In fact, the exercise was completed with a reflection on the correlations between data obtainable from LAs and how their analysis could allow the organization to monitor and to assess activities and make improvement decisions based on evidence. The students thus suggested how some local authorities can identify areas for organizational improvement in the analyzed courses. Some examples are shown in the following table (see Table 4).

About the learning outcomes achieved by students and related to their ability to define an assessment plan based on the EFQM model to organize the LAs, the analysis of their products indicates that they understood how:

Table 1. Learning analytics identified related to the CAF Criterion "Citizen/Customer-oriented Results"

CAF Evaluation Criterion and Sub-Criterion	Learning analytics
Evaluation criterion 6: Citizen/Customer-oriented Results *Evaluation sub-criterion 6.2:* *Performance assessment*	**Results regarding the involvement:** Total connection time to complete the course for each User Average time to complete the course per User Average timing of use of LUs and other resources provided Duration of each course session per user Average duration of each course session No. of actions performed by each User in a single work session No. Accesses of Users to the platform in a selected period of time No. of Users never connected to the platform % of Users never connected to the platform on the total of enrolled Users % of Users who have used the forum, chat and messages No. of comments of each User on the forum, chat and messages No. of downloads of learning materials (pdf, e-book, video, link, etc.) No. of tasks delivered on time % of tasks delivered on time on the total of those required **Results regarding the quality of delivery of products or services:** No. of complaints received Average response time on complaints received Average complaint handling time No. of clarification requests Average response time for clarification requests Average clarification request handling time No. of accesses to FAQs and other technical support tools No. of Users dropped out No. of Users never connected to the platform % of Users never connected on the total of subscribers Average of the results obtained by structured feedback on the quality perceived by the users

- the data available in an e-learning system can be used for the purposes of LAs processes
- LAs may produce evidence about different CAF criteria and/or sub-criteria

Table 2. Learning analytics identified related to the CAF Criterion "People results"

CAF Evaluation Criterion and Sub-Criterion	Learning analytics
Evaluation Criterion 7: People Results *Evaluation Sub-criterion 7.2:* *Performance assessment*	No. of requests for clarifications and information by Users on the forum, chat and messages No. of responses for clarifications and information by teachers and tutors on the forum, chat and messages % of questions/requests on forum chat and messages that were answered Average response time of clarification requests by teachers and tutor Average clarification requests handling time Average response time of each tutor, teacher and other staff member Average time for uploading the learning materials on the platform by each staff member No. of tasks delivered on time % of task delivered on time on the total of those required % of Users never connected to the platform on the total of enrolled Users % of Users who complete the course out of the total number of connected No. of characters typed by user/staff in forums and other tools requesting clarification and sending comments Ratio of the average of connection time to the platform to the expected course usage time Ratio of the average of connection time of the staff (teachers, tutors, etc.) to the expected delivery time Ratio of the per capita cost of the course to the average of the learning results obtained by the users

- criteria, sub-criteria, and indicators are used to define data collection tools (checklists, questionnaires or other), to organize LAs
- the definition of improvement plans and actions could always be verified through the use of LAs.

Finally, the students' works highlight some critical issues related to assuming a systemic perspective in the analysis of training and education services as well as to lead to consistency levels and fields of the system with the analysed processes, and the collected data.

Table 3. Learning analytics identified related to the CAF Criterion "Key performance Results"

CAF Evaluation Criterion and Sub-Criterion	Learning analytics
Evaluation Criterion 9: Key Performance Results *Evaluation Sub-criterion 9.1:* External results: outputs and outcomes to goals *Evaluation Sub-criterion 9.2: Internal results: level of efficiency*	Results of the mid-term and final evaluation tests Average of the results obtained in the mid-term and final evaluation tests % of tests/tasks delivered on the number of enrolled Users No. of feedbacks required on the assessment tests Average time to provide feedback on assessment tests Time spent running the quiz per User No. of failed attempts per user and total Average time to run each mid-term and final evaluation test Ratio between the per capita of the course cost and the average of the learning results obtained by the users

Table 4. Improvement areas detected by the students through using LAs combined with the CAF model

CAF Sub-criterion	LAs	Improvement area identified by the master students
Evaluation sub-criterion 6.2: Performance assessment	No. of comments of each User on the forum, chat and messages	"It provides information on the level of participation and involvement of the students, but also on the difficulties encountered during the course. If aimed at request clarifications, they would indicate that the information provided is not clear/sufficient. It would be useful to be able to divide the interventions aimed at collaboration from those with requests for information"

(*continued*)

Table 4. (*continued*)

CAF Sub-criterion	LAs	Improvement area identified by the master students
Evaluation sub-criterion 6.2: Performance assessment	Number of complaints received (via email, forum, etc.); Average time of response Average complaint handling time	"With these data it is possible to verify whether it is necessary to improve the time and response capacity of the staff for improving various aspects of the course delivery"
Evaluation Sub-criterion 7.2: Performance assessment	Average time for uploading the learning materials on the platform by each staff member	"It allows you to assess whether the organization of the course was well structured (does it take a long time because the material was not ready? And why? Has something been changed in the organization in progress to meet the needs of the students or for incorrect programming?); if the addition of the material is easy and immediate (the times are long because it is difficult to enter the material from a technical point of view?)"
Evaluation Sub-criterion 9.1: External results: outputs and outcomes to goals	% of tests/tasks delivered on the number of enrolled Users	"A low percentage of tests/tasks delivered could indicate problems in scheduling tasks or a too complex task that generates frustration and abandonment. In this case, it is possible to evaluate whether to reduce the complexity of the task or divide it into smaller tasks or provide more information to the students"

4 Conclusion

The culture of quality needs a change in the paradigm of knowledge and the vision of teachers and educators, overcoming the focus on assessment skills of learning processes towards managerial assessment skills of the complex educational context. The integration between the perspective of LAs and QA devices seems to offer a supportive reference. In fact, the use of learning analytics in the framework of quality devices supports the development skills and abilities for using and managing data provided by the e-learning system for evaluation and self-evaluation of actions, in order to improve the quality of the teaching and learning processes, the learning environments and outcomes.

On the other hand, an appropriate use of LAs can help professionals working in education and training services to better reflect and plan activities, based on objective data, gaining greater awareness of the different factors that intervene in teaching/learning processes according to a systemic perspective [18]. The research carried out starting from the training practice within the master has produced some initial results that seem to confirm the usefulness of the quality devices for typesetting the LAs and also seem to confirm the possibility that a conscious and critical use of LAs can contribute to the development of a culture of quality within organizations. From these results, further research paths emerge for the definition of new skills that must characterize the professionalism of the teacher and the educator who works on e-learning platforms.

References

1. Taylor, A., Hill, F.: Quality Management in Education. Qual. Assur. Educ. **1**(1), 21–28 (1993)
2. Tsai, Y.-S., Gašević, D.: The State of Learning Analytics in Europe – Executive Summary – SHEILA (2017). http://sheilaproject.eu/2017/04/18/the- state-of-learning-analytics-in-europeexecutive- summary/
3. Rogers, E.M.: The Diffusion of Innovations. The Free Press, New York (1995)
4. Salih, T.: Total quality management in education. Zanco J. 36 (2008)
5. Brookfield, S.D.: Self-Directed Learning. In: Maclean, R., Wilson, D. (eds.) (a cura di), International Handbook of Education for the Changing World of Work, pp. 2615–2627. Springer, Dordrecht (2009)
6. Larson, J., Jordan, S.S., Lande, M., e Weiner, S.: Supporting self-directed learning in a project-based embedded systems design course. IEEE Trans. Educ. **63**(2), 88–97 (2020)
7. Ehlers, U.D.: Understanding quality culture. Qual. Assur. Educ. **17**(4), 343–363 (2009)
8. Candy, L.: Practice Based Research: A Guide. University of Technology, Sydney (2006)
9. Skains, L.: Creative practice as research: discourse on methodology. J. Media Pract. **19**(1), 82–97 (2017)
10. Vanhoof, J., Van Petegem, P.: Matching internal and external evaluation in an era of accountability and school development: lessons from a Flemish perspective. Stud. Educ. Eval. **33**, 101–119 (2007)
11. OECD: Reviews of evaluation and assessment in education, OECD, New Zealand (2012)
12. Levina, E.Y., Kamasheva, Y.L., et al.: A process approach to management of an educational organization. Rev. Eur. Stud. **7**(4), 234–240 (2005)
13. Hattie, J.: Horizons and whirlpools: the well-travelled road of national standards, cognition institute (2009)
14. Pellegrini, M., Vivanet, G.: Evidence-based policies in education: initiatives and challenges in Europe. ECNU Rev. Educ. **4**(1), 209653112092467 (2020)
15. Shum, S.B.: Learning analytics. policy brief. UNESCO Inst. Inform. Technol. Educ. 12 (2012)
16. Ferguson, R., et al.: Research evidence on the use of learning analytics - implications for education policy. In: Vuorikari, R., Castaño Muñoz, J. (eds.). Joint Research Centre Science for Policy Report (2016)
17. de Waal, P.: Learning analytics for continuous learning-processes improvement through dynamic data-informed decisions. Formazione Insegnamento, X V/2, 43–51 (2017)
18. Becker, B.: Learning analytics: insights into the natural learning behaviour of our students. Behav. Soc. Sci. Libr. **32**(1), 63–67 (2013)

19. Scheffel, M., Drachsler, H., Stoyanov, S., Specht, M.: Quality indicators for learning analytics. Educ. Technol. Soc. **17**(4), 117–132 (2014)
20. Endsley, M. R., Garland D. J (Eds.): Situation awareness analysis and measurement. Lawrence Erlbaum associates, Mahwah, NJ (2000)
21. Weick, K.E.: Sensemaking in Organizations. Sage, Thousand Oaks, CA (1997)
22. Whalen, T.: Factors affecting quality culture. Qual. Manag. J. **11**(4), 43–55 (2020)
23. Kairiša, I., Lapiņa, I.: Analysis of factors influencing quality culture and their impact on organizational development. In: Proceedings of the International Scientific Conference, vol. VI (2019)
24. Del Gobbo, G., Valutazione di sistema e cultura della qualità: itinerari di ricerca e formazione per le università. Nuova Secondaria, vol. XXXVIII, pp. 99–110 (2021). ISSN: 1828–4582
25. APEC: quality assurance of online learning. University of Melbourne: Melbourne centre for the study of higher education (2017)
26. Reed Scull, W., Kendrick, D., Shearer, R., Offerman, D.: The landscape of quality assurance in distance education. Continuing High. Educ. Rev. **75**, 138–149 (2011)
27. European commission: learning analytics (Key messages) (2016). https://ec.europa.eu/education/sites/education/files/2016-pla-learning-analytics_en.pdf
28. Tsai, Y.S., Moreno-Marcos, P.M., Tammets, K., Kollom, K., Gašević, D.: SHEILA policy framework: informing institutional strategies and policy processes of learning analytics. In: Proceedings of the 8th International Conference on Learning Analytics and Knowledge, pp. 320–329 (2018)
29. Tsai, Y.-S., Poquet, O., Gašević, D., Dawson, S., Pardo, A.: Complexity leadership in learning analytics: drivers, challenges and opportunities. Br. J. Edu. Technol. **6**, 2839–2854 (2019)
30. European institute of public administration: improving public organisations through self-assessment. CAF 2013 (2013). http://qualitapa.gov.it/sitoarcheologico/fileadmin/mirror/crcaf/documenti/CAF_2013.pdf
31. European foundation for quality management. business excellence model (2006). www.efqm.org
32. European foundation for quality management: assessing for excellence. European foundation for quality management, Brussels (2003)
33. European institute of public administration: improving public organisations through self-assessment. CAF 2020 (2019). https://www.eupan.eu/wp-content/uploads/2019/11/20191118-CAF-2020-FINAL.pdf
34. Mukhopadhyay, M.: Total quality management in education. Sage, Thousand Oaks, California (2005)
35. Sullivan, G.: Making Space: The purpose and place of practice-led research. In: Smith, H., Roger, T., Dean. Practice-Led Research, Research-Led Practice in the Creative Arts, pp. 41–65. Edinburgh University Press, Edinburgh (2009)
36. Whitelock-Wainwright, A., Gašević, D., Tejeiro, R.: What do students want? Towards an instrument for students' evaluation of quality of learning analytics services. In: Proceedings of the Seventh International Learning Analytics & Knowledge Conference, pp. 368–372 (2017)

Legalisation Issues and Reconfiguration of Education? Challenges for Nordic Teacher Education in the Digital Age

Eyvind Elstad(✉)

University of Oslo, Oslo, Norway
eyvind.elstad@ils.uio.no

Abstract. The purpose of this paper is to discuss new challenges and growing demands on teacher education in Nordic countries (Norway, Sweden, Denmark, Iceland and Finland, which have a history of close links). These challenges are linked to increased legalisation and digital adaptions promoted by several discourses. The questions are thus: What does this legalization trend entail? When will the digital revolution occur in the Nordic countries' teacher education programmes? What will this mean for the content and the structural character of the teacher education programmes today? The developmental features of today's Nordic teacher education programmes are very complex and partly characterised by inherent tensions between contradictory considerations, but one vital question is: will increased legalisation and digital adaptions promote more instrumentalism in teacher education programmes? These questions are discusses.

Keywords: Legalisation · Digitisation · Instrumentalism

1 Introduction

This study focusses on teacher education in the North. The five current Nordic countries – Norway, Sweden, Denmark, Iceland and Finland – have a history of close links. As independent states, the Nordic countries have educational systems with not only clear similarities but also some differences. Nordic countries rely on a comprehensive school model that values equity, no streaming, and easy passage between levels. Some of these educational systems have attributes of the so-called Nordic model of education [1]. The similarities among Nordic educational systems may be partly due to similar social developments, equivalent cultures and so on and also because of the mutually inspired politics and social debates of these independent states; indeed, the Nordic countries borrow ideas about policy development from one another [2]. However, the focus among politicians is often quality measured by international large-scale surveys: Pupils' learning is measured, inter alia, by international large-scale surveys, to which each Nordic country's politicians attach great importance. The league table of student performance has become central in both the political sphere and the public conversation about school and teacher education in the North. To succeed better, the focus is also often on successful solutions

M. Ranieri et al. (Eds.): ATEE 2021, CCIS 1649, pp. 116–123, 2022.
https://doi.org/10.1007/978-3-031-20777-8_9

for teacher education ("the world's best"); [3] that can serve as inspirations and hence the bases for policy funding. In this context, transnational organisations are important in promoting development towards their desired direction. The five-year Finnish teacher education programme, with its school-oriented research thesis, has received substantial attention and inspired policymaking in other Nordic countries (notably Norway and Iceland). Experts have described Finnish teacher education as "outstanding" and "excellent" [4–6].

On the hand, teacher education ought to be adapted to the kind of school for which the aspiring teacher wants to qualify, which may (and likely will) involve different national characteristic [7]. On the other hand, global trends are driving forces towards greater convergence regarding the structure and the mechanisms of European higher education, including teacher education. Thus, teacher education reforms are influenced by both global and national forces, creating instances of "vernacular globalisation" [8], which describes the processes by which international and national educational systems coalesce to create distinctive versions of teacher education within different nation states [9]. Thus, teacher education in each Nordic country can be carried out differently even though the basic structure is almost the same. The purpose of this paper is to discuss new challenges and growing demands on teacher education in Nordic countries. These challenges are linked to increased legalisation and digital adaptions promoted by several discourses. The questions are thus: What does this legalization trend entail? When will the digital revolution occur in the Nordic countries' teacher education programmes? What will this mean for the content and the structural character of the teacher education programmes today? The developmental features of today's Nordic teacher education programmes are very complex and partly characterised by inherent tensions between contradictory considerations, but one vital question is: will increased legalisation and digital adaptions promote more instrumentalism in teacher education programmes?

2 Increased Legalisation of Matters Related to School Activities

One trend in especially Scandinavian countries is the increased legalisation of matters related to school activities [10]. For example, legalisation can be manifested through strengthened student rights. Strengthened student rights affect the balance of power between teachers and students, where the teachers' transactional position is weakened. Several examples are found in [11]. Enhanced student rights have been and appear to be further institutionalised. This new legalisation trend schools has implications for the teacher role and content of teacher education; teachers of the future must be extremely cautious about exhibiting behaviours that can provide a subjective experience of student discomfort. This offers guidance in the direction of a more facilitating teacher behaviour. Is this facilitating role also promoted by teacher education programmes?

Another premise for discussing the future of teacher education is the Nordic countries' emphasis on equality values. The school should provide students with equal learning opportunities [1]. One implication is that the shortage of qualified teachers will make it difficult to achieve such a goal. The shortage of teachers with adequate qualifications poses a challenge in the Nordic countries, to varying degrees, with the greatest challenges in Sweden, but this trend is emergent in this decade also in Norway and Iceland [11]. In the worst-case scenario, teacher shortages can weaken the work of providing students with equal learning opportunities in school. One question is: Is Sweden a frontrunner or an outlier?

3 From Nation Building Towards Transnational Governance

The school as an institution has historically been important in particular countries, such as Norway, Iceland and Finland, in their efforts to create national identities, that is, nation building under the auspices of the school. It is an open question whether nation building will be replaced by supranational visions of a future where each country's situation heavily depends on those of other countries. Thus, contributing to the formation of a national identity under the auspices of the school can be replaced by forming world citizens [12] or possibly European citizens [13]? In that case, we moves away from the nation and devalues national citizenship in favour of globalism and minority and human rights based on the ideas of universal altruism. If this happens, a distinctive change in the Nordic countries' school systems will occur – the enrichment of the national welfare for the benefit of the global welfare. One possible inference is that the world citizen vision has increasingly been raised as an idea, but it is too early to tell whether this kind of thinking will be consolidated further. One possible scenario is that a balance will be sought between maintaining some national features and widely opening the door for globalised influence. Continued liberalisation of the labour market in European countries can be expected, which can contribute to market mechanisms in the labour market for teachers. There is a rapid increase in international mobility [14]. It seems likely that the labour market for teachers and teacher educators and study situation for preservice teachers will also be Europeanised more strongly than is the case today. Further harmonisation of requirement specifications seems inevitable. The globalisation trend may create additional needs for tailored solutions for complementary teacher education.

Practices might nourish a wider process of reconfiguration of school education and teacher education into an instrumental commodity state, which strongly contrasts with the notion of Nordic education as a collective public good. The latest examples of instrumentalism in Norway are linked to actors outside the teacher education community who call for a system for sharing quality-assured and research-based teaching and learning programs for student teachers [11]. This example is part of a pervasive international trend. For example, the OECD is in the process of building Global Teaching InSights, which is a global video library of teaching [12]. Learners gain access to a bank of educational content that they can use in a flexible way. This can free up time for more individual or group-based guidance in teaching situations. Thus, instrumentalism can go hand in hand with the digitisation trend in schools [15]. The teacher role might become more and more seen as the executive technician who implements ready-made arrangements. This is not the main trend yet, but an instrumentalist trend might affect schooling as well as teacher education, but the range and the depth of such a change impulse are uncertain.

4 Two Extreme Cases

There are multiple tendencies. Here, I discuss two extreme cases as illustrations: the new Kvibergsskolan and Michaela Community School.

The intentions behind the new Kvibergsskolan in Sweden can serve as an anchor for discussing the changes required in response to teacher education's need to qualify future teachers to work in in this type of school. The Municipality of Gothenburg describes the school as 'a school of the future'. The traditional 'grammar of schooling' [16] is based on the idea of teaching different subjects in relatively short blocks (typically 45 min) in classrooms for age-appropriate classes. At Kvibergsskolan, however, this scholastic 'grammar' is broken down for more individualized solutions. Classrooms are considered outdated; instead, students instead work with iPads in open work areas. A 'maker-space' (a kind of information and communications technology [ICT] workshop) is arranged in which students learn how to work with 3D printers and use their own iPads to communicate with teachers and other students. Each student should have a personal work schedule, and students work in age-matched groups. The school's idea is based on the four C's: 'communication, collaboration, creativity and critical thinking' [17]. Content knowledge is not among these C's. At the intention level, this type of school development can be thought of as extremely individualized facilitation of learning, where students primarily work with their own iPads in a kind of network model that changes both the roles of both teachers and students. In principle, it is conceivable that a student could sit at home and carry out all the learning activities and associated communications on purely virtual channels. There are many analogous cases of school development in the Scandinavian countries.

In contrast to the modernization of the school exemplified by the Kvibergsskolan, Michaela Community School in London [18] was launched as a protest against school development trends amidst riots and social problems in one of London's poorest areas. Here, the 'grammar' of the traditional school is restored as a counter-reaction to disciplinary slippages; there should be calm during school hours. The learners – unless told otherwise – sit at their desks. Teaching takes place in clearly separated time blocks in classrooms for learners divided into age cohorts. Michaela Community School seeks solutions based on teacher authority and control. The timetable has fixed weekly lessons for teaching the various subjects, with teaching carried out in classrooms where the desks are arranged in rows. The school focuses on academic knowledge and discipline throughout the school day. Its 'no excuses' strategy means that even minor misconduct has consequences [18]. All teachers at Michaela are committed to this strategy. The school year starts with practicing common rules. An example of a goal is for students to remain in their seats for 30 s after the bell rings.

Every day, lunch is served to both students and teachers. All students are assigned places to prevent cliques from accumulating around the lunch tables. Students also have duties; one serves the food to everyone around the table, another pours water for everyone, a third clears the table after the meal and so on. The lunch is led by a teacher at each table. The topic of conversation may be current events, literature or natural phenomena. The purpose of conversation during lunch is to cultivate a repertoire with stimulation of factual arguments, learning to take responsibility for common tasks and so on. The school has received a lot of positive attention for its outstanding results and student performance [19]. It is mentioned here because some schools in the Nordic countries are following similar ideas of strict regulations, such as students shaking the teacher's hand when entering the classroom. How strongly the conservative restoration of an old-fashioned school model will spread in Nordic countries remains to be seen, but the restoration of teacher authority may be reinforced, given the number of discipline problems and incidents of violence against teachers in Nordic schools.

Between these two extreme cases, other examples show a continuum of approaches. The question is whether the emphasis in school development will be towards a progressive modernization of the type represented by Kvibergsskolan or towards a conservative restoration where traditional subjects, knowledge acquisition and discipline are emphasized. If the development moves towards dissolving what we know as fixed structures in the school (subject-specific schedules, teaching in classrooms with the teacher leading the session, exams, etc.), we may witness the beginning of the end of the institution that we have long known as school. If that happens, there will be profound implications for teacher education. The former headmaster of Kvibergsskolan has stated that teachers recruited for the new school would have to be urged to become pioneers. This signals that the school administration wants to appoint a specific type of teacher. Can teacher shortages be alleviated by individualizing and digitizing teaching? Every student receives a work plan with his or her expected progress laid out. Students are given digital learning opportunities, with teaching sequences available in an online portal. Virtual (but still somewhat 'intelligent') feedback and guidance can be provided through digital platforms. Such solutions may also include feedback from real mentors. Anyone who envisages a forced development of the school in this direction will have to recognize that such a school will be a long way from what we have hitherto understood as school.

It is part of the story of Kvibergsskolan and other pioneering schools that new ideas elicit counterarguments from parents and politicians and incite community debates. How radical school development will be is an open question. [20] analyses a case of school development (through a focus on computers for all students) that went in reverse, while [21] explains a case of school development that has been a continual process of in-depth digitization. On one hand, several types of mechanisms can occur through modernization that combines ICT with the new working methods. On the other hand, new trends have also been replaced by the restoration of established school practices. In other words, the implications of modernization for teacher education are uncertain. Either way, the digitization of school activities is something for which teacher education must prepare to an even greater extent. Political rhetoric expresses the expectation that teachers should develop their own professional digital literacy skills, and teacher education programmes in all Nordic countries are concerned about this issue. It is difficult to have an overview of how the idea of a computer for each student will break down in Nordic countries, although further forms of digitization seem plausible.

5 Discussion

In this study, I have mentioned complex and dynamic relationships and tensions, transnational trends, national policy practice and teaching practice. The impact through globalisation processes has prevailed in education in general, including teacher education, but certain national characteristics still exist at a time when the globalisation pressure is exerted to its fullest extent. The pace of change is rapid, but it is uncertain whether the development trajectory will behave as a linear process. A complete eradication of national peculiarities is difficult to imagine.

It is worth recalling a digital revolution has not yet been fully implemented in teacher education in the Nordic countries. The question is: when will the digital revolution occur in the Nordic countries' teacher education programmes? What will this mean for the content and the structural character of the teacher education programmes today? Today we do not have the answers to these questions, but an economic recession can force rationalisations. A promotion of instrumentalism in schools might also depend on how this digitisation of teacher education unfolds.

Despite the criticism against the university-based teacher education models, university-based teacher education appears to be victorious on virtually all fronts in the Nordic countries, except Denmark. This trend means that the campus component of teacher education is becoming increasingly academic. While the previous recruitment of teacher educators often came from the training schools, a new cadre of teacher educators with academic merits has entered the teacher education institutions. Many of these new teacher educators have never practised as teachers themselves, but they often have their doctorate degrees to refer to. The teacher education offered by the universities thus stands with one leg on each camp.

On one hand, the university units must adapt to the virtues, expectations and norms of the university domain. These expectations are related, among other things, to target figures for production of publication points, citation indices and the international orientation of research. On the other hand, in the long term, university teacher education cannot succeed without the people of the school, and those who are educated as teachers perceive the content of the education as relevant to a reasonable degree. Success in being relevant to the school world, that is, to students who judge the quality of education from their perspective, while being successful in the increased scope of relevant research in international channels, is a balance between contradictory desires. One potential danger that cannot be overlooked is that it is possible to bridge the gap between the campus teaching theory base and the field of practice theory to a limited degree. However, the two-part career paths for teacher educators can mitigate the challenges when calling for more methodology in teacher education's campus teaching.

Partnership solutions can also alleviate the internal tensions between teacher education academics and the consideration of pragmatic closeness to the school's core business [22]. However, a retreat back to teacher seminars does not seem very likely (but similar solutions for school-based teacher education introduced in England cannot be completely excluded). The English government has yet [23] decided that there are issues of quality with initial teacher education programmes, and a new market review arrangement arises in 2024. The term university obviously has prestige in the Nordic countries. The Finnish teacher education model for research-based practice appears to be a strong source of inspiration for other Nordic countries. An exception is Iceland, where problems with the dropout rate of student teachers lead to a policy shift that helps to avoid the research-based master's thesis with school issues.

Despite globalisation processes, the decision-making framework for policy-making remains national. The Nordic countries' teacher education programmes have distinct national features. Moreover, considerable variations exist within each Nordic country. Nevertheless, it is possible to envisage a convergence in the direction of increasingly university-based teacher education institutions. Teacher seminaries have been turned into colleges, which have been incorporated into universities. Among politicians and key decision makers in the university domain, there is a strong belief that large entities are favourable, and synergy processes are expected to create large, powerful entities through mergers. Furthermore, there is an increase in profiled institutional initiatives as a consequence of institutional leadership. Such profiled initiatives may build up during an institution's branding, but this tendency does not appear to be strong for teacher education.

6 Limitations of the Study

The current study has limitations from a methodological approach because of the small sample of cases obviously limits the generalizability of the results. At a methodological level, the presentation of only two representative cases of the school realities of the North could be reductive. The cases presented are from a methodological point of view the sample is not representative and the examples described risk to be reductive. The two cases are extreme cases. Extreme cases can be useful for us to be able to better understand some key mechanisms in school development. The weakness is of course the lack of generalizability. I must also acknowledge that the chosen concepts in the analysis may be a possible shortcoming. Nevertheless, the terms used are a contribution to the professional discussion. I acknowledge these shortcomings and argue that they can serve as a point of departure for future research.

References

1. Imsen, G., Blossing, U., Moos, L.: Reshaping the nordic education model in an era of efficiency: changes in the comprehensive school project in Denmark, Norway, and Sweden since the millennium. Scand. J. Educ. Res. **61**(5), 568–583 (2016)
2. Hadzialic, A., Skarheim, P., Wilhelmsson, T.: Framtida Nordiskt Utbildningssamarbete: Svar på dagens och morgondagens utmaningar. Nordic Council of Ministers, Copenhagen (2017)
3. Barber, M., Mourshed, M.: How the World's Best-Performing Schools Systems Come Out on Top. McKinsey & Company, London (2007)
4. Darling-Hammond, L.: Teacher education around the world: what can we learn from international practice? Eur. J. Teach. Educ. **40**(3), 291–309 (2017)
5. Mourshed, M., Chijioke, C., Barber, M.: How the World's Most Improved School Systems Keep Getting Better. McKinsey and Company, London (2010)
6. The British educational research association: the role of research in teacher education: reviewing the evidence. Interim report of the of BERA-RSA Inquiry, London (2014)
7. Menter, I., Flores, M.A.: Teacher education, teacher professionalism and research: international trends, future directions. Eur. J. Teach. Educ. **44**(1), 1–4 (2021)
8. Rizvi, F., Lingard, B.: Globalizing Education Policy. Routledge, London (2009)

9. Menter, I.: The Interaction of Global and National Influences. In: Tatto, M.T., Menter, I. (eds.) Knowledge, policy and practice in learning to teach: A cross-national study, pp. 268–279. Bloomsbury, London (2019)
10. Karseth, B., Møller, J.: Legal regulation and professional discretion in schools. Scand. J. Educ. Res. **64**(2), 195–210 (2020)
11. Elstad, E.: Lærerutdanning i nordiske land. Universitetsforlaget, Oslo (2020)
12. Organisation for economic co-operation and development: teaching for global competence in a rapidly changing world. Organisation for economic co-operation and development, Paris (2018)
13. Ritzen, J., Haas, J., Neeleman, A., Teixeira, P.: European Identity and the Learning Union. IZA Policy Paper No. 121. IZA Institute of Labor Economics, Bonn (2016)
14. Porte, C.D.L., Heins, E.: A new era of European integration? Governance of labour market and social policy since the sovereign debt crisis. In: Porte, C.D.L., Heins, E. (eds.) The sovereign debt crisis, the EU and welfare state reform, pp. 15–41. Palgrave Macmillan, London (2016)
15. Selwyn, N.: Teachers vs technology: Rethinking the digitisation of teachers' work. Ethos **25**(3), 10–13 (2017)
16. Tyack, D.B., Cuban, L.: Tinkering Toward Utopia: A Century of Public School Reform. Harvard University Press, Cambridge MA (1995)
17. Municipality of Gothenbourg (homepage): Kvibergsskolenan F-9. https://goteborg.se/wps/portal/enhetssida/kvibergsskolan. Accessed 22 Jul 2022
18. Birbalsingh, K.: Michaela: The power of culture. John Catt Educational, Woodbridge (2020)
19. The office for standards in education, children's services and skills. School report: Michaela community school. The office for standards in education, children's services and skills, London (2017)
20. Elstad, E.: Why is There a Wedge Between the Promise of Educational Technology and the Experiences of a Technology-rich Pioneer School? In: Elstad, E. (ed.) Digital expectations and experiences in education, pp. 77–96. Sense Publishers, Rotterdam (2016)
21. Hauge, T.E.: On the Life of ICT and School Leadership in a Large-Scale Reform Movement: A Case Study. In: Elstad, E. (ed.) Digital expectations and experiences in education, pp. 97–116. Sense Publishers, Rotterdam (2016)
22. Mutton, T., Burn, K., Hagger, H., Thirlwall, K.: Teacher Education Partnerships: Policy and Practice. Critical Publishing, St. Albans (2018)
23. Department of education: Initial teacher training (ITT) market review report. Department of education, London (2021)

The Training of Teachers in Citizenship Education Through Theatre and Dialectical Method

Francesco Fabbro[1(✉)] and Colin Isham[2]

[1] University of Rome Tor Vergata, Rome, Italy
francesco.fabbro@uniroma2.it
[2] Isham Education and Community Ltd., Walsall, UK
cisham@ishamedu.com

Abstract. This paper presents the results of an evaluation of a professional development programme to promote teacher skills in fostering young students' active participation in democratic society through the dialectical method and drama techniques. The blended training has been designed within the framework of the Erasmus+ project EAR (*Forming active European Citizens through the dialectical method and theater*) that addressed about 500 teachers in five European Countries.

Data collection tools such as questionnaires addressing the trainees and focus groups with pupils provided quantitative and qualitative pre- and post-data to evaluate the training programme. The discussion of findings focuses on the educational value of EAR pedagogical approach, teachers' perceptions of changing dynamics in the classrooms where EAR methodology was implemented and their confidence in teaching and evaluating citizenship education.

Keywords: Teachers' professional development · Citizenship education · Evaluation research

1 Background and Aims of EAR Project

The EAR project *(Forming active European Citizens through the dialectical method and theater)* was proposed in response to the EACEA call 10/2018 – Erasmus+, KA3 – Support for policy reform. EAR set out to address the call objectives of:

- Enhancing the acquisition of social and civic competences, fostering knowledge, understanding and ownership of values and fundamental rights
- Enhancing critical thinking and media literacy among learners, parents and educational staff

The ethos of EAR has been to promote the values of peace, democracy, freedom and tolerance, which are at the heart of European integration. The EAR project was conceived on the premise that these values are at risk in an era of social media, where young people are exposed to diverse and fragmented information that is difficult to

M. Ranieri et al. (Eds.): ATEE 2021, CCIS 1649, pp. 124–135, 2022.
https://doi.org/10.1007/978-3-031-20777-8_10

form into a coherent whole. Education, and in particular, citizenship education, have an important role to play in supporting the young generation to understand their role in maintaining the values which underpin democratic, tolerant and peaceful societies, and to equip them with the competences to achieve this.

The project took place against the backdrop of a concerted effort by the Council of Europe and European Commission to strengthen citizenship education in Europe under the umbrella of the Democratic and Inclusive School Culture in Operation (DISCO) joint programme for cooperation projects[1]. Underlying projects within the scope of this programme was the reference framework of competences for democratic culture (RFCDC) [1], which sets out in detail the values, attitudes, skills, and knowledge and critical understanding necessary 'to be responsible citizens in modern, diverse, democratic societies' [2].

Within the DISCO programme, a series of curriculum interventions and accompanying practitioner guides and resources have been developed to support students to develop citizenship competences. These depart from the traditional knowledge-based curricula, and shift responsibility to the student to navigate their learning and relationships. And so, for example, service learning features as a key intervention, where students are required to make decisions and problem solve, in ways which have real world consequences [3].

Other interventions under the DISCO programme supported students to navigate controversial issues [4]. Such approaches are of particular value in regions which had seen conflict, but also of increasing relevance universally, where students experience extreme views online, and in an era of increasing migration. Added to this, were digital resistance interventions, which explicitly set about equipping young people with knowledge and tools to deal with misinformation online.

While not a DISCO funded programme, EAR nevertheless fitted well within this direction of travel of citizenship education. At the centre of the EAR intervention is the dialectical method - discourse between two or more people holding different points of view about a subject, but seeking to establish the truth through reasoned arguments [5–7]. This pedagogical focus was chosen because of its potential to promote the four competence areas of citizenship of: interacting effectively and constructively with others; thinking critically; acting in a socially responsible manner; and acting democratically [8].

Students are supported in developing skills in dialogue through theatre techniques. These provide modes of interaction which significantly aid children and pupils' communication and ability to express themselves [9, 10]. In this way they provide an engaging element to encourage discourse, and as such are an appropriate accompaniment to the dialectical method.

The project used a cascading approach consisting of multipliers, trainers, and teachers, and sought to enable teachers to implement EAR practice with fidelity and encourage changemakers in each partner country to embed practice in training for future teachers and trainers.

The training of teachers was critical to the success of the project, because of the intricate, 7-step design of the methodology. In addition, teachers require particular support to develop skilful, open questioning. Findings from research indicates teachers

[1] https://www.coe.int/en/web/education/disco.

tend to dominate talk in the classroom, preferring closed questions [11]. Furthermore, while the presence of theatre techniques was intended to provide scaffolding, and a way into dialogue and Socratic questioning, there was a danger that, as the more accessible, and immediately enjoyable, activity, trainers and teachers may focus primarily on theatre techniques. Without appropriate professional development activity, there was a risk teachers would lose sight in the training of the central role of questioning, and not adequately hone this skill for application in the classroom.

The evaluation of the project was designed to help support the training and implementation process to ensure fidelity with the EAR methodology.

2 The Value of EAR in an Era of Demographic Change in Europe

Country situation analyses were carried out in Greece, Italy, Portugal, Spain and the United Kingdom and synthesised into a project situation analyses [12].

The situation analyses identified nine challenges and constraints of citizenship education from teachers' perspectives. These are set out below, along with an indication of how the project was able to help address these.

A key finding from the situation analysis, was that teachers across participating countries often felt there was a tension between the democratic ethos promoted by schools and less favourable attitudes externally, including in the media and many family homes. By providing a structured forum to discuss issues and norms, along with coaching in the necessary skills of communication and cooperation, EAR ensures pupils develop agency to critically evaluate external messages, as well as what they learn at school, and so position themselves in relation to both. In this way too, teachers should be reassured that the methodology avoids an indoctrination approach to citizenship – telling pupils what to think – but rather, equips them to engage critically with information and opinions.

The introduction of the methodology and teacher guides for a range of scenarios, addressed the second issue identified by teachers: limited resources for teaching citizenship.

With regard to issues around time: limited time to implement citizenship education and teachers' workload, it was important that partners promoted the EAR methodology as a key strategy to develop pupils' learning to learn skills. Effective questioning is a critical skill for both teachers and their pupils across all learning situations, and a method for developing this is what EAR provides. The methodology also provided the potential for pupils to learn important cooperation and communication skills, as well as a disciplined approach to enquiry and critical analysis. These are essential skills for pupils' wider learning, higher education and the world of work. Where partners helped teachers and school leaders make links between EAR and other areas of the curriculum and pupils' learning, they also addressed the perception of marginality of citizenship education, expressed by several respondents in the situation analysis.

The professional development element of the project addressed the lack of training in citizenship education, as well as the gap between the intended democratic curriculum and education practices. EAR modelled good continuing professional development practice, and so added value to schools' participation in the project. This raised teachers' confidence in teaching citizenship education. While for the purposes of the project a single methodology is presented, the professional development design had the potential to support teachers' identity and skills as professional learners, building a culture of seeking out and trialling other approaches.

Finally, teachers found evaluating learning in citizenship education a challenge. This issue was addressed through collaboration between the external evaluator and partner organisations to create and implement the competence ladder tool. The competence ladder enabled teachers to assess progress in particular competences related to the teaching resources, and also generated data for the external evaluation.

3 The Educational Scenario

The main organizing tool for the methodology is the educational scenario. This provides a 7-step framework, by which practitioners can plan the delivery of EAR, adapting it to the needs of their students, while keeping fidelity to the process. The stages of the scenario are set out below, with examples of activities teachers implemented to illustrate practice at each stage:

Warm Up

- Brainstorming words and ideas associated with the topic of the lessons – using a ball or handheld cards to regulate contributions
- Miming actions
- Formulating questions around a topic to be revisited later in the lesson
- Frozen images – pupils created tableaux with their bodies to represent ideas and concepts

Discussion to Explore Topic

- Response to stimulus materials with reference to the topic in various formats (video, pictures, written texts, etc.)
- Creation of mind maps to establish starting points

Binary Oppositions to be Explored

- Must we always comply with the law or are there times when it is ok to disobey the law?
- Should we change our body appearance to impress our friends?
- Is it always helpful to help others?

Using Theatre Techniques

- Acting a character written on a slip of paper for others to guess
- Simulation of scenes/interaction related to the topic, e.g., victim and aggressor
- Forum theatre

Dialectical Discussion to Understand Topic in Depth

- Response to statements about the topic
- Questions to bring to the surface points of view, prompt deeper thinking, and re-evaluate assumptions, e.g.: Is x something to worry about? Do you agree with the statement?
- Facing each other, pupils formed inner and outer circles, which moved to enable alternation of discussion partner.

Personalising the Topic

- Allowing pupils to choose the focus for lessons
- Recreating events which had happened in the school/lives of pupils which related to the topic, for example an incident of racist bullying in a playground.

4 The EAR Training Model

The training model consisted of 20 h of face-to-face workshops in which theory and practice of the Dialectic Method and theatre techniques for learning were introduced. This was supported by a specially compiled handbook for the EAR methodology [9], and the educational scenarios planning template. Teachers were also introduced to 'competence ladders'. These guided focused assessment of students' developing CDC development. Based on earlier work carried out on behalf of the Royal Society of Arts Opening Minds programme [13].

During implementation, practitioners maintained teacher logs to support reflection, and were engaged in debriefing activities at the end of implementation, to embed practice further.

To ensure a collaborative approach to the professional development in Italy, in-service teachers and teachers in training were formed into quads. Each teacher planned a series of lessons with a group of three teachers in training, who in turn would observe and debrief the lessons with the teacher.

5 Research Methodology

The research was designed for the purposes of the EAR project, and so was informed by the project objectives. The general objective was to improve the acquisition of four key competence areas related with citizenship education, i.e., Interacting effectively and constructively with others; thinking critically; acting in a socially responsible manner; acting democratically.

The specific objectives were: 1) enhance the ability of the teachers to teach citizenship education in a more effective way; 2) mainstream the dialectical method (with the support of theatre techniques in mainstream education).

The objectives were then operationalised into evaluation questions, and measures formulated in accordance with the intended pedagogical foci: social responsibility, critical thinking, understanding of concepts related to democracy and human rights. The

Council of Europe Competences for Democratic Culture (CDC) framework [1] was drawn on to define relevant pupil outcomes and provide indicators for data analysis for each of these areas.

Data collection tools provided quantitative and qualitative pre- and post-data relevant to the evaluation questions, and as close to implementation as possible. These consisted of:

- teacher pre- and post-questionnaires
- teacher logs, for completion after the implementation of a lesson and/or peer observation
- focus groups schedules for pupil feedback at the end of implementation
- competence ladders.

The teacher questionnaires included a combination of quantitative and qualitative items. In both pre- and post-surveys, teachers indicated using a 5-point likert scale their confidence in teaching the four aspects of citizenship education which were the focus of EAR. They also indicated the prevalence of six aspects of students' learning behaviour in EAR classes in comparison with regular classes. These were followed by prompts to provide examples of student behaviour, and explain in what ways EAR lessons differed from regular lessons.

Teacher logs/observation schedules prompted practitioners to provide contextual information, approaches to planning, a description of student activity, an indication of which competences students developed in the session, with justification, and of their learning, and finally what the teacher themself had learned from the lesson.

The competence ladders were an additional reflective tool for teachers whereby they focused on the actions and talk of an individual student in the lesson and assessed where the student was in terms of mastery of the competence. This was a four-stage model, beginning with recognising examples of the competence in others, being able to describe examples themself, explaining the nature of the competence, and explaining why it is important. Figure 1 shows the competence ladder for 'respect' from the RFCDC.

Given the nature of the project, teacher participation was encouraged throughout the two years of the project, and partners in each country needed the freedom to implement training and oversee classroom delivery at times and durations which were suitable for them. This meant that there was uneven participation among teachers, which it was impossible to control for research purposes. Instead, teachers were encouraged to complete data collection tools at each stage. The pivotal sample were the 216 participants who completed both pre- and post-surveys, enabling a comparison of quantitative items. Table 1 shows the number of practitioners who received training in EAR, and implemented the methodology in some for in their setting, completing each data collection tool by country.

For the analysis, where quantitative data were collected, a comparison of scores was run for those practitioners who had completed both pre- and post-questionnaires to indicate trends in increased confidence in relation to four areas of citizenship education.

For the qualitative data a content analysis was carried out, the coding aligning to the evaluation questions, and data grouped accordingly. Texts were then subject to a content

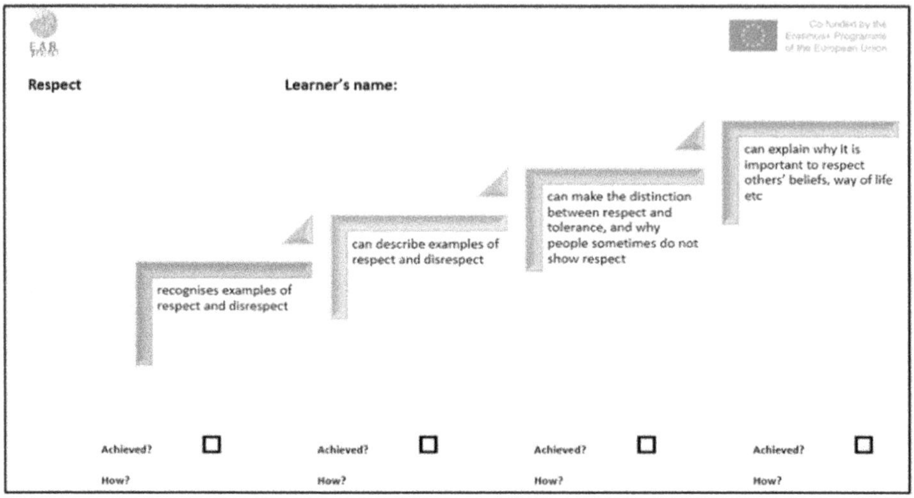

Fig. 1. Example competence ladder: respect.

Table 1. Data collected by tool and by country.

Country	Pre- & post survey	Pre-survey	Post-survey	Training evaluation	Teacher logs	Focus group	Observation	Competence ladders
Total Partner	**216**	**532**	**230**	**243**	**53**	**21**	**10**	**57**
Greece	35	88	43	6	25	19	0	0
Italy	151	198	155	158	15	2	0	39
Portugal	7	139	7	45	3	0	3	4
Spain	8	40	9	10	9	1	7	9
UK	15	32	16	20	1	1	0	5

analysis [14] to identify the key messages emerging from the qualitative data, and these used to answer the evaluation questions.

This paper presents the outcomes of the data analysis which focused on how teachers implemented EAR, and its impact on their confidence in teaching and assessing citizenship skills. The focus is on teacher professional development, in terms of changes in confidence in teaching citizenship skills.

The results are presented for the whole project, for which pre- and post-data were collected for 216 participating practitioners. A particular focus in reporting qualitative findings is on the cohort of Italian practitioners who participated.

6 Teacher Perceptions of the Changing Dynamics in the EAR Classroom

A recurring theme prevalent across all teacher logs was the use of theatre activities and stimuli to provoke thinking and discussion. The impact of this can be seen in the changes in the balance of teacher talk vs pupil talk (see Fig. 2 below).

In EAR lessons:

- The balance between teacher talk-time and pupil talk-time shifted, so pupils were more actively involved in learning conversations
- Pupils were more likely to listen to each other
- Pupils worked more independently (less dependent on teacher), and in greater collaboration with each other.

Given the emphasis in EAR on pupil activity, both through drama techniques and dialogue, changes in classroom dynamics would be expected. This turned out to be the case. For most teachers, their talk-time was lower and pupil talk-time higher in EAR lessons. Good learning behaviours of independent learning, pupils working together, and pupils listening to each other were all more prevalent in EAR lessons compared with regular lessons.

At the same time as providing the lesson structure – drama and dialogue – which would naturally ensure greater pupil talk, the focus on binary oppositions and questioning skills also had a positive impact on the quality of talk. For example, in Italy both pre-service and in-service teachers acknowledged how dialectical discussions resulted into an opportunity to consolidate and develop students' analytical and critical thinking skills.

> *During the discussions the boys often did not repeat the same things as their classmates but gave original and personal answers. Each time they took up their companion's speech it was to analyze it or to make a personal reflection.* (teacher in training, Italy)

Interestingly, in the Italian context, practising teachers have different views about their relationship with students when adopting EAR methodology in the classroom. On the one hand, many teachers observed how students' active role in the learning process and the simultaneous presence of pre-service and in-service teachers in the classroom enabled them to stand back, observe and listen young people from a novel perspective.

> *At first I was tempted to correct the students' answers but then I held back, I took a "step to the side" to make the children express more freely and then they positively surprised me with their insights on the topic of solidarity* (Practising teacher, Italy)

On the other hand, for some teachers EAR methodology was not an impetus to change teacher practice, but in those cases where teachers were already promoting learner interaction, it reinforced and provided new activities for that practice.

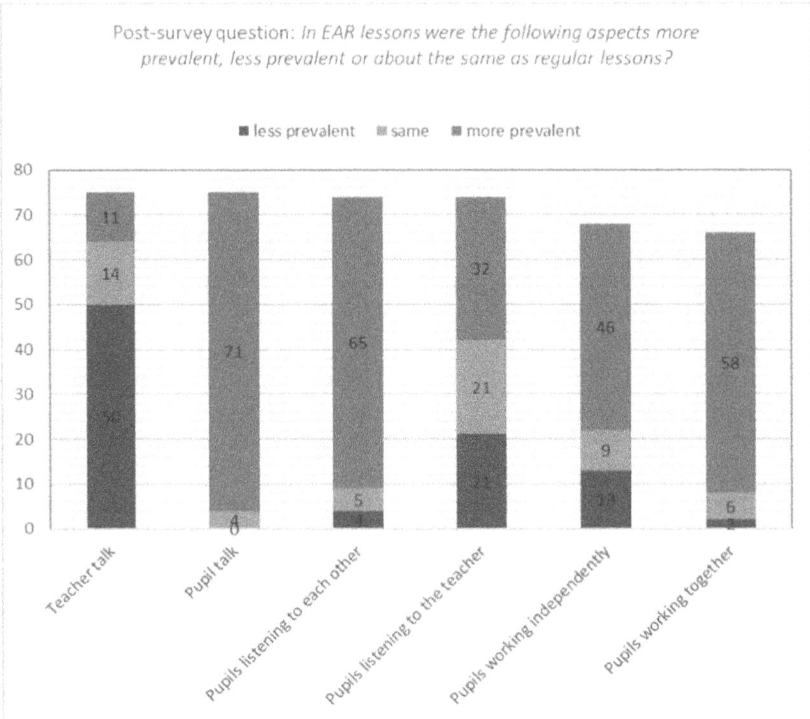

Fig. 2. Prevalence in EAR lessons of teaching and learning interaction.

7 Teachers' Confidence in Teaching and Evaluating Citizenship Education

At the end of the implementation period teachers generally noted improved confidence in teaching pupils the core competences of EAR. Because a far larger number of Italian participants completed pre- and post-surveys, this also skewed the statistics across the project (Tables 2 and 3).

Table 2. Trends in practitioner confidence in teaching the foci of EAR.

How confident are you about teaching young people the following?	Pre-	Post-
Critical thinking	3.4	3.7
How to behave in a socially responsible way	3.8	3.8
Concepts related to democracy	3.3	3.5
Concepts related to human rights	3.6	3.8

(Respondents scored 1-*not at all confident* to 5-*very confident*, the scores here are the average for those who completed both pre- and post-survey)

Table 3. Country in practitioner confidence in teaching the foci of EAR.

How confident are you about teaching young people the following?	Greece N = 28	Italy N = 150	Portugal N = 5	Spain N = 8	UK N = 15
Critical thinking	+0.3	+0.3	+0.1	+0.9	+0.9
How to behave in a socially responsible way	+0.2	0.0	0.0	+0.5	+0.5
Concepts related to democracy	+0.3	+0.2	+0.5	+0.6	+0.8
Concepts related to human rights	+0.4	+0.1	+0.4	+0.4	+0.7

The positive trends were less pronounced among Italian participants. This may be due to the fact that a large number of participants were teachers in training and may have encountered the challenges of teaching at the same time as implementing EAR. Indeed, in the Italian context, practising teachers experienced a larger increase in confidence in teaching citizenship competences than teachers in training. Teachers' in training comments reflect the more uncertain stage of career they are in, and more tentative judgement on progress in their professional learning and development:

> *I do not feel like giving the highest rating as I think that to feel confident that you can promote these skills requires long and intense work... The EAR project was definitely a good start. (Teacher in training, Italy)*

Overall, it is also noticeable that the trend in confidence to teach pupils how to behave in a socially responsible way is also less pronounced than in the other three areas. Qualitative data indicates that opening the classroom up at times presented classroom management difficulties in the early stages of implementation. In some cases, in particular in reports from Italy, the setting up of collaborative activities was initially accompanied by disruptive behaviour. Likewise, the opening up of the classroom, and allowing greater space for pupils to talk and interact on also brought occasional problems around behaviour. However, the structure of the activities and their certainty of next steps, enabled teachers and students to manage this well. Where teachers reported having to deal with inappropriate behaviour, pupils tended to respond well. This was also a part of their learning. In Italy, when some small conflicts occurred students actively managed them peacefully.

The pupils interacted in the working groups recognizing and respecting the various points of view, providing their own contribution to the realization of the common task. Sometimes small conflicts arose within the class group but also in these occasions the pupils proved capable of resolving them independently without the intervention of the teacher. (Teacher in training, Italy)

An important strand of the project was trialling ways teachers could assess competences. For this purpose, competence ladders and a section on the training logs drew teachers' attention to specific aspects of citizenship learning. The post-survey indicated that in the area of assessment teachers had indeed developed confidence. Analysis of the scores participants gave on the confidence scale of 1-*not at all confident* to 5-*very confident*', no participants scored '1', and of the 23 who scored '2', 19 were teachers in training in Italy. At such an early stage in the profession, this cohort can be expected in any case to question teaching and assessment skills (Table 4).

Table 4. Practitioner confidence in assessing citizenship competences.

How confident are you about assessing young people's competences in citizenship?	
EAR/N = 231	**3.5**
Greece/N = 43	4.0
Italy/N = 156	3.3
Portugal/N = 7	4.6
Spain/N = 9	3.9
UK/N = 16	3.7

(Respondents scored 1-*not at all confident* to 5-*very confident*, the scores here are the average for the whole project, and by country)

Practitioner comments on assessment were generally positive.

The competency ladders were an excellent framework and progression model on which to judge pupils' responses as well as how to scaffold and extend. (practising teacher, UK)

As I work on issues that have to do with human rights, I will have more confidence in evaluating the competencies of young people. (Practising teacher, Spain)

The variation in quality of teachers' thinking about the progress of their pupils was reflected in the variety of detail different teachers went into in completing the reflective tools. Nevertheless, the shift of focus from teacher actions, to pupil learning was evident across competence ladders and tools, and was at times forensic.

In Italy, only one teacher stated explicitly the benefit of the training programme in relation to the understanding of how to use the competence ladder. However, several participants mentioned the capacity to observe – and reflect on – episodes of learning and participation during classroom activities as an important achievement in their training path.

They [classroom activities] gave the possibility to the pupils to interact differently on issues that were previously addressed. In this way I was able to ascertain what had been understood and reworked by the students. (Practicing teacher, Italy)

8 Conclusions

Citizenship education can often be seen as a less important element of the curriculum, but the focus in EAR in developing questioning and communication skills demonstrated how it can have broader pedagogical value. Opening the classroom up to student questions so they are truly leading their own learning, can be a risky strategy if it leads to behaviour management problems. The EAR model and approach to training demonstrated that it provides an adequate framework to enable this to happen, and that the result is changing, more favourable dynamics in the classroom.

References

1. Council of Europe: Competences for democratic culture: living together as equals in culturally diverse democratic societies. Council of Europe, Strasbourg (2016)
2. Council of Europe: Reference framework of competences for democratic culture. Volume 2: Descriptors of competenctes for democratic culture. Council of Europe Publishing, Strasbourg (2018)
3. Council of Europe: Schools for the benefit of the community: guide for carrying out service-learning projects. Council of Europe, Strasbourg (2021)
4. Kerr, D., Huddleston, T.: Learning how to handle controversial issues in schools and other education settings: a good practice guide. Council of Europe, Strasbourg (2020)
5. Bloom, A.: The Republic of Plato. Basic Books, New York (1968)
6. Plato: The Republic. Aris & Phillips, Oxford (1991)
7. Freire, P.: Pedagogy of the Oppressed. Continuum, New York (2001)
8. Education, Audiovisual and Culture Executive Agency: Citizenship education at school in Europe, 2017. EACEA, Brussels (2017)
9. Boal, A.: Games for Actors and Non-actors. Routledge, London (1992)
10. Clark, R.: Drama techniques. IPC, Exeter (2013)
11. Paramore, J.: Questioning to stimulate dialogue. In: Building Skills for Effective Primary Teaching, Learning Matters, London (2017)
12. Fabbro, F., Ranieri, M., Cuomo, S.: Analysis of Current Situation on Citizenship Education. University of Florence, Florence (2019)
13. Isham, C., Cordingley, P.: Opening Minds Action Research: Teaching, Learning and Assessment on Competence Based Programmes. RSA, London (2012)
14. Krippendorf, K.: Content Analysis: An Introduction to Its Methodology. Sage, Los Angeles (2019)

Educating Students at Teacher Education Faculties in Art Fields (Visual Arts and Music) in the Online Environment

Svetlana Novaković[1], Jelena Blasković[1](✉), and Zlata Tomljenović[2]

[1] The Faculty of Teacher Education, University of Zagreb, Zagreb, Croatia
jelena.blaskovic@ufzg.hr

[2] The Faculty of Teacher Education, University of Rijeka, Rijeka, Croatia

Abstract. During the crisis caused by the COVID-19 pandemic, the instruction at faculties in Croatia was realised mostly online. Online teaching exclusively has proven inadequate due to the specificities of realising art courses regarding their practical part normally implemented in specialised art studios and music cabinets, that provide special equipment, tools and means, and due to the importance of monitoring and supporting students by their mentors in the creative learning process itself. Students' didactic-methodical practice with children in preschools and schools can be realized in a quality manner only through direct work in their natural surroundings where, besides teaching the subject area, social contact and the preschool teacher/child and teacher/student interactions play an important role. This research was carried out at faculties of teacher education in the academic year 2020/2021. The research goal was to determine the satisfaction with online instruction in art courses (visual arts and music) and technical readiness of students at teacher education faculties. The participants evaluated the quality of studying and support in the online environment in the art fields. Research results have shown that students of teacher education are satisfied with the implementation of art practice in online teaching as well as with their own work results. As was manifested, they are not satisfied with didactic-methodical practice nor regard themselves competent enough to perform art activities with early and preschool age children independently. The participants have expressed their satisfaction with the feedback from teachers, which positively influenced their motivation and encouraged them to work further.

Keywords: Art field (visual arts and music) · Faculty of teacher education · Satisfaction with the quality of online teaching · Technical readiness · Support to students

1 Introduction

Nowadays we live in the information age in which information, technology and knowledge play the central role. New technologies and new media govern all activities, economy and education. Creating knowledge is no longer tied exclusively to formal environment such as schools and faculties but to e-learning, online education and web learning,

M. Ranieri et al. (Eds.): ATEE 2021, CCIS 1649, pp. 136–148, 2022.
https://doi.org/10.1007/978-3-031-20777-8_11

which are increasingly present. The implementation of information and communication technology in the learning/teaching process entails carefully selected digital contents responding with the context of the course and the teaching activities. Digital contents should be founded on quality instructional design, respecting the principals of cognitive learning theory, information processing theory, cognitive load theory and the integrative model of understanding text and image [24]. Digital technology can make the education process more efficient and economic [3, 35], but the improvement of the education process is not the result of solely technology [14]. Many studies point to the fact that students are aware of both positive and negative side of instruction in the online environment [21, 25]. Decoding and understanding these positive and negative sides, especially in the time marked by the COVID-19 pandemic, can help professors in creating new educational policy, i.e. strategies for a more efficient realisation of classes, ensuring undisturbed learning process for the students. Greater flexibility concerning time and space is regarded positive by students [11]. They also consider as benefits the availability of teaching materials [32] and independent learning pace and financial feasibility, because they do not have to commute to university [16]. The research in the field has also confirmed that, when evaluating the individual learning process in digital environment, students position in the first place the possibility to choose their own learning tempo and the opportunity to decide between different learning strategies [9, 22, 30]. According to the students' opinions, the principal flaw of online teaching is lack of socialisation [1, 7, 16]. Despite the availability of online forums, electronic mail and chat rooms, students express the feeling of loneliness [10]. One of the mentioned faults of online teaching is insufficient personal contact with other students and mentors [10, 20]. Social isolation causes inadequate learning motivation in students, which is an important factor for success in web learning [18]. Besides, technical difficulties are also very often mentioned in online surroundings, whether be it insufficient technical infrastructure or deficient students' technical knowledge [2, 15]. Croatian students consider online teaching is flexible with regard to time and place, and it provides faster information exchange. Equally so, they are of the opinion they possess the technical knowledge and skills for online classes [16].

2 Methodology

2.1 Research Sample

During the crisis caused by the COVID-19 pandemic, courses at Croatian facultieswere carried out mostly online. The transition from contact learning and teaching, which entails direct professor-student contact, to distant teaching implemented exclusively with the use of ICT has pointed out some drawbacks, especially in the art field (visual arts and music). The realisation of classes in art fields has its specificities, such as specialized art studios and music cabinets, equipped with adequate tools and means. When compared to contact teaching, performing classes and monitoring and supporting students by their mentors have not proven to be efficient enough in the online environment. Furthermore, due to social contacts and interaction between the participants, the only way of implementing the practical part of teaching methodology courses with children in kindergartens and pupils in schools in a quality manner is through direct work in their natural surroundings. The goal of this research was to establish students' satisfaction with online instruction in art courses (visual arts and music), and the level of technological readiness, i.e. competences of teacher education students. Research participants have assessed the quality of studying and support in the online environment in the art fields.

The following hypotheses ensue from the above:

H1: There are differences in the satisfaction with online classes considering the knowledge on e-learning technologies.

H2: It is assumed that teacher education students (preschool teachers, teachers) are not satisfied with online teaching within the art courses (visual arts and music).

H3: It is assumed that teacher education students are not satisfied with the realisation of teaching methodology courses in the online environment.

2.2 Research Sample

The research was carried out in the academic year 2020/2021. It included students of undergraduate studies of early preschool education (N = 215) and teacher education students (N = 126) at the faculties in Zagreb and Rijeka. In total, 341 students participated in the study. 10,3% of the participating students attended online courses for one semester, 37,2% for two, 47,5% attended online classes for three semesters, and 5% of them had online classes for all four semesters.

2.3 Instrument

An author questionnaire was designed for the needs of the research. The questionnaire entailed objective questions of dichotomous nature (type of study, year of study) and the questions of subjective nature, wherein the participants expressed their own opinions on a five-degree scale about the set claims. Likert scale and other ordinal scales for expressing degrees of agreement with the claims were used. The instrument's validity was determined via the procedure of main components factorisation, and it yielded 5 factors with characteristic roots over 1, which together explain 60,02% of the variance (KMO = 0,872; Bartlett's test: p = 0,000). There are five factors in total based on 25 claims. The content of the first factor regards the advantages of online classes, and it entails seven claims. The factor loadings for this factor are in range from 0,44 to 0,85. The second factor regards the technological conditions of online classes, for which the factor loadings are in range from 0,29 to 0,66 (Inter – Item correlation is 0,35). The third factor, i.e. satisfaction with the quality of classes, entails 4 claims, and the factor loadings are in range from 0,73 to 0,86. The fourth factor is quality of instruction in art courses based on 5 claims, and the factor loadings are in range from 0,74 to 0,89. The fifth factor is the quality of support based on five claims, with factor loadings from 0,33 to 0,87. The coefficients of internal consistency for each obtained factor are in range from satisfactory to high. For the factor advantages of online classes, it is $\alpha = 0{,}84$, and for technological conditions of online classes $\alpha = 0{,}62$ (Inter - Item correlation je 0,35), for satisfaction with the quality of classes $\alpha = 0{,}84$, for the quality of instruction in art courses $\alpha = 0{,}89$ and for the quality of support for students $\alpha = 0{,}76$.

2.4 Data Analysis and Statistical Processing

The gathered data were processed in the statistical programme SPSS 21.0. For descriptive statistics of nominal and ordinal variables, the following measures were calculated: frequencies (f), relative frequencies (%), arithmetic mean (M), dominant value (mode), median (Md), standard deviation (SD), and the measures of the distribution's normality (skewness, kurtosis). The normality of the distribution was checked with Kolmogorov-Smirnov test, and parametric Student's t-test was used for testing the hypothesis.

3 Interpretation of the Results

3.1 Advantages of Online Teaching

The participants have assessed classes in the online environment according to a five-degree scale and it was shown that online classes, according to their opinions, have many positive sides. More than half of the participants, 60,4%, consider they have better availability of the materials (M = 3,70; SD = 1,18) because by transferring to online classes, teachers have enriched the learning contents with a series of tools the students could use. 79,8% of the students emphasize the advantage of flexibility in choosing the place and time for learning (M = 4,18; SD = 1,00), and 66,9% of them consider that the exchange of information and knowledge with other students is swift (M = 3,96; SD = 1,02). This way of learning and teaching presents a challenge for the students (72,8%) and the opportunity to improve their digital competence (M = 4,01; SD = 0,96). On the other hand, lower assessments can be observed on the variable *realisation of better learning outcomes and acquiring knowledge in online class* (M = 2,74; SD = 1,15), agreed upon by 43,7% of the participant, whereas, 31,7% partially agrees with it. As little as 23,4% of the participants feels such form of classes encourages active participation. 28,4% of the participants consider online environment diminishes the teacher's role, while 40,2% of them disagree with this claim, and one third of the participants (31,4%) partially agrees with it (M = 2,83; SD = 1,27). On some variables, the participants do not take a determined stand, but are in doubt. For example, 37, 9% does not agree, and 33,4% partially agrees that online learning contributes to faster content matter acquisition (M = 2,90; SD = 1,22). Almost a third of the students (32,9%) consider online teaching enhances their creativity and desire for further exploration (M = 3,00; SD = 1,20), whereas almost equal number, 34,3% of them, disagrees with the claim. 42,3% of the students do not feel that online classes are appropriate for the needs of today's students (M = 3,34; SD = 1,03).

3.2 Technological Conditions of Studying

In the online environment, it is important to own appropriate technological equipment for performing classes [6, 16, 23]. In this research, most students (87,1%) possess their own equipment necessary for active participation in online learning. It entails the knowledge on applying technologies of online learning. The success of learning and teaching depends on knowing how to apply online learning technologies. More than half of the students (61,6%) rate their own knowledge on online learning technologies as very good (M = 3,59: SD = 0,58). Out of the tools needed for online classes, 95,9% of the participants used office tools and tools for working on the computer (operation system, e-mail, Internet, MS word, Excel, PowerPoint and others), while the least used were tools for cooperative work (blog, wiki...) (12,3%) and social networks (Facebook, Twitter, LinkedIn...) (22,9%).

The claim of basic informatics literacy being essential for online learning is agreed upon by 93% of the participants. 86,5% of them feel that the use of e-learning technology is necessary for online learning, as well as knowledge on digital tools for using and finding video and audio contents, and knowledge on digital tools for searching professional and scientific literature.

Within this research, hypothesis H1 was set presuming the existence of difference in students' satisfaction with online teaching with regard to their knowledge on e-learning technologies (see Table 1).

Table 1. Students' satisfaction with online classes and their knowledge on e-technologies (N = 341)

Knowledge in the field of online learning technologies' application		N	M	SD	T (df = 327)	p
Advantages of instruction in online environment	Good	115	3,40	0,70	-2,562	**0,011**
	Very good	214	3,62	0,79		
The quality of instruction in art courses	Good	115	3,34	0,98	1,478	0,140
	Very good	214	3,16	1,08		
Quality of support for students	Good	115	4,22	0,71	0,086	0,932
	Very good	214	4,21	0,70		
Satisfaction with the quality of instruction	Good	115	3,44	0,82	-4,179	**0,000**
	Very good	214	3,84	0,86		
Technological conditions of studying	Good	115	3,97	0,78	-4,168	**0,000**
	Very good	214	4,33	0,67		

$p \leq 0.05$

The results of the t-test show statistically significant differences in the arithmetic mean of the compared groups. The participants who know e-technologies better notice more advantages, are more satisfied with the quality of instruction and have good equipment, i.e. good technological conditions for studying. This *confirms* the hypothesis of the existence of differences in the satisfaction with online teaching considering the knowledge on e-learning technologies.

3.3 Quality of Support to Students

During online classes, an important role is played by support to students on behalf of their professors. A research [4] points to the problem of the lack of communication between students and certain professors, and the lack of feedback. Students are isolated from each other in online class, and they need teacher support.

The participants feel that in online learning, feedback from the teacher is important because it motivates and encourages students to work (f = 88,2%; M = 4,49; SD = 0,77). 66,2% of the students consider the aspect of nonverbal communication lacking (M = 3,93M SD = 1,13). That organisation and economic time management is important in the online environment is agreed upon by 88,3% of the participants (M = 4,48; SD = 0,77), whereas 82,7% of the students feel that a lot of independent work is needed (M = 4,31; SD = 0,95). 68,9% of the students need additional motivation for online learning (M = 3,39; SD = 1,20). 61,6% of the students in total are satisfied with the given feedback about the realisation of assignments (M = 3,74; SD = 1,09).

3.4 The Quality of Teaching Art Courses

Art courses are an indispensable formative part of gaining professional competences of preschool teachers and teachers since visual art and music contents are an integral part of compulsory primary education in Croatia. Instruction of art courses is realised through theoretical courses, practical exercises and teaching methodology courses. Online classes have disabled undisturbed implementation of those forms of work that demand additional equipment or mentor approach in the course of practice.

In accordance, hypothesis H2 was set, which assumed that teacher education students (preschool teachers, teachers) are not satisfied with online classes in performing practice in art courses (visual arts and music). The results are presented in Table 2.

Table 2. The quality of online art courses teaching (N = 341)

	Mode	Md	M	SD	SK	KA
I am satisfied with the availability of class materials on digital platforms	4	4,00	3,86	0,98	-0,56	-0,08
I am satisfied with the quality of class content's presentation via the use of various electronic tools	4	4,00	3,89	0,93	-0,48	-0,13
I am satisfied with mastering the assigned practical exercises in Music course	5	4,00	3,91	1,13	-0,80	-0,14
I am satisfied with the mastery of assigned practical exercises in Art course	5	4,00	4,16	0,90	-0,79	-0,08
I am satisfied with the work results considering the invested time and effort in the realisation of visual art practice	5	5,00	4,31	0,92	-1,24	0,98
I am satisfied with the work results considering the invested time and effort in the realisation of music practice	5	5,00	4,25	1,03	-1,46	1,63

(*continued*)

Table 2. *(continued)*

	Mode	Md	M	SD	SK	KA
I am satisfied with the professor taking technical problems in online classes into consideration (poor sound, Internet connection, poor image, visual processing of class content…)	5	4,00	4,12	1,06	-1,16	0,74
I am satisfied with the realised individual communication with the professors (e-mail, forum, whats app…)	5	4,00	4,16	0,94	-0,99	0,47

The results presented in Table 2 show that students are satisfied with the quality of online teaching of art courses, both in visual arts and music field. They are also satisfied with the availability and quality of the teaching contents, with the mastery of the practical part of the course, and with teacher support and teacher-student communication. The basic purpose of teacher education faculties is to educate future preschool teachers and teachers for working with children. Hence, didactical courses are a fundamental part of teaching at teacher education faculties. Teaching methodology courses in certain educational fields at teacher education faculties in Croatia are realised at higher years of teacher education and early preschool education studies. The assessment of satisfaction with the implementation of teaching methodology courses in the art fields in the online environment has been done by students of the fourth and fifth year of their teacher education studies and the students of the second and third year of early and preschool education studies (N = 295). Less than half of the participants are satisfied with the quality of methodical readiness, i.e. acquiring competences for working in kindergarten or school (47,8%). *In the preparation and education for working with children, mentor, i.e. individual work with professors is necessary* is a claim deemed true by 61,9% of the participants, whereas a small number of them (8,5%) do not have a need for teacher's help in the preparation for working with children (8,5%). During the COVID-19 pandemic, the practical part of teaching methodology courses in kindergartens and schools has been organised under special conditions. The usual practice before the pandemic was that one students performed a methodical exercise, and the other colleagues (in groups up to 15 students) observed and evaluated the implemented activity, i.e. school lesson. The newly-created situation under COVID-19 measures has resulted with special measures in educational institutions as well, wherein only one student was allowed in class alongside a mentor preschool teacher/teacher, and the rest of the group observed the recorded activity online (not in contact with children). Performing art courses methodology (visual art and music) during the pandemic has hindered the overall insight into all dimensions of mentor work with children, which is agreed upon by 49,2% of the participants and partially agreed on by 22,9%.

Considering the problem, a hypothesis was set assuming teacher education students are not satisfied with the implementation of the practical part of teaching methodology courses in the online environment. The results are presented in Table 3.

Table 3. Assessment of student satisfaction with the realisation of art courses teaching methodology in the online environment (N = 295)

	Mode	Md	M	SD	SK	KA
I am satisfied with the quality of methodical preparation for working in kindergarten/school in the online environment	3	4,00	3,62	1,09	-0,46	-0,35
Work with mentors, i.e. individual work is necessary in the preparation of students for working with children in kindergarten/school	5	4,00	3,94	1,10	-0,95	0,35
The realisation of art and music methodology in special conditions during the pandemic does not reflect the true image of future work with children	5	4,00	3,67	1,22	-0,55	-0,66
The realisation of methodology courses in professional-pedagogic practice in the online environment does not provide adequate qualification for working with children	5	4,00	3,68	1,22	-0,57	-0,61

Looking at the results of arithmetic means, more than half of the participants agrees with the claim that visual arts and music teaching methodology in special conditions during the pandemic does not paint a true picture of future work with children (f = 56,9%; M = 3,67; DS = 1,22). Somewhat more than half of the participants (57,6%) agree with the claim that performing teaching methodology courses through professional-pedagogic practice in the online environment does not provide quality training of students for working with children (M = 3,68; DS = 1,22). Therefore, the hypothesis that students are not satisfied with the implementation of teaching methodology courses in the online environment is *confirmed.*

4 Discussion

Introducing distant instruction during the Covid-19 pandemic has led to the recognition of this field and the importance of such type of education at all levels, including high education, but also to the need of acquiring new ways of work and communication between students and teachers [33]. Some faculties have managed the situation better than others [12, 13]. For implementing online instruction, the most important thing is to secure a stabile internet connection, appropriate computer and other equipment, and access to electronic literature (availability of university textbooks and other study matter) [4]. Technological problems may cause intense frustration [34] so technical support by the faculty's staff is needed. Technical and pedagogic readiness of professors is paramount to performing instruction in the online environment. Students emphasized the choice of place and time for learning as benefits of online teaching, which is confirmed in other studies as well [34]. They regard the possibility of swift information and knowledge exchange with other students important, as well as the chance to improve their digital competences, which this form of teaching provides. On the other hand, almost half of the participants feel online instruction does not secure faster matter acquisition nor efficient attainment of the learning outcomes or knowledge gain. They are aware that self-organisation, time management and independent work are key to efficient online learning, but they also consider they need support and additional motivation from their professors. In research [8] students named significant, constructive, textual feedback, and video recordings that explain the course matter as the most important elements in their learning and motivation during online instruction. They also appreciated timely feedback (within 12–24 h). This research has pointed out the problem of nonverbal communication's absence in the online environment, which is corroborated by some other research [4]. The students have shown satisfaction with the realised individual communication with teachers, wherein they used various electronic and digital models for establishing the connection, which was proven successful in some other cases as well [19, 28]. They have also expressed their satisfaction with teachers' understanding for experienced technical problems in online classes (poor sound and image, internet connection, visual processing of class content, etc.). The results of the implemented research regarding the technological conditions of studying show that teacher education students in Croatia possess the necessary equipment for participating in online learning, that their knowledge of online learning technologies is very good, and that they use various tools for attending classes and doing homework. On the other hand, there are differences in student satisfaction with online classes regarding the knowledge on e-learning technologies. Participants with better knowledge of e-technology notice more positive sides of online teaching, they are satisfied with class quality and have good technological conditions for studying, which is also confirmed by other studies [23]. The focus of this research was the instruction of art courses in the online environment. Art classes have their specificities since they include practical exercises done in specialised art studios and music cabinets fitted with special equipment, tools and means, which can lead to problems in realising these classes in the online environment [5]. The need for individual monitoring and support to students by their mentors during the creative process itself is also characteristic of art instruction. Due to the introduced measures regarding the COVID-19 pandemic, students could have also been faced with the problem of procuring the basic materials and means necessary for artistic expression, i.e. performing class assignments [26]. A research done in Uganda [31] showed that art and design professors face motivational challenges with regard to the use of digital technologies (concerning the negative attitude towards digital technologies, lack of self-confidence and time, insufficient digital competence and the fear of losing creativity). Moreover, they struggle with the lack of adequate approach to modern technologies (i.e. hardware, software and the Internet). In a research that sought to determine the opinions of undergraduate students about the art and design class taught via distant education during the COVID-19 pandemic, it was found that students lost their motivation. They did not satisfy their socialisation needs nor sufficiently develop some knowledge and abilities regarding certain contents that require practical exercise in art classes [2, 27]. Online way of work gives students the opportunity to acquire theoretical knowledge in the frame of art courses. However, instruction in visual arts teaching methodology without classroom practice does not realise its basic purpose nor develops student competence, whose attainment the course aims for [17].

5 Conclusion

Students at teacher education faculties acquire professional and expert competences in the frame of art courses by gaining knowledge and skills through theoretical and practical instruction and didactic-methodology courses. This research has shown that students are satisfied with the implemented practical training in the frame of visual arts and music courses and with their work results. Didactical practice in teaching methodology has not provided students with complete insight into working with children nor do they consider themselves competent enough for independent implementation of art activities with preschool and school age children. Most participants (55,4%) consider hybrid or mixed teaching method as the most optimal form of instruction in visual art courses at teacher faculties, which is confirmed by some other research [29]. Some studies suggest [4] that online teaching is applicable for theory transfer and less practical or non-applicable for practical work and art classes, wherein physical contact is irreplaceable. Owing to innovations in the field of technology and its greater and greater availability, changes occur in the methods of learning and teaching in the overall educational hierarchy, i.e. new forms of interaction and cooperation between teachers and students. However, this does not mean that the overall traditional curriculum should be changed. Research results show that the combination of traditional didactical approaches and online teaching is some sort of a most contemporary direction in art education. Quality interactive communication between students and teachers can provide the sense of social presence and in greater measure prevent the isolation due to the lack of direct interpersonal contact. A change in the educational programs for preschool teachers and teachers is also necessary regarding the acquisition of digital competence indispensable for implementing technologies in working with children and students.

6 Recommendations for Further Research

Research in the field could be expanded by including additional instruments that would utilize focus groups or interviews with participants. In such a way, a deeper insight into the experience of online learning would be acquired within the art courses students attend. Additionally, the research could encompass teachers' standpoints and views on online learning in art courses, and examine their opinion on their digital competence and possible problems in the course of online teaching.

References

1. Adnan, M., Anwar, K.: Online learning amid the COVID-19 pandemic: students' perspectives. Online Submission **2**(1), 45–51 (2020). https://files.eric.ed.gov/fulltext/ED606496.pdf. Accessed 10 May 2021
2. Babakova, L., Kolovska, T., Konstantinidu, K.: Influence of distance learning on the academic motivation of students from specialties in the field of arts. Proc. CBU Soc. Sci. **2**, 22–26 (2021). https://ojs.cbuic.cz/index.php/pss/article/view/197/369. Accessed 06 Aug 2021
3. BECTA: Primary schools – ICT and standards: an analysis of national data from Ofsted and QCA by Becta. Coventry. British Educational Communications and Technology Agency, UK (2003). https://dera.ioe.ac.uk/1700/1/becta_2002_ictstandards_analysisreport.pdf. Accessed 01 Feb 2021

4. Bezjak, S., Đorđević, M., Plužarić, Ž.: Izazovi u visokom obrazovanju za vrijeme pandemije bolesti COVID-19 i socijalne izolacije: iskustva i potrebe studenata i djelatnika visokih učilišta. Agencija za znanost i visoko obrazovanje (2020). https://www.azvo.hr/images/stories/novosti/Rezultati_istra%C5%BEivanja_Izazovi_u_visokom_obrazovanju_za_vrijeme_pandemije_bolesti_COVID19_i_socijalne_izolacije.pdf. Accessed 08 May 2021
5. Bigham, B.S., Fannakhosrow, M., Safipour, A., Jafari, M., Chenari, K.: E-learning model for art education: case study in Iran. 1–11 (2021). https://arxiv.org/ftp/arxiv/papers/2110/2110.03904.pdf. Accessed 01 Sep 2021
6. Brumini, G., Mavrinac, M., Brumini, M., Špalj, S., Blagović, B.: Oblikovanje i validacija upitnika kojim se mjeri stav studenata prema e-učenju. Med. Flum. **48**(1), 48–56 (2012). https://hrcak.srce.hr/file/119307. Accessed 07 June 2021
7. Bunn, J.: Student persistence in a LIS distance education program. Aust. Acad. Res. Libr. **35**(3), 253–269 (2004). https://www.tandfonline.com/doi/pdf/10.1080/00048623.2004.10755275?needAccess=true. Accessed 01 June 2021
8. Conklin, S., Garrett Dikkers, A.: Instructor social presence and connectedness in a quick shift from face-to-face to online instruction. Online Learn. Consortium **25**(1), 135–150 (2021). https://doi.org/10.24059/olj.v25i1.2482. Accessed 01 May 2021
9. Conole, G., De Laat, M., Dillon, T., Darby, J.: 'Disruptive technologies', 'pedagogical innovation': what's new? Findings from an in-depth study of students' use and perception of technology. Comput. Educ. **50**(2), 511–524 (2008). https://citeseerx.ist.psu.edu/viewdoc/download?doi=10.1.1.466.587&rep=rep1&type=pdf. Accessed 01 June 2021
10. Ćukušić, M., Jadrić, M.: E-učenje: koncept i primjena. Školska knjiga, Zagreb (2012)
11. Fraj-Hussein, R., Barak, M., Dori, Y.: Lifelong learning at the technion: graduate students' perceptions of and experiences in distance learning. Interdiscip. J. E-skills Lifelong Learn. **8**, 115–135 (2012). https://www.researchgate.net/publication/266827984_Lifelong_Learning_at_the_Technion_Graduate_Students'_Perceptions_of_and_Experiences_in_Distance_Learning. Accessed 01 June 2021
12. Goin Kono, K., Taylor, S.: Using an ethos of care to bridge the digital divide: exploring faculty narratives during a global pandemic. Online Learn. Consortium **25**(1), 151–165 (2021). https://doi.org/10.24059/olj.v25i1.2484. Accessed 01 June 2021
13. Hart, C.M.D., Xu, D., Hill, M., Alonso, E.: COVID-19 and community college instructional responses. Online Learn. Consortium **25**(1), 41–69 (2021). https://doi.org/10.24059/olj.v25i1.2568. Accessed 01 June 2021
14. Higgins, S., Xiao, Z.M., Katsipataki, M.: The impact of digital technology on learning. Full Report. Durham University (2012). https://larrycuban.files.wordpress.com/2013/12/the_impact_of_digital_technologies_on_learning_full_report_2012.pdf. Accessed 04 Apr 2021
15. Jæger, M.M., Blaabæk, E.H.: Inequality in learning opportunities during Covid-19: evidence from library takeout. Res. Soc. Stratif. Mobil. **68**, 100524 (2020). https://www.ncbi.nlm.nih.gov/pmc/articles/PMC7301805/. Accessed 05 Sep 2021
16. Jukić, D.: Tehnička pripremljenost i motiviranost studenata hrvatskih sveučilišta za online oblik nastave. Život i škola: časopis za teoriju i praksu odgoja i obrazovanja **LXIII**(1), 103–115 (2017). https://hrcak.srce.hr/file/286047. Accessed 05 Nov 2021
17. Kuščević, D., Tomaš, S., Mornar, I.: Primjena sustava Moodle u metodici nastave likovne kulture [The Application of Moodle in the Didactic of Teaching Art]. Zbornik radova filozofskog fakulteta u Splitu **6/7**, 55–63 (2014). https://hrcak.srce.hr/file/227804. Accessed 05 Nov 2021
18. Lim, D.H., Morris, M.L., Kupritz, V.W.: Online vs. blended learning: differences in instructional outcomes and learner satisfaction. J. Asynchronous Learn. Netw. **11**(2), 27–42 (2007). https://files.eric.ed.gov/fulltext/EJ842695.pdf. Accessed 30 May 2021

19. Martin, F., Wang, C., Sadaf, A.: Facilitation matters: instructor perception of helpfulness of facilitation strategies in online courses. Online Learn. Consortium **24**(1), 28–49 (2020). https://doi.org/10.24059/olj.v24i1.1980. Accessed 01 May 2021
20. McMurtrie, B.: How to reconnect with students and strengthen your remote course (2020). https://www.chronicle.com/article/How-to-ReconnectWith-Students/248461? Accessed 30 June 2021
21. Miziuk, V.: Distance learning in higher education institutions in modern conditions: advantages, disadvantages, prospects. In: Nestorenko, T., Pokusa, T. (eds.) Education During a Pandemic Crisis: Problems and Prospects, Monograph, pp. 163–170. The Academy of Management and Administration in Opole, Opole (2020). https://www.wszia.opole.pl/wpcontent/uploads/2020/09/2020_education_during_pandemic_crisis_problems_and_prospects-1.pdf. Accessed 03Aug 2021
22. Paechter, M., Maier, B.: Online or face-to-face? Students' expectations of and experiences in e-learning: their relation to learning achievements and course satisfaction. Comput. Educ. **54**(1), 222–229 (2010). https://www.sciencedirect.com/science/article/abs/pii/S0360131509003029?via%3Dihub. Accessed 01 June 2021
23. Peytcheva-Forsyth, R., Blagovesna Yovkova, B., Aleksieva, Lj.: Factors affecting students' attitudes towards online learning - the case of Sofia University. In: Pasheva, V., Popivanov, N., Venkov, G. (eds.) Proceedings of the 44th International Conference on Applications of Mathematics in Engineering and Economics, vol. 2048, pp. 1–9 (2018). https://aip.scitation.org/doi/pdf/10.1063/1.5082043. Accessed 01 June 2021
24. Rončević, A.: Uvjerenja učitelja o multimedijima i ishodi učenja kod učenika. In: Cindrić, M., Domović, V., Matijević, M. (eds.). Pedagogija i Društvo Znanja, Učiteljski fakultet Sveučilište u Zagrebu, Zagreb, pp. 315–324 (2008). https://www.bib.irb.hr/398761. Accessed 05 Oct 2021
25. Rudenko, Y., Naboka, O., Korolova, L., Kozhukhova, K., Kazakevych, O., Semenikhina, O.: Online learning with the eyes of teachers and students in educational institutions of Ukraine. TEM J. **10**(2), 922–936 (2021). https://www.temjournal.com/content/102/TEMJournalMay2021_922_931.pdf. Accessed 15 Aug 2021
26. Sabol, F.R.: Art education during the COVID-19 pandemic: the journey across a changing landscape. Arts Educ. Policy Rev. (2021). https://www.tandfonline.com/doi/full/10.1080/10632913.2021.1931599. Accessed 25 Sep 2021
27. Sehran, D.: Students' opinions about the distance education to art and design courses in the pandemic process. World J. Educ. **10**(3), 113–126 (2020). http://wje.sciedupress.com. Accessed 01 June 2021
28. Sheridan, K., Kelly, M.A.: The indicators of instructor presence that are important to students in online courses. J. Online Learn. Teach. **6**(4), 767–779 (2010). https://files.eric.ed.gov/fulltext/EJ1108404.pdf. Accessed 30 May 2021
29. Smidt, E., Bunk, J., McGrory, B., Li, R., Gatenby, T.: Student attitudes about distance education: focusing on context and effective practices. IAFOR J. Educ. **2**(1), 40–64 (2014). https://files.eric.ed.gov/fulltext/EJ1080350.pdf. Accessed 01 June 2021
30. Sun, P.C., Tsai, R.J., Finger, G., Chen, Y.Y., Yeh, D.: What drives a successful e-learning? An empirical investigation of the critical factors influencing learner satisfaction. Comput. Educ. **50**(4), 1183–1202 (2008). https://www.researchgate.net/publication/260001547_What_drives_a_successful. Accessed 01 June 2021
31. Tusiime, W.E., Johannesen, M., Björk Gudmundsdottir, G.: Teaching art and design in a digital age: challenges facing Ugandan teacher educators. J. Vocat. Educ. Train. 1–22 (2020). https://www.tandfonline.com/doi/full/10.1080/13636820.2020.1786439. Accessed 14 Oct 2021
32. Yaghoubi, J., Malekmohammadi, I., Iravani, H., Attaran, M., Gheidi, A.: Virtual students' perceptions of e-learning in Iran. TOJET: Turkish Online J. Educ. Technol. **7**(7), 89–95 (2008). https://files.eric.ed.gov/fulltext/ED502679.pdf. Accessed 10 May 2021

33. Yefimenko, I.V., Yakymchuk, O.M., Kravtsova, N.Y., Sotska, H.I., Korol, A.M.: Art education development in the context of global changes. Linguist. Culture Rev. **5**(S2), 501–513 (2021). https://doi.org/10.37028/lingcure.v5nS2.1386. Accessed 12 Sep 2021
34. Wasserman, E., Migdal, R.: Professional development: teachers' attitudes in online and traditional training course. Online Learn. Consortium 23(1), 132–143 (2019). https://olj.onlinelearningconsortium.org/index.php/olj/article/view/1299/790. Accessed 01 June 2021
35. Wenglinsky, H.: Does it compute? The relationship between educational technology and achievement in mathematics. Princeton: Policy Information Center, Research Division, Educational Testing Service, New York (1998). https://www.ets.org/Media/Research/pdf/PICTECHNOLOG.pdf. Accessed 04 Apr 2021

Digital Technology and Equity for Inclusive Teaching

"La scuola si Nutre del Territorio nel Quale Alberga" "The School is Nourished by the Local Context"

Alessandra Anichini(✉), Giuseppina Cannella(✉), and Rudi Bartolini(✉)

INDIRE, Florence, Italy
{a.anichini,g.cannella,r.bartolini}@indire.it

Abstract. During the 2020/21 school year the "Small and rural schools" (Piccole Scuole) INDIRE research team set up a research activity with a group of teachers active in the Madonie area (Sicily) grouped as RESMA network. The research topic dealt with planning a didactic unit linked to the enhancement of the territory.

Recorded interventions, projects, logbooks produced by teachers during their experimentation in the classroom are the basis for documentation analysis which attempts to describe the ways in which schools have tackled activities centred on the relationship with the territory. Meetings and interactions have been carried out entirely at distance due to the pandemic.

This article aims at proposing ideas for analysing the relationship between contextual curriculum, emerging curriculum and national curriculum in the context of small Italian schools. It also gives some insights into the theme of the relationship between the local and global dimensions of the curriculum in order to overcome subject boundaries according to three parameters borrowed from Morin's work: the need to carry out "disciplinary encroachments", i.e., multidisciplinarity able to restore meaning to learning pathways. To establish a balance between the micro and macro dimensions, between the context and the global, to reconnect the observation of reality with "high" knowledge. Refine and provide students with the "complexity" (sociological, political, psychological, affective, mythological, etc.) of the vision that affects reality.

The findings of the investigation can be identified into the richness of the teachers' journeys and are also analysed in relation to the awareness they have gained.

Keywords: Small schools · Context · Local curriculum

1 Introduction

Piccole Scuole has been dealing for years with the small schools located throughout Italy. Recently, research carried out by a group of researchers [1, 2] has been able to conduct a census, revealing surprising data: the overall number of small and rural in Italy schools are 8.848. Among them, 7.204 are primary schools and 1.644 lower secondary. The small and rural schools have 591.682 students enrolled and 1.460 schools have

M. Ranieri et al. (Eds.): ATEE 2021, CCIS 1649, pp. 151–160, 2022.
https://doi.org/10.1007/978-3-031-20777-8_12

multigrade classes. Small primary schools are 45,3% of all the Italian primary schools. Small lower secondary schools are 21,7% of all the Italian lower secondary schools.

Approximately 54% of small schools are located in inland areas of the country, which are characterized by problems of isolation, remoteness and cultural marginalization.

Small schools are therefore a very important reality in our country [3]. One of the main features deals with the multiage classroom which usually also includes a reduced number of teachers. Moreover, some of Italy's small schools are in areas at risk of depopulation. These areas present economic difficulties: younger generations move away in search of job opportunities as well as cultural stimuli. Often the school is the only cultural institution and a functional element in the life of the community and society [4, 5].

These schools usually establish a strong relationship with their territories, for the aim of this study they represent a privileged observatory. The theme of the relationship between school and territory is not a new one: it belongs to a pedagogical tradition that draws its main inspiration from the John Dewey's thoughts [15], who advocated a strong link between school institution and reality outside, understood as a small community (the family, the neighborhood) and as society in its entirety. The school, as well as its components, teachers, and students in particular, as Bronfenbrenner reminds us, are at the center of a system of concentric circles which, starting from the family nucleus, reaches the organization of planetary government and the media [6] (Fig. 1).

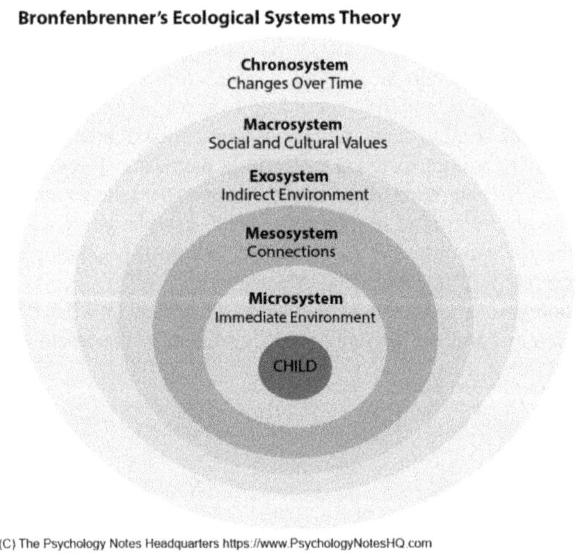

Fig. 1. Bronfenbrenner ecological system theory.

The model proposed by Bronfenbrenner represents an "ecosystem" made up of different levels (Macrosystem, Exosystem, Microsystem and Chronosystem) in which the individual is rooted. The ecosystem is the environment necessary for the development of the person in his or her entirety.

This approach must be accompanied by the constructs of "environment", "context" and "territory" [7]. If the "environment" can easily be traced back to the "learning environment" in which spaces, objects, materials and didactic (and not) tools are aimed at achieving educational objectives, the "context" is given by the set of expert relationships that involve subjects among themselves and are always in progress [8]. In these relationships, the physical space is a *pedagogical object* [9] because it is a medium that transfers meanings as a) it is a structured system, b) it acts by means of functions, c) with communicative purposes.

And finally, as far as the "territory" is concerned, it has recently become the main character of educational activities carried out outside the classroom. In late sixties in Italy pedagogist such as De Bartolomeis (2018) have identified the territory as an "extended schooling system" which could offer opportunities to avoid educational poverty and at the same time to strengthen students' identity. More recently, there have been an increasing number of reflections and experiences connecting education and territory, also with reference to natural spaces and the environment [11, 12].

The relationship between local and global dimension is at the heart of today's reflections on the theme of ecology in its broadest sense.

Edgar Morin (2000), theorist of complexity, has placed it at the centre of his thinking, indicating the importance of a closer connection between elements often considered antithetical as the Indicazioni Nazionali (National Curriculum) promotes: "There is an ever-increasing inadequacy between our disjointed, fractionated knowledge, divided into disciplines on the one hand, and increasingly multidisciplinary, transversal, multidimensional, transnational, global, planetary realities or problems on the other. (...) More and more, all particular problems can only be correctly posed and thought of in their context, and the very context of these problems must increasingly be placed in the planetary context. (...) Relevant knowledge is that which can place all information in its own context and, if possible, in the whole of which it is part. It can also be said that knowledge progresses primarily not through sophistication, formalisation and abstraction, but through the ability to contextualise and globalise" (*ivi*, p. 5)[1] tracing the idea of an ecosystem-world, of a "community of destiny" that is inevitable today. Morin's work invites us to reconnect dimensions and knowledge in a horizon of meaning that aims at answering the great questions of our time, often prompted by questions arising from contingent and local needs, but which have an obvious correspondence with the more general questions that concern society in its entirety.

---

[1] English translation from Italian version by the authors: "C'è un'inadeguatezza sempre più ampia tra i nostri saperi disgiunti, frazionati, suddivisi in discipline da una parte, e realtà o problemi sempre più polidisciplinari, trasversali, multidimensionali, transnazionali, globali, planetari, dall'altra. (...) Sempre più, tutti i problemi particolari possono essere posti e pensati correttamente solo nel loro contesto, e il contesto stesso di questi problemi deve essere posto sempre più nel contesto planetario. (...) La conoscenza pertinente è quella capace di collocare ogni informazione nel proprio contesto e se possibile nell'insieme in cui si inscrive. Si può anche dire che la conoscenza progredisce principalmente non con la sofisticazione, la formalizzazione e l'astrazione, ma con la capacità di contestualizzare e globalizzare" (Morin, 2000, p. 5).

2 The Project

It is precisely the relationship between micro and macro dimensions that our research is interested in, approaching a privileged observatory such as that of small schools. We present a research project carried out with a network of small Italian schools (The Resma Network) located in the Madonie area, in Sicily. The RESMA Network has been active for a few years and aims to activate and encourage exchanges between schools in this area in the province of Palermo. The project, which assumes the model of action-research, has involved researchers and teachers for a few months of the 2020/21 school year, in the middle of the pandemic time. Schools, represented by primary and lower secondary school teachers, were involved in the design and development of digital educational content, with the aim of enhancing the territory and the relationship with it, to include it in the curriculum.

Considering the study of the territory as an important part of the curriculum, we often speak of a "contextual curriculum" by referring to the possibility offered by the law which allows schools to devote 20% of the total quota to subjects identified by the school as being linked to territorial needs.

The project aims to start a reflection on the theme of the relationship between "standard" curriculum (the macro dimension) and "contextual" curriculum (micro). The use of contextual curriculum is an established practice in schools involved in the network but, sometimes they run the risk of celebrating localism, removing the connections between local contexts and globalization. The research has sought to study the two dimensions (local and global) towards a reconnection between them.

The teachers that participated in the research activities were asked to design a teaching activity closely linked to their teaching subject considering elements of interdisciplinarity and transdisciplinary connected to the theme of the territory. The course started reading several passages from Morin's work [13, 14], which served to emphasize the concept of "relevant knowledge". The subject of reflection was also the nature of interdisciplinary practices.

3 Methodological Design

The project was designed using an action-research methodology and included a training-mentoring activity, which consisted in listening to the teachers in order to understand their needs and their opinions. The course included a series of meetings in which teachers were invited to discuss some concepts. We used theoretical cues that addressed the issue of the relationship between micro and macro, in a perspective of revisiting the curriculum in a contextual key. The National Curriculum [17] was also a constant reference for our work. Reflection was also fueled by cues of a practical nature, through the analysis of learning products already realized by some schools and based on in-depth work on the theme of the territory. The online conversations were recorded and constitute an important source of analysis, along with the documentation that the teachers designed such as teaching plans, logbooks kept by those who were able to experiment with the planned pathway and, lastly, the content produced (which not all of them were able to complete in the planned time frame, partly because of the worsening of the pandemic situation). The initial meetings served to bring the teachers closer to the theme in question, through the analysis of products (CDDs) already realized by colleagues. Each meeting allowed us to reflect on the relationship between institutional and contextual curriculum, on the role of the student in a process of designing and producing digital educational content, and on their function within a training program. Teachers were then invited to produce a class design, which was then discussed by the group. Finally, a collective analysis of the products was carried out.

The material collected constitutes a very rich source of analysis and allowed us to investigate teachers' approach to activities linked to the territory. An initial reading of the recorded conversations, diaries and plans led us to define an analysis grid which was then applied to a second careful reading of the materials in question. The grid is structured in the following dimensions: Curriculum & Territory, Didactic contents, Effects (on students), Teacher professionalism. Each dimension, which has subdimensions, has been identified after Morin and Guerra's approach to the relation with the territory.

4 Findings

The research activity started with a problem-based approach. The whole group of teachers agrees on a problem: too often students, children, and young people, show a superficial knowledge of the area where they live. They do not know territory traditions, as well as the native language, partly forgotten or removed by young people. According to teachers' opinion, regaining possession of a shared memory can help students to build their own cultural identity. "Cultural identity is built through the process of discovering reality" teachers told us. It is not enough to say that "the learning environment is the child's experience", we can go further to try to establish how much of the experience of each pupil is now made up of elements belonging to the immediate reality (the family, the school, the village, the neighborhood, the city) and how much instead is linked to an imaginary that include, for example, the whole symbolic horizon experienced through the media. "The question starts from close up, but the answer comes from far away" says one teacher, describing almost a method that was implemented in the development of the projects. The projects were designed from the "choice of a topic that motivates the pupils, linked to cultural and social themes, allows an interdisciplinary approach, and opens up collaboration with the territory".

In proposing the themes, the teachers listened to the students, trying to intercept what the authentic questions are, taking care to ensure that the adults' needs do not overlap with those of young inhabitants of the Madonie: "Are our narratives the same as those of the young?" wonders one of the teachers. And how can we be sure that we are not attributing to them a need that is instead felt by generations still tied to tradition? The problem exists. It is a question, then, of seeking "the pupils agency in a work of tradition" as another teacher said.

Teachers admit the awareness that the school cannot close itself up in a dangerous horizon of self-referentiality: "The school cannot remain closed within four walls". Its task is also to recover traditions that would otherwise be lost, a cultural and social world to be defended: the theme of memory is therefore the leitmotif for many of the planned activities. "Starting from my teaching subject, English, and having emphasized the main language, as the language of the heart, of emotions and primary affections because it is spoken from birth, we shift the focus and reflect on our mother tongue, the language that Sicilians speak with old relatives. It is with regret that I learn that the pupils do not identify their mother tongue, but rather think of Italian or even Latin". So, one of the teachers wrote. She has chosen to work on "Siculish", the perfect blend of English and Sicilian. The course will allow the analysis and discovery of a language that is unknown to most people, but still widespread in the United States.

The same aim is supported by a group of teachers who are collecting stories and proverbs from the Sicilian tradition: the chosen topic is, in fact, "the rediscovery of 'cunti' and proverbs from popular tradition, combined with the intention of appreciating the expressive value of the dialect and protecting our roots from oblivion".

Teachers denounce a sort of "uprooting" taking place: the students sometimes show that they inhabit the territory without taking possession of it. This happens by many were not born in the inhabited area, but it also happens to those belonging to families who have lived in the area for generations.

The school, moreover, has a varied population today: "It finds itself operating in a heterogeneous and articulated social reality. On the one hand, it welcomes pupils from families that are attentive to the emotional and cultural growth of their children; on the other hand, it has pupils who, regardless of their family background, present situations of hardship, including pupils from a family home for minors". The situation requires attention to diversity, the ability to include and also to deal with the complex issue of identity: "inclusion has become more difficult and the school has had to open up to new strategies, more flexible and more adaptable to new situations in order to meet the needs of all pupils, especially those who, for different reasons, require special attention".

This is one of the aims of the projects: to transform the undefined space of everyday life into a place full of personal and collective meanings: "The project ties in well with the themes linked to the school's local area, since it rediscovers and highlights the most important aspects of it, reinterpreted and 'experienced' by the pupils in a personal way; this is how a 'non-place' becomes a 'place' for them. Our school believes strongly in the value of the history of its territory, which it has enhanced over time in the vertical curriculum".

Some projects intend to work on themes that automatically contain a sort of progression from personal events to planetary, social and political issues, passing precisely through the relationship with the territory to which they belong: "What the project proposes is a difficult journey around man, in a labyrinth that begins in the folds of the soul of the boy who, as he grows up, discovers he is different. (…) The role of the community becomes important, whether it is understood as a school, family or civil society, because it must be able to tell the boy's story, to give him roots, to comfort him in his search for himself, consoling his loss'. A sort of 'sentimental education', as one teacher defined it, which is nourished by relationships with the world".

The projects carried out by teachers therefore aim to make the students more familiar with the area in which they live and at the same time to build connections between elements of the surrounding reality and other areas, other dimensions. This knowledge of the area also serves to illuminate several experiences that operate in the direction of enhancing the area itself, of a commitment to the recovery of resources, cultural enrichment and development. One of the schools has, for example, intercepted the experiences of professionals who have chosen to invest their professionalism in the area, in some cases renouncing attractive opportunities that would have made them move away from their land. "We first worked on the creation of the video 'ReStare' concerning the collection of interviews that the children had posed to young Madonie entrepreneurs, and from which emerged, significant positive and encouraging messages and enthusiasm for the life choices made".

"We put in place paths that we could call 'the courage to stay': the knowledge of the territory underlies the idea of creating a strong relationship with the territory. Alongside these reflections comes the bitterness of being forgotten by small and large-scale politics" writes the teacher, revealing her profound civil sensitivity.

The activities proposed by the teachers are structured in such a way as to start from stimuli linked to the reality close to the children, but with subsequent openings that establish a bridge between particular and general horizons of meaning. The fairy tale, for example, represents an emblematic element of this relationship between local and global, between a common structure and the variant linked to different contexts: "I have, at this stage, broadened the horizon by reflecting on the fact that these stories were perhaps born in Gangi or near our village but that there are similar stories which, although told in the same period, have been heard by a large number of people and for this reason have been saved to a greater extent from the wear and tear of time and we often find them in children's storybooks". Thus, the connections we have referred to several times are established.

5 Conclusion

Through our research, we tried to analyse the relationships between school and territory, investigating the different perspectives, in relation to (a) the curriculum, (b) teaching, (c) the effects on students, (d) teacher professionalism.

a. In relation to the *curriculum*, the territory emerges in different ways:

    1. In many cases *the territory is covered in some school activities*. The curriculum is thus enriched with themes that cannot be found in textbooks or general texts but require research in the field or from a variety of sources.
    2. In some cases, *the territory becomes a "sounding board" for the school's activities*. The school comes out of its own walls and communicates some of its activities to families and the village, taking on a proactive role in relation to the territory itself.
    3. More rarely, *school and territory fully cooperate through community alliance* drawn up between school and administration, associations and other bodies present in a certain area.

b. In relation to *didactics*, from the diaries and conversations, as well as from the analysis of the products produced by the schools, we were able to verify how the work on the territory carried out in the classes opened didactic opportunities in different directions. In particular, the learning paths followed were characterised by:

1. *Interdisciplinarity*, involving teachers from different disciplines in common projects.
2. The paths are also characterised by *a close relationship established between local aspects and more general issues.*
3. Paths designed and implemented are also characterised by that "*complexity of vision*" so often called for by Morin, which means looking at problems from different perspectives such as psychological, social, anthropological, scientific, and political.

c. In relation to *students*, from the analysis of the teachers' diaries the research has limited itself to recording the teachers' perceptions in this area; it would be interesting to deepen the data collected with observations, focus, and interviews to be administered to the students themselves [see Design Documentation]. Teachers state that within training courses that envisage the development of digital teaching contents centred on the territory's themes, *students develop transdisciplinary competences*; among these, above all *digital competence and citizenship competence.* Teachers also note a general increase in *motivation* on the part of the students, who are more involved in the training courses.
d. In relation to the development of teaching professionalism, some important elements have emerged:

1. Some teachers stated that they had become aware of a kind of "ecology of action", that is, of conceiving the circularity of their work and the need to establish connections between different teaching actions. The keyword is "planning".
2. Teachers stated that they give more importance to the development of a strategy, rather than emphasising the importance of a programme to be completed. The use of the contextual curriculum legitimises the possibility of "choosing" certain themes, in the direction of essentialising the curriculum, which is one of the frontiers of research today.
3. Teachers show a greater willingness to take a "gamble" attitude, that is to say according to Morin's lexicon, the attitude of being able to grasp, within didactic paths, that extemporaneity that characterises every authentic and virtuous educational path.

Finally, looking more deeply into the theme of the relationship between the local and global dimensions, we can summarise the following:

- At the basis of authentic knowledge there is always a question that is solicited by contexts and situations. Reality tasks (but also what someone has called "unreality" tasks if they are linked to imaginary dimensions) start from questions raised in classroom by one or more students, from questions or problems arising in the everyday context or prompted by readings.

- The answer to these questions, the search for solutions, triggers paths that are a real opportunity to learn a research method that consists of learning how to read sources (of various kinds), compare information, select and evaluate them.
- Research that explores neighbouring realities enables students and teachers to open up a clearer knowledge of territories, but also to connect local issues with the more general questions at the centre of contemporary interest.
- Knowledge can be said to be "solid" if it is re-read and systematised through operations of 're-writing' carried out by the learner.
- Knowledge is solid if it is shared, i.e. it is generated by a comparison with knowledge mediated also by the synthesis of different points of view, of multiple reflections.
- Knowledge is sound if it is rooted in context, if it develops a method that can be applied to knowledge in general. If it proceeds from the micro to the macro, if it combines near and far.
- In a process of reading and reinterpreting elements of the territory, the school performs the fundamental task of "memory archive", working in this way on the concept of cultural identity, a concept which is as controversial as it is topical today.

Summarising, we can conclude that "What did the children experience with this activity? The aim was to fill the children with hope" as a teacher wrote in her diary.

We make our thanks to the teachers with whom We have carried out the resarch: Maria Concetta Bongiorno, Mirella Cefalù, Antonella Cerami, Michele Cerami, Carmela Di Pasquale, Leonarda Dino Grazia, Elisabetta Duca, Maria Santa Duca, Anna Maria Ferraro, Francesca Giunta, Anna Rita Lio, Giuliana Longo, Maria Mascellino, Elisa Migliazzo, Loredana Scavuzzo, Santina Scavuzzo, Francesca Sottile.

References

1. Bartolini, R., De Santis, F., Tancredi, A.: Analisi del contesto italiano. Piccole scuole: dimensioni e tipologie. In: Mangione, G.R.J., Cannella, G., Parigi, L., Bartolini, R. (eds.) Comunità di memoria, comunità di futuro. Il valore della piccola scuola, pp. 249–260. Carocci Editore, Roma (2020)
2. Mangione, G.R.J., Bartolini, R., Chipa, S., De Santis, F., Tancredi, A.: Piccole Scuole in Italia: identificazione, mappatura e analisi dei territori. Rapporto di ricerca Indire-Ministero dell'Istruzione (2021)
3. Mangione, G.R.J., Cannella, G., Parigi, L., Bartolini, R. (eds.): Comunità di memoria, comunità di futuro. Il valore della piccola scuola. Carocci Editore, Roma (2020)
4. Anichini, A., Bartolini, R.: Curricolo locale e curricolo istituzionale: viatici per un rapporto virtuoso. In: Mangione, G.R.J., Cannella, G., De Santis, F. (eds.) Piccole scuole, scuole di prossimità. Dimensioni, strumenti e percorsi emergenti. I Quaderni Della Ricerca, vol. 59, pp. 155–164. Loescher Editore, Torino (2021)
5. Anichini, A., Bartolini, R.: Curricolo e territorio. In: Mangione, G.R.J., Cannella, G., Parigi, L., Bartolini, R. (eds.) Comunità di memoria, comunità di futuro. Il valore della piccola scuola, pp. 249–260. Carocci Editore, Roma (2020)

6. Bronfenbrenner, U.: The Ecology of Human Development: Experiments by Nature and Design. Harvard University Press, Cambridge (1979)
7. Cerri, R.: Quando il territorio fa scuola. Da un'indagine sulle pluriclassi a un'idea di scuola. Franco Angeli, Milano (2010)
8. Mangione, G.R.J., Cannella G.: La scuola di prossimità: alleanze territoriali per la realizzazione di nuove forme educative nella piccola scuola. Archivio di studi urbani e regionali **132**(suppl./2021), 86–109 (2021). Franco Angeli, Milano
9. Gennari, M.: Pedagogia degli ambienti educativi. Armando, Roma (1997)
10. De Bartolomeis, F.: Fare scuola fuori della scuola. Aracne, Roma (2018)
11. Farné, R., Bortolotti, A., Terusi, M. (eds.): Outdoor Education: prospettive teoriche e buone pratiche. Carocci Editore, Roma (2018)
12. Cagol, M., Calvano, G., Lelli, C. (eds.): Esperire l'ambiente. Tra natura e contesti di vita. Zeroseiup, Bergamo (2020)
13. Morin, E.: Enseigner à vivre: Manifeste pour changer l'éducation. ACTES SUD, Paris (2014)
14. Morin, E.: La testa ben fatta. Raffaello Cortina, Milano (2000). (orig. ed.: Morin, E.: La tète bien faite. Seuil, Paris, 1999)
15. Dewey, J.: The school as a social centre. The elementary school Teacher (1902). https://chipbruce.files.wordpress.com/2008/09/dewey_1902_school_as_social_center.pdf
16. Guerra, M.: Fuori. Suggestioni nell'incontro tra educazione e natura. Franco Angeli, Milano (2015)
17. Ministry of Education: Indicazioni nazionali per il curricolo della scuola dell'infanzia e del primo ciclo d'istruzione. Annali della Pubblica Istruzione, Numero speciale. Le Monnier, Firenze (2012). http://www.indicazioninazionali.it/wp-content/uploads/2018/08/Indicazioni_Annali_Definitivo.pdf

Teaching in Upper Secondary Schools with High Migratory Complexity: The European Project QuaMMELOT

Raffaella Biagioli(✉) and Maria Grazia Proli

University of Florence, Via Laura 48, Florence, Italy
{raffaella.biagioli,mariagrazia.proli}@unifi.it

Abstract. The necessity to support secondary school teachers for the educational needs of migrant minors, organize the reception of unaccompanied minors, improve their scholastic-performance, detect their knowledge, and decrease school drop-out, requires methodologies and tools which can develop basic skills through targeted disciplinary paths.

The QuaMMELOT Project (Qualification for Minor Migrants Education and Learning Open access - Online Teacher-training) Erasmus KA2, developed an e-learning structured path in training-modules around eight topics within the Moodle platform of the University of Florence that enabled teachers from partner countries (Greece, Denmark, Spain, Italy) to create, develop and adopt innovative teaching methodologies in the school-contexts of reference.

In this way we want to respond to the complexity of the school and rethink the role of the teacher as a person capable of reflecting on himself and on society, of doing research as a tutor for inclusion, of carrying out concrete action against discrimination and of promoting active citizenship. Distance learning allows the participation of European teachers within an interconnected system in order to confront everyone with a reality that cannot be avoided for a long time and that must be oriented towards dialogue and cooperation. The paper aims to describe the QuaMMELOT project through the main objectives achieved and the methodological approaches implemented, and to present some significant data from the survey carried out at the end of the training course.

Keywords: Migrant minors · e-learning training for European teachers · Inclusion · QuaMMELOT

1 Teaching in School with High Migratory Complexity

Since 2015, the number of refugees and migrants seeking asylum in Europe has increased significantly[1]. This development poses new challenges and opportunities for European Member States at administrative and practical levels, such as housing capacities, asylum procedures, health issues, employment opportunities and schooling. One of the

[1] Eurostat, *Asylum Statistics*, September 2020.

M. Ranieri et al. (Eds.): ATEE 2021, CCIS 1649, pp. 161–173, 2022.
https://doi.org/10.1007/978-3-031-20777-8_13

main reasons for the existence of a pluralistic society is related to the phenomenon of emi/immi-gration. For several decades, Europe has been one of the main geographical areas receiving immigrant and refugee populations, and this trend has increased in recent years. Threats to a pluralistic, democratic and inclusive society come from racism, xenophobia and discrimination. These movements of rejection hinder democratic coexistence and social inclusion, fostering discourses and practices based on fear, hatred and the idea that European cultures are hierarchically privileged and hegemonic.

Education is a key tool to promote diversity and inclusion. Schools are crucial contexts in which to learn tolerance, coexistence, equality and democratic values. The coexistence of students can foster socialisation without prejudice, within a democratic society that seeks to ensure that all children and young people have the same rights and opportunities.

For this reason, rather than integration, we talk about inclusion, since it is a matter of ensuring that the educational system gives answers to the needs of all, as a strategy to engage the real participation of students, both immigrants and natives [1]. Recognition of diversity does not mean homogenizing the student body. It is not about transitional or temporary measures for people with specific educational needs, but rather about generating a curricular model that facilitates shared learning, in the recognition of diversity. In this sense, attention to diversity engages all of us as a society, and is not exclusively about the school. This commitment involves a dialogical relationship in the process of seeking a shared culture, both in school and in society. A pluralistic and tolerant society implies overcoming assimilation (understood as the passive adaptation of minority or immigrant cultures to that of the host society) and segregated multiculturalism (conceived of as the mere coexistence of different cultural or national groups in isolation), in order to develop a critical, tolerant, inclusive, dialogical and human rights-based intercultural approach. The intercultural model is based on the recognition and horizontal relationship between different cultural perspectives. The new decolonial and critical approaches propose a radical perspective of the intercultural model, conceived as a political project, which considers a joint process of decolonization, transformation and creation. In this sense, the aim is to question power structures and conventional epistemes, to foster social and cultural practices based on justice, equity and diversity. This question is addressed by the socio-critical educational paradigm, which poses the need for the school curriculum to be sensitive to social, economic and political issues, with the aim of making people aware of reality, as a fundamental principle in the process of social transformation.

The QuaMMELOT project is set in a cooperative and international intercultural perspective. It is a training proposal that seeks to improve the educational focus on immigrant students and minors, innovating the in-service training of teaching staff in secondary schools, since teachers are a decisive factor in the educational success and social inclusion of immigrant and refugee students.

In order to be able to respond to the complexity of the School – as an institution, rethink the role of the teacher as a person capable of professional reflection as well as reflecting on society, promoting inclusion, carrying out a concrete action against discrimination and promoting citizenship, it becomes necessary to deepen our knowledge of the needs of these adolescents who, from ongoing research [2], reveal an unexpected need to talk, to tell about themselves, about their life path, from the past in their family and land of origin, to their arrival in the host country, and their more or less adventurous or dramatic journey. In the search for points of reference, the minor who emigrates finds himself in a more problematic condition than others, aggravated by the fact that, first in the country of origin, then in the country of arrival, he has not had family, social and cultural experiences that have allowed him to form and maintain his roots, but has experienced a form of fracture. The affirmation of one's own ethnic identity not only appears as an expression of a defensive attitude, but often becomes a symbolic manifestation, of which the community of arrival knows little or nothing. This involves many difficulties, including the coherent upholding of the constitutive elements of the cultural model of origin, with possible consequences at the level of the individual's psychological wellbeing. But growing up between two cultures, as happens for the children of immigrants in our country, can also be a great opportunity: they know a "before" and an "after" that they have to connect, and this is not always easy; for this reason the school, as a welcoming environment, can be fundamental.

With regard to the interventions addressed to unaccompanied minors, there are different steps of complexity at the level of organization, services and activities addressed to users, as well as specific planning influenced by different methodological approaches. For this reason, Universities, Regional Education Authorities and educational institutions and training agencies from the four project partner countries DK, ES, GR, IT, cooperated for 36 months to offer teachers new tools based on network synergies and ICT to improve their skills for inclusive education. The project fostered cooperation between the educational and social worlds, as inclusion problems, if not solved in the educational process, have immediate repercussions in the social sphere, generating school drop-out or increasing Not in Education, Employment or Training (NEET) rates. Since reception facilities, in addition to their primary task, also deal with school, training, work and foster-care, the QuaMMELOT project set-out to respond to the need to increase the level of awareness and sensitivity on the themes of integration and social inclusion, as well as to improve the possibilities of integration of minors in the school context. In the latter context, the need has emerged to open up to sharing, as well as to meet those who are able to give voice, testimony, recognition and dignity to their identity (NEETs). Indeed, the world of schooling often lacks the tools to facilitate the education of a growing number of migrants, many of whom are Unaccompanied Foreign Minors (UAMs), who have the right to education. The presence of migrant minors has multiplied in recent years in line with growing migratory waves characterized more and more by young people under 16 years of age who are unaccompanied. More specifically, Italy, Greece and to a lesser extent Spain, as landing destinations, are countries of arrival of migrants i.e. *reception countries*, and have to deal with the problems of reception and education of minors, while the countries of Northern Europe, such as Denmark, are *destination countries* which, over time, have developed quite solid integration tools and processes.

Schools in Greece, and especially in the Attica region, have welcomed a large number of students with immigrant and refugee backgrounds over the last decade, as the movement of populations from countries such as Syria, Iraq, Iran, Afghanistan, Kurdistan, Egypt, etc. has meant that thousands of school-age people are in urgent need of access to educational facilities, both primary and secondary education.

With reference to secondary education, an age-group in which a large number of refugees were unaccompanied, the challenge of their integration into the educational system was accompanied by the difficulty of their inclusion in school, their equal participation in the educational process and their effective involvement in the learning process. Thus, the priority of the Attica Regional Directorate for Primary and Secondary Education (PDE), as regards the education of refugees, was not only their reception and integration into the Greek educational system, but also their continuous support so that they could respond psycho-emotionally and cognitively to their learning obligations.

Consequently, the involvement of the Regional Directorate for Primary and Secondary Education (PDE) of Attica in the QuaMMELOT Project coincided with the effort of the Greek Ministry of Education and Religious Affairs to organize educational facilities for the reception of refugee and migrant students and training programmes for their more effective and smooth integration into the Greek educational system. Inclusive education was a priority for the Ministry of Education and thus for the PDE of Attica, which was administratively and pedagogically responsible for the proper functioning of refugee reception, their education facilities and the implementation of responsible inclusive pedagogical practices in its schools.

Together with other educational and training programmes implemented by the Ministry of Education and Religious Affairs (YPAITH), the Institute of Education Policy (IEP) and the Regional Educational Planning Centres (PEKES) of Attica, the QuaMMELOT project was an innovative educational and training programme that allowed all school leaders and teachers involved to study in depth the institutional framework regulating the education of refugees and, more specifically, that of unaccompanied refugees in secondary education. It also enabled the comparison of the organization and implementation of the reception and education of students with a migrant background in different European educational systems, mainly in the partner countries of the Project. Moreover, it allowed project partners to study, exchange and apply good/best educational practices in the field of the reception of refugee and migrant students and in the field of the development of language skills, in order to successfully meet the requirements of secondary education and to implement didactic scenarios with special attention to interdisciplinary approaches (mainly language and mathematics)[2], which favour the active participation of students in the educational process (with inclusive practices such as theatre, digital technologies, art in education, debate) and collaborative group-work approaches.

There were two main objectives that the PDE of Attica set out to achieve through its involvement in the QuaMMELOT Project. One was to raise awareness and educate teachers participating in the Project's activities in relation to the extremely complex issue of integrating refugee students into the education system. What emerged from QuaMMELOT is that there are different types of integration of foreigners in school and that the great challenge is that the type of integration does not lead to assimilation or marginalization of refugee and immigrant students, but adopts a pluralistic approach for successful social interaction, solidarity, and equal opportunities for all. Therefore, the goal of inclusive education must be the awareness-raising in citizens who, through their active citizenship, contribute to the development of social cohesion and, above all, democracy. The school leaders and teachers who participated in the actions developed

[2] E.g. CLIL-based interdisciplinary approaches.

by the Attica EDP in the framework of the QuaMMELOT Project seem to have adopted these principles and tried to apply them in the fulfilment of their duties, according to their role in refugee education.

The second main objective was to enable secondary school teachers to design, develop and implement educational activities that would allow refugee and immigrant students to develop skills in a variety of subjects without necessarily requiring a high level of host-country language proficiency, something that these students did not acquire during the first years of their school life. This goal seemed to be the big challenge, especially in secondary education, as Greek schools generally speak of a "language centre". The low level of language proficiency of refugee and immigrant students is often an insurmountable obstacle to developing a good learning path. For this reason, the teaching material used in the high school (lower secondary school) and high school (upper secondary school), both in the reception classes (RC) and in the general classes, had to be adapted to the new conditions, taking into account the heterogeneity observed in the general classes with the coexistence of non-Greek and Greek-speaking students. The training carried out in the framework of the QuaMMELOT Project was very useful in this sense, as it has "armed" teachers with adequate teaching tools that can be used in teaching students with a migrant background, but also in classes with heterogeneity in terms of Linguistic Competence Levels.

Integration is possible only in the name of reciprocity and, therefore, of the constitution and recognition of the identity of the other. In the dynamics of reciprocity that characterizes identity and integration, it is not enough for the "different" person to learn to do something, but it is necessary for him to integrate his possibilities with those of others in a relationship of exchange and collaboration. If we really want to practice equality of educational opportunities, we must plan based on the basis of differences.

The added-value of diversity must not be misunderstood: that is, it must not serve to emphasize inequalities, but to create the necessary conditions to respect the originality of each individual. In addition to the challenges of the developmental tasks of all adolescents, young immigrants face specific challenges that have to do with migration fatigue and the need to fit in without losing their history [3]. It is necessary to act on two levels: cognitive-knowing, and informative-affective, regarding mutual representations, relationships and emotional experiences. But cognitive openness is the first step, the necessary but not sufficient condition to establish relationships and encounters based on mutual exchange. It is important that, alongside the cognitive dimension, there is the ability to approach others, to open and maintain contacts, the ability to manage negotiations and conflicts, to tolerate uncertainty, to put oneself in the shoes of others for a while to try to see things from different points of view.

The European project QuaMMELOT supported teachers in their professional development to prepare them to curb early school-leaving, cultural diversity and facilitate the learning process(es) of unaccompanied foreign minors, seeking to strengthen teachers' competences in the face of the multi-ethnic composition of classes, with a view to supporting all students, including migrant students in their access to learning and their inclusion. Distance learning has allowed the participation of European teachers within an interconnected system to enable everyone to come to terms with a reality that cannot be avoided for long and that must be oriented towards dialogue and cooperation.

Moreover, it gave pedagogical and methodological-didactic answers through experiences carried out in secondary school classes in Denmark, Greece, Italy, and Spain. The training-course modules addressed to European secondary school teachers in multicultural contexts facilitated the strengthening of the teacher-skills necessary for school inclusion of migrant children, to avoid abandoning studies (drop-out) and the difficulties in learning disciplines. Thus, best-practiced based research from states was implemented through a training course in Open-access Online Learning for "Tutors involved in the reception and inclusion of foreign minors within secondary schools in European countries" regardless of the teaching disciplines. This experience marks the beginning of a new chapter in the history of secondary school to actively support it and help it overcome obstacles and challenges: a model that encourages the educational and training value of experience and reflection, with the opportunity to 'cultivate' a double richness, that of two worlds that can enrich each other.

2 The Training-Course Modules

The online training-course modules for the professional figure of "Tutor for the reception and inclusion of foreign minors in secondary schools in European countries" is divided into eight training modules on specific topics (legislation, first reception, citizenship, relational communication, mathematics, L2, artistic-creative laboratory, computer science). The modules were placed on the e-learning platform managed by the Centro Linguistico di Ateneo of the University of Florence and allowed the eighty teachers selected in schools with a strong immigrant presence to train and apply the methodologies and tools proposed in each module: video lessons, texts, discussion forums, interactive tools, examples and tests. The training modules are available in the languages of the partner countries (ES, DK, GR, IT) as well as in English.

Secondary school teachers learned, applied in their classrooms, elaborated and produced new ways of using the proposals, which they then posted on the same e-learning platform and forum, to share with all the other participants. The course was experimented with 80 secondary school teachers and 1312 students were involved in the activities proposed and carried out in class, of these 1312 students 518 were migrant students (a much higher number than the 300 migrant students envisaged by the end of the project). The total number of students reached directly and indirectly was 1797.

The QuaMMELOT Project favoured the exchange in peer learning activities between teachers and 60 social operators (educators/mediators/services employees/families) in tables for discussion. Moreover, in mobility, it involved 23 staff members in the partner countries, more than 200 people in 3 multiplier events and international seminars, it saw 5 transnational meetings for cooperation between partners and it expected to be useful for all European teachers because it contains methods, processes and contributions of the experimentation carried out as well as materials useful for innovative approaches because these materials manage to bring together training/learning and social education - as they manage to combine instruction and social education.

The QuaMMELOT Project made it possible to achieve the following macro-objectives which are subsequently detailed in the "objectives achieved" section:

- strengthening teachers' skills and enhancing their professionalism with innovative tools;
- improving the school learning of migrant and UAMs students;
- fostering integration between education and the social/reception systems;
- building more inclusive educational practices;
- promoting the full enjoyment of rights and the inclusion of disadvantaged groups.

With regard to the modules designed and coordinated within the QuaMMELOT Project, monitoring of the online course-modules was carried out by all partners using the e-learning platform reporting system which enabled partners to see-at-a-glance course progress, and quantitatively determine in real time the number of activities carried out by the teachers in training, as well as the gradual completion of the training modules. This automatic detection system also made it possible to identify, quickly, any delays or trainee-difficulties in completing the activities, thus allowing course designers/providers to intervene with targeted support actions.

From a qualitative viewpoint, it was possible to get information about course progress by viewing the tasks and products delivered by the participants based on what each module required participants to achieve including the expected knowledge, skills and abilities. A further way of qualitatively surveying the outcomes of the online course was the assessment of the trainee contributions submitted in the forums dedicated to each training module.

The quantitative survey of the course outcomes was carried out using a questionnaire administered to the teachers involved at the end of the course.

Eighty completed questionnaires were returned by the 80 teachers who competed the online course. The quantitative and qualitative analysis of the data from the questionnaires was presented in the Online Course Monitoring Report (IO4) focusing on the results related to the educational issues faced by teachers working in secondary schools with a high presence of migrant and refugee students. Quantitative results were collected using descriptive statistical methods, such as frequency tables and bar graphs.

The aim of the QuaMMELOT Project was to train students from all cultural groups, including, of course, immigrants, so as to enable them to adapt, develop and be competent, both in the context of the host culture and in that of their culture of origin. This implied overcoming assimilationist and reductionist approaches. True intercultural education builds on dialogue and shared encounter-spaces, based on the respect and appreciation of students, teachers, families, associations and other stakeholders, through a dynamic of participation and confrontation. To achieve this goal, educational institutions must open up to society, creating the best conditions so that families, both native and immigrant, can be involved in the life of the school. The QuaMMELOT Project, therefore, was not limited to the cognitive development of students, but also addressed other aspects of the educational process: the legislative framework, educational facilities, reception, school climate, psycho-emotional support of students, cooperation, mutual understanding and acceptance. It did not approach knowledge in a partial way, but allowed the horizontal connection of different disciplines and encouraged a transversal and interdisciplinary approach as well as synergies between teachers.

The QuaMMELOT Project activities, transnational meetings and multiplier events were well-organised, included quality content and used innovative methodologies. The project's comprehensive approach facilitated complex but necessary work to integrate the multiple dimensions related to migration and the education of migrant and refugee students, with attention to the legal framework, national cultures, the Common European Framework, public institutions and private entities established for the pursuit, without profit, of civic, solidarity and socially useful purposes.

3 Methodological Approaches

In designing and developing online training for secondary school teachers, the QuaMMELOT Project adopted a flexible, innovative, complex and integrated approach in relation to the curriculum and the different social actors involved in schools (students, teachers, management team, professionals, families, intercultural mediators, social workers, associations, social and local authorities). Based on the implementation of multimodal approaches, teachers, as trainees, are stimulated to design and implement a series of activities to encourage their students to understand mathematical ideas and abstract mental constructs, in a foreign language. Teachers involved in the education, training and instruction of students with a migrant background, in fact, need skills in relating to different languages and cultures in order to build an adequate pedagogical-didactic environment to support and encourage all those in training. From this perspective, it is necessary that the relationship between school and social development be conceived as a recognition of the handing-down to younger generations of existing cultural heritage and as a source of innovation, through the integrated development of all aspects of students' personalities (Biagioli 2015). It is important, moreover, "to promote students' ability to make sense of the variety of their experiences, in order to reduce the fragmentation and episodic character that risk characterizing their lives" [4].

The modules of the online training course QuaMMELOT present innovative approaches that have been tested by teachers in the *piloting* phase of the Project (2018–2019), with the aim of facilitating the inclusion of all students involved, as well as the improvement of learning to mitigate the phenomena of failure and school dropout. These methodologies mostly refer to the teaching of L2, the promotion of positive attitudes towards cultural diversity, the introduction of contents from the cultures of origin of students with migrant background in the ordinary curriculum (QuaMMELOT 2020 Guidelines).

The construct underlying the designed instructional activities is collaborative learning which emphasizes cooperation and experimentation among different participants leading to mutual learning and potential new ideas and exchanges among participants [5]. In this way, in the teaching-learning processes everyone participates actively and pupils learn to engage in social contexts. Collaborative learning is a way to work for and with social inclusion, where learning of content, models, and ways of thinking occur in a continuous and incessant co-construction [1].

3.1 Narrative, Artistic and Multimedia Approaches

Storytelling, art and multimedia are now considered winning strategies in teaching-learning processes especially in multicultural contexts where they are used to foster communication, learning of knowledge and disciplines through self-knowledge and knowledge of the world. Through the processes of knowledge of self and other, teachers and students can tune in and creatively dialogue, this in support of motivation to learn and for the achievement of communicative well-being [6]. In this sense, educational communication and intercultural communication are intertwined in the process of growth and evolution of the subjects in training.

Education at school is enriched by artistic practices that stimulate emotions and creativity as a means of promoting deep and positive learning in the areas of communication, interpersonal relations and more [7]. Similarly, the mix of artistic, narrative and multimedia approaches give rise to opportunities for self-experimentation that, as in the case of digital storytelling, allow the emergence of one's experiences and emotions through a story of the self that can be addressed through different languages that make it possible to overcome language barriers. Autobiographical narration is an important component to create a multi-voice dialogue ([8], where the writer is the protagonist of the story with its construction in the relationship with the world and its perspectives [9].

In school contexts, storytelling can be considered as a transformative tool that contributes to the added-value of cultural origins and the construction of the future of native and migrant learners. Self-narration opens-up the boundary between inside and outside; at the same time it helps to alleviate fears, the state of anxiety due to separations from places or loved ones.

Narrative methodology and digital storytelling allow people to express their experience and emotions through different languages that also allow them to overcome language barriers. Unlike storytelling in the classical sense, digital storytelling includes the use of multimedia tools and new technologies that can improve its ease of use as an educational methodology, as well as being easily available and reproducible (QuaMMELOT 2020 Guidelines [19]). Creating a multimedia product becomes a meaningful task that can contribute to a sense of belonging to a group, and help create self-esteem, and self-confidence [10].

The telling of one's own life-story represents an important educational opportunity for everyone. Self-writing, used as a means of expression of autobiographies, becomes a significant practice of school and social inclusion.

The pedagogical perspective of the autobiographical method makes central the theme of acceptance of otherness, of different worldviews, of different experiences. The construction of an autobiographical space becomes a priority, writing about oneself alone or with others, in fact, encourages one not to fear the judgment of others and allows everyone, regardless of the diversity of approaches and experiences, to take care of their own identity "wounded", offended, hidden [11].

For students whose mother tongue is different from that of the host country, collaborating with their classmates through the digital languages of mobile learning is an opportunity to meet on common ground for all digital natives in every part of the world [12].

The galaxy of free share applications and Creative Commons licenses offers many possibilities to create original projects that can stimulate all the members of the class group to put their previous skills into play, and to engage in collaborating on common projects. In this way it is possible to try to overcome various learning difficulties related to the disciplines and to linguistic competence, especially in relation to the language of study, helping students to feel more capable in a very popular and familiar field.

So, it is in this pedagogical perspective that students can create their own products by processing materials and information through editing operations that become real narratives, even of their own experience, to be shared in class and in the family by fostering an important aspect of intercultural competence, namely the ability to critically evaluate, practices and products of their own and other cultures and countries [13].

Below are some examples of creative activities carried out in the European classes involved in the *piloting* phase of the QuaMMELOT project.

Narratives and Objects of Memory. Objects allow for the exploration of culture and cultural identities as evoking objects also means evoking human actions and activities in their unlimited variety and meaning [14].

Culture is made up of material practices, but also of symbols, values and beliefs. We inhabit a world of objects that characterize our daily lives and, even if they have an instrumental function, they are always invested symbolically and emotionally by human beings. We cannot avoid producing meaning by interacting with things. It should be emphasized that this meaning is not only an individual production, but that meaning develops within a cultural framework, mediated by socially and linguistically shared activities [15].

The teachers participating in the QuaMMELOT Project involved their students in the "Objects and materials of memory workshop" (Module 2 - *First reception*) to work on biographical objects, and asked them to choose objects that were important or significant for their personal history. After choosing the objects and communicating to the other classmates why they chose them, the students were asked to describe the selected objects with short texts, underlining their importance, meaning and potential relation to the values, symbols and people involved. Material objects can be a relevant way to access biographical complexity.

A Greek teacher wrote in the forum of the e-learning QuaMMELOT platform that the pupils in her class (secondary school in Athens), including some from Turkey, Afghanistan, Georgia, Bulgaria and China, chose to design "memory bottles". At the end of the workshop all the students in this class presented their work to their classmates (mostly in English), thus having the opportunity to talk about their own origins and compare themselves with others. The teacher pointed out that, through this activity, she was able to get to know her students better, and she plans to repeat the experience as an *ice-breaking* activity in the future.

Linguistic Portrait. Language autobiography is a writing exercise that stimulates learners to reflect on their own linguistic and cultural experiences. The *language portrait* has been proposed in the QuaMMELOT training project (Module 4 - *L2 language*) by Danish partners to facilitate the process of teaching-learning of Language 2 by students with migrant backgrounds and also to encourage cross-contamination between linguistic heritages and cultures. Through language portraits, in fact, it is possible to visualize one's linguistic repertoire using the outline of a body silhouette. Linguistic portraits were originally developed as an exercise in linguistic awareness in education, and are now increasingly used as a research tool to investigate how speakers themselves experience and interpret their heteroglossic practices and repertoires [16]. In linguistic portraiture, the image functions as a means of opening up a conversation and as a point of reference within it, thus facilitating the evocation of (biographical) narratives. The purpose of the linguistic portrait is to be an important signal, to foster awareness and visibility, to configure itself as a didactic tool for the teacher, to solicit the potential for learning across languages [17].

Multimedia: Video-Curriculum and Recipes on the Radio. In Denmark, in a third class of the secondary school, teachers wanted to experiment the realization of the video-curriculum (Module 8 - *Multimedia Art Laboratory*). The activity stems from the idea of teachers who propose to students an innovative way to introduce themselves and talk about themselves, so as to have a better chance of finding a job by sending a video curriculum to potential and future employers. Using ICT as a means of creating a multimedia product, students were introduced to specific uses of digital technologies at school with the aim of supporting newcomer students who do not yet have sufficient Language 2.

Combining narrative methodology and artistic-creative expression with the use of technology, the Danish students, both native and with migrant backgrounds, involved in the QuaMMELOT project wrote a *story line* for their video curriculum, focusing on how to present themselves, they experimented with different *apps* on tablets so as to record and edit the film, and they benefited from the language and digital skills of the members of the teaching team involved in the activity.

The experience of radio-recipes, included in the same training module, allowed students from the four partner countries, both native and with migrant backgrounds, to tell their stories through typical recipes of their places of origin or through traditional family dishes: radio podcasts were made (radio programs recorded and available on the web as podcast) where the same recipe was presented in the language of the country of residence (host) and in the mother tongue of the country of origin. The activity fostered the rediscovery of cultural roots and the improvement of language skills related to L2 [17].

4 Findings

The QuaMMELOT project led to an implementation of the skills of the 80 teachers involved in the online training course and at the same time to an improvement in the learning outcomes of the 1312 students involved through the teaching activities that the trainee teachers carried out in their classrooms, according to the methodologies learned. These results, summarised here, were deduced from the analysis of quantitative[3] and

[3] The analysis of the quantitative results was carried out using descriptive statistical methods such as frequency tables and bar graphs. Due to the small sample size, hypothesis testing and inductive statistical methods (e.g. factor analysis by country of origin) could not be applied. Data analysis was performed with the statistical package for the social sciences IBM SPSS Statistics 23.

qualitative[4] data collected from 80 self-assessment and satisfaction questionnaires filled in by the teachers involved at the end of the training course delivered via the e-learning platform.

In particular, through the analysis of qualitative data it was understood that the training course was useful, that most of the activities were of high quality and appropriate for mixed, multilingual and multicultural classes with a high number of students with a migrant background. Indeed, the inclusive educational practices implemented contributed to improving the social and linguistic skills of all students involved [18]. Furthermore, the analysis of the qualitative data showed that the methodologies proposed by the QuaMMELOT project improved the social inclusion conditions of students with a migration background, increased their ability to become socially active in their country of residence and optimised opportunities for school integration. The analysis of the quantitative data revealed the educational problems faced by teachers working in multicultural contexts with a strong migratory presence, the teachers acquired skills to increase the effectiveness of their educational work with children with a migratory background and improved the reflective dialogue through meetings and multiplier events.

The project course demonstrated the need to recognise the existing skills and competences of pupils with a migration background instead of focusing on the competences that may be lacking when they enter school. The analysis of contexts was confirmed as indispensable for the creation of curricula that attempt to respond to the need to establish an effective link between subject content and the individual linguistic and cultural baggage that each pupil brings with him or her.

The positive feedback provided by the teachers through their answers to the open-ended questions in the questionnaire administered confirmed the importance of ongoing teacher training to foster the educational success of all students and the development of their human potential; to build a relational network in an intercultural dimension; and to understand different ways of representing the world and acting reality [17].

Authors' notes. The present contribution is the result of shared reflections by the authors but, for the purposes of authorship attribution, Raffaella Biagioli is the author of the abstract and of paragraphs 1 and 2; Maria Grazia Proli is the author of paragraphs 3 and 4.

References

1. Biagioli, R.: La ricerca pedagogica tra prassi e pratiche. In: Biagioli, R., Proli M. G., Gestri S. La ricerca pedagogica nei contesti scolastici multiculturali. Formazione e accompagnamento dei docenti. ETS, Pisa (2020)
2. Biagioli, R., Gonzáles-Monteagudo, J., Petruzzi, C.: Ruolo e formazione degli educatori. Pedagogia e metodologie per le comunità di accoglienza dei minori stranieri. L'Harmattan Italia, Torino (2018)
3. Demetrio, D.: Educare è narrare. Le teorie, le pratiche, la cura. Mimesis, Sesto San Giovanni (2013)

[4] The qualitative data are obtained from the answers to the 6 open-ended questions of the questionnaire. Brief comments on the teachers' answers were included in the analysis, interpreting the meaning of the content of the textual data. A flexible approach to content analysis was used, in which coding categories were derived directly from the textual data.

4. Indicazioni Nazionali per il Curricolo 2012, Gazzetta Ufficiale del 5 febbraio 2013, Serie Generale, n. 30 (2012)
5. Smith, B.L., MacGregor, J.T.: What Is collaborative learning?. In: Ann Godsell et al (eds) Collaborative Learning: A Sourcebook for Higher Education. North Carolina Tutoring & Learning Association – NCTLA, Chicago (1992)
6. Boffo, V.: Comunicare a scuola. Autori e testi. Apogeo, Milano (2007)
7. Planalp, S.: Communicating Emotion: Social, Moral, and Cultural Processes. Cambridge University Press Cambridge. https://doi.org/10.1017/CBO9781316257012
8. Demetrio, D., Favaro, G.: Didatticainterculturale. Nuovi sguardi, competenze, percorsi. FrancoAngeli, Milano (2018)
9. Biagioli, R.: Traiettorie migranti. Minori stranieri non accompagnati. Racconti e storie di vita. ETS, Pisa (2018)
10. Elias, N., Lemish, D.: Spinning the web of identity: the roles of the internet in the lives of immigrant adolescents. New Media Soc. **11**(4), 533–551 (2009)
11. Biagioli, R.: I significati pedagogici della scrittura e del racconto di sé. Liguori, Napoli (2015)
12. Ranieri, M., Pieri, M.: Mobile learning. Dimensioni teoriche, modelli didattici, scenari applicativi. Edizioni Unicopli, Milano (2004)
13. Ranieri, M., Fabbro, F., Nardi, A.: La media education nella scuola multiculturale. Teorie, pratiche, strumenti. Edizioni ETS, Pisa (2019)
14. Lani-Bayle, M.: Taire et transmettre: Les histoires de vie au risque de l'impensable. Chronique Sociale, Lyon (2006)
15. González-Monteagudo, J.: Travail biographique en formation par les objets: entre exérience, identité et culture. In: González-Monteagudo (ed), Les Histories de vie en Espagne. Entre formation, identité et mémoire, pp. 199–221. L'Harmattan, Paris (2011)
16. Busch, B.: The language portrait in multilingualism research: theoretical and methodological considerations. Working Pap. Urban Lang. Literacies, **236**, 1–13 (2018)
17. Biagioli, R.: Proposte per l'insegnamento della lingua 2 nelle classi multiculturali delle scuole secondarie europee. Epale J. **6**, 18–24 (2019)
18. Proli, M.G.: La formazione e-learning per gli insegnanti della scuola secondaria in contesti multiculturali nel progetto europeo QuaMMELOT. In: S., Polenghi, F. Cereda, P. Zini, La responsabilità della pedagogia nelle trasformazioni dei rapporti sociali. Storia, linee di ricerca e prospettive, pp. 264–271. Pensa Multimedia, Lecce (2021)
19. AA.VV.: Linee guida QuaMMELOT 2020. ETS, Pisa. http://www.edizioniets.com/scheda.asp?n=9788846759245&from=Libri&fk_s=0

Accessible School Textbooks for Students with Hearing Impairments

Cristina Gaggioli[1](✉) and Moira Sannipoli[2]

[1] University for Foreigners of Perugia, 06100 Perugia, Italy
cristina.gaggioli@unistrapg.it
[2] Perugia University, 06100 Perugia, Italy
moira.sannipoli@unipg.it

Abstract. How can ICT (Information Communication Technologies) help in facilitating comprehension of school textbooks for students with hearing impairments?

Text comprehension is a very difficult task for students with deafness. Hearing impairments may hinder or impede (depending on the severity of hearing loss) the reception of acoustic signals, even of their own native language. Accessibility to available textbooks does not guarantee understandable texts: if this is the case, the obstacle occurs at the time the child with deafness learns to read. Instead, even if all children with deafness learn to read and write, many of them do not understand what they are reading and text comprehension often remains an unattainable goal. According to the Universal Design for Learning approach, learning is impossible if the information is not perceptible or difficult to comprehend for the student. In order to reduce learning barriers, it is important to assure that key information is equally perceivable for all students.

This research study has analyzed, through 177 support teachers, some textbooks and has defined the main obstacles in comprehension.

The barriers have been divided into three aspects: graphic, linguistic and cognitive. An analysis carried out on each obstacle resulting from the study, has led to a classification of each aspect in favor of improving the comprehension of available texts.

The study has shown that the adaptation of texts through the use of the most common word processor software, may already result in a simple solution to remove the most common obstacles.

Keywords: Accessibility · Reading comprehension · Student with deafness · Information communication technology

1 Theoretical Framework

In Italy, as in in other European countries, the attention paid by public institutions and the community at large towards students with disabilities has steadily grown in recent decades, which has resulted in a significant improvement in terms of health conditions, independent living and social integration. Policies centred on institutionalization and

M. Ranieri et al. (Eds.): ATEE 2021, CCIS 1649, pp. 174–184, 2022.
https://doi.org/10.1007/978-3-031-20777-8_14

welfare have been gradually eliminated, to be replaced by initiating and promoting policies of participation and social inclusion, equal opportunities and good practice, thanks to which a progressive empowerment of institutions, associations and the private social sector has developed. The focus on inclusion has allowed for a widening of the perspective, shifting the focus from needs to desires, from assistance to care, and from rehabilitation to building a genuine life project, in a dance of mutual recognition and continuous reciprocal existential arrangements. "All citizens have the right, founded on justice, to enjoy all their capabilities, up to an appropriate threshold level: if people fall under this threshold in any capacity, fundamental justice becomes less effective, and how well they are able to exercise their other capacities is of no importance" [1]. It should be added that the Convention on the Rights of Persons with Disabilities (December 2006) emphasizes in the Preliminary article (e) that "disability is an evolving concept, and disability results from the interaction between persons with impairments and the attitudinal and environmental barriers that hinder their full and effective participation in society on an equal basis with others".

By 2050 nearly 2.5 billion people are projected to have some degree of hearing loss and at least 700 million will require hearing rehabilitation. Over 1 billion young adults are at risk of permanent, avoidable hearing loss due to unsafe listening practices. An annual additional investment of less than US$ 1.40 per person is needed to scale up ear and hearing care services globally. Over a 10-year period, this promises a return of nearly US$ 16 for every US dollar invested.

Over 5% of the world's population – or 430 million people – require rehabilitation to address their 'disabling' hearing loss (432 million adults and 34 million children). It is estimated that by 2050 over 700 million people – or one in every ten people – will have disabling hearing loss.

'Disabling' hearing loss refers to hearing loss greater than 35 decibels (dB) in the better hearing ear. Nearly 80% of people with disabling hearing loss live in low- and middle-income countries. The prevalence of hearing loss increases with age, among those older than 60 years, over 25% are affected by disabling hearing loss.

A person who is not able to hear as well as someone with normal hearing – hearing thresholds of 20 dB or better in both ears – is said to have hearing loss. Hearing loss may be mild, moderate, severe, or profound. It can affect one ear or both ears, and leads to difficulty in hearing conversational speech or loud sounds.

'Hard of hearing' refers to people with hearing loss ranging from mild to severe. People who are hard of hearing usually communicate through spoken language and can benefit from hearing aids, cochlear implants, and other assistive devices as well as captioning.

'Deaf' people mostly have profound hearing loss, which implies very little or no hearing. They often use sign language for communication [2].

In recent years, experimental research on deafness, developed in Italy and abroad, on effective and inclusive teaching practices for students with deafness, has been enriched by contributions from other know-hows such as ICT (Information and Communication Technologies), linguistics and glottodidactics. The Italian school system has welcomed an increasing number of pupils with disabilities. 2.3% of the total number of pupils with disabilities attending state and non-state schools, of all orders and grades, have a hearing disability [3]. Independent of the choice of the oralist and/or bilingual method, research evidence within the framework of reading comprehension for people with deafness [4] indicates the need to treat the language of the country, in which you live, as a second language. The indications given to teachers suggests using the principles of glottodidactics. The support that ICT can give in this area is significant, not only to promote communication [5, 6] but also in the field of learning [7, 8, 9]. The latest data published by the European Agency for Special Needs and Inclusive Education [10] shows that the degree of inclusion of pupils with disabilities differs from country to country. With regard to the "inclusive system" Italy stands out with a low percentage of pupils with disabilities enrolled in special schools, the majority of students with disabilities attend the public-school system. The contribution provides an example of how it is possible to promote school integration of students with hearing disabilities by adapting school textbooks.

2 Research: Methodological Design and Results

The contribution proposes a review of the main obstacles faced by students with deafness with reading comprehension and the possible facilities that can be proposed, to adapt the school textbooks, through the help of ICT.

177 primary and secondary school teachers who attend the specialization course for support activities for students with disabilities at the University of Perugia (2017/2018), were involved in an analysis activity of the school textbook, intended as the main tool employed in daily educational activities, through the use of a pre-structured grid [11].

The grids have been compiled by teachers to analyse different textbooks and cover three aspects: graphic, linguistic and cognitive.

The teachers have compiled the grids by inserting, for each aspect, the elements of potential obstacle for the learning of students with deafness and possible facilities.

The grids were compiled in small groups of two or three teachers (to encourage comparison and discussion between them). The analysis of the collected data is qualitative and was carried out with the Nvivo software, first categorizing the answers in the three aspects and then calculating the frequency of the words used for each aspect. The criteria used for calculating the most frequent words are: minimum word length of 4 letters, exclusion of prepositions, verbs and adverbs, grouping by synonyms, and searching for the 50 most frequent words. The results identified the 10 most frequent words for each aspect.

Table 1. The ten barriers to reading comprehension in textbooks, for graphic aspects.

Graphical aspects	
Word	Weighted Percentage (%)
Images	4,39
Font	2,85
Text	2,26
Line spacing	1,89
Words	1,66
Graphic elements	1,31
Pages	1,31
Keywords	1,19
Dimension	0,83
Bold	0,71

As far as the graphic aspect (Table 1) is concerned, the use of images (4.39) and graphics (1.31) is often inappropriate, as is the graphic setting of text (2.26) and page (1.31). Even the font (2.85) does not always promote readability and there is a barrier in the failure to find keywords, (1.19) highlighted in bold.

Table 2. The ten barriers to reading comprehension in textbooks for linguistic aspects.

Linguistics aspects	
Word	Weighted Percentage (%)
Vocabulary	4,00
Glossary	3,70
Syntax	3,09
Text	2,06
Simplification	1,95
Shortness	1,60
Comprehension	1,15
Paragraphs	1,14
Subordinate sentences	0,91
Sub-paragraphs	0,34

Regarding the language aspects (Table 2), the vocabulary (4.00) is often difficult and without glossary support (3.70). Syntax (3.09) are also often complex and with too many subordinate sentences, (0.91) thus limiting understanding (1.15). Paragraphs (1,

14) are often too long and there are few sub-paragraphs (0.34). Simplification (1.95) and a reduction in text length (1.60) would be needed.

Table 3. The ten barriers to reading comprehension in textbooks for graphic cognitive aspects.

Cognitive aspects	
Word	Weighted Percentage (%)
Metacognition	3,36
Questions	3,02
Concept Maps	2,01
Information	1,34
Self-evaluation	1,01
Promote understanding	1,00
Reflection	1,01
Synthesis	1,01
Exercises	0,67
Inferences Control	0,50

Cognitive operations (Table 3) defect to activities that stimulate metacognition (3.36): questions (3.02), exercises (0.67) for reflection (1.01) and self-evaluation (1.01). More conceptual maps (2.01) and synthesis (1.01) would be needed.

3 Discussion and Operational Proposals

Although digital technologies specifically created for people with deafness impairments are not referred to in literature, this experience shows that ICT can help teachers adapt or build tools that not only provide access to information for students with hearing impairments, but also remove barriers to understanding texts within a classroom.

Even though the use of ICT is seen as an emerging opportunity for deaf students and their families [6], it is essential that the same barriers are not replicated in digital material, as already present in textbooks. The technology offers the possibility of customizing text from a graphic point of view (font, bold, line spacing), calculating the readability of a text (readability statistics), facilitating linguistic access and creating quizzes, interactive tests or conceptual maps.

Today, the most common word processor software is sufficient to not only adapt the graphic aspects of the text, but also to calculate the readability indexes in the accessibility settings and insert graphic elements. This type of software, grants the users the possibility to create their own formatting templates, allowing them to define a file in which the title, heading, paragraph, and other element designs differ from the standard templates.

Among its features, this software includes a built-in spell checker, a thesaurus, a dictionary and utilities for manipulating and editing text (see Fig. 1).

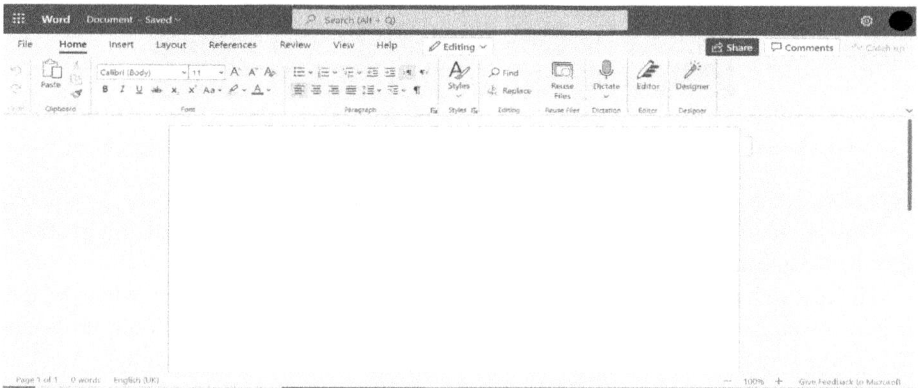

Fig. 1. Example about utilities for manipulating and editing text in Microsoft Word software.

Additionally, you can run the Accessibility Checker to make sure the content of your document is easy for all users to read and edit (see Fig. 2). This option identifies most of the accessibility problems and explains why each of them could be a potential problem for users with disabilities. It also offers tips on how to solve each problem.

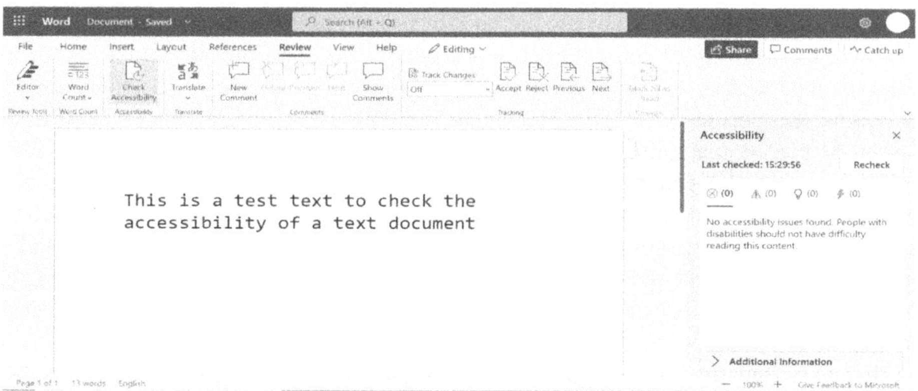

Fig. 2. Example about utilities for identifies the accessibility problems in a Microsoft Word document.

Finally, images, graphics and diagrams can be inserted in a document (see Fig. 3).

Fig. 3. Example about utilities for insert imagines in a Microsoft Word document.

This is the simplest example, just one of the opportunities that technology has to offer for adapting a text to facilitate its understanding.

The research study was carried out during the 2018–2019 school year, when didactic activities were primarily carried out in-classroom with the use of traditional textbooks. The Covid 19 pandemic and its subsequent school closures forced the adoption of new educational methods. On one hand, such methods have brought about a considerable use of new technologies, with more family participation on the other.

Therefore, many didactic guidelines in favour of learning for students with deafness [12–15] had to be transformed in order to guarantee online participation. The need for educational reform, throughout this pandemic, has undoubtedly led to contemplation on both in-class learning and online learning. In truth, online education has only drawn attention to the limits of traditional education, which is more oriented towards conveying information than facilitating the learning process. Thus, forcing us to rethink teaching, in a way that is more centred around the students and their involvement [16, 17].

Despite the guidelines set by the Italian Ministry of Public Education regarding inclusion and accessibility of content [18], students with Special Educational Needs (SEN) demonstrated the most difficulties during online learning. The scientific study carried out during this period [19, 20] has shown the main obstacles faced by SEN students represented by: technical family difficulties (37,7%), insufficient teacher training (28,3%), inadequate school organization (26,4%), lack of family support (18,9%) and teachers with technical difficulties (9,4%). Further studies [16] performed on elementary school teachers and online teaching management [21] have shown that all teachers used digital technologies during the pandemic period, regardless of the fact that (89%) of them had never used them before, thus further showcasing the strong lack of technological tools in the Italian school system [22, 23].

In conclusion, the importance of digital material is a transversal element that closely impacts many of the aspects mentioned above.

In fact, in view of further studies we are impelled to further elaborate on such topics, taking into consideration the creation of adapted material as a key competence for teachers, so to offer accessible content not only in class, but online as well.

4 Conclusion

In order to define itself as inclusive, school should be able to accept diversity and differences of each one, regardless of the presence or not of students with deficit and set accessibility and participation of all [24] as priority goals.

Research has shown that in most cases deaf students have difficulties in school results because they are placed in an inadequate communicative context and in a learning environment, that does not know how to implement strategies individualization and personalization. Future research perspectives could concern other types of disabilities and other available resources.

The didactic proposal, despite of numerous research evidences [25], often remains anchored to a traditional way of promoting learning, which does not take into account the different cognitive styles, interests, modulation of the curriculars proposals. Differentiating the teaching offer could then become necessary to allow each subject to have equal access to education.

"Differentiation is not a set of strategy, but rather a way of thinking about teaching and learning" [26]: the challenge is to help teachers build a methodology capable of providing differentiated learning opportunities.

The Universal Design for Learning (UDL) approach is now part of this framework, which aims to identify a set of principles that allow the construction of a curriculum able to ensure equal learning opportunities and at the same time allow all students to experiment themselves as competent actors.

In fact, the UDL [27] provides a model for the creation of objectives, methods, materials and assessment tools that take shape according to the needs and capabilities of targeted subjects. It overcomes the question of the retrospective accessibility of learning-teaching processes for certain categories of pupils, highlighting how every teaching that provides "a single level" raise, even if involuntarily, the barriers of learning for all.

The approach brings together some recent research in the neuroscientific and psychopedagogical field that for some time now, from a constructivist point of view, support the centrality of the recognition of subjective variability in learning.

Starting from these studies, UDL identifies the interconnected brain networks that take action in learning: the recognition network, the strategic network and the emotional network.

The principles developed by CAST derive from these networks to provide:

- multiple means of representation, options for perception, language, symbols and understanding;
- multiple means of action and expression linked to physical action, expressive skills, fluidity and executive functions;
- multiple means of involvement to arouse interest, to activate a sustainable effort and perseverance, to promote self-regulation.

UDL combines a systemic and constructivist conception of the teaching-learning relationship where success or failure do not depend only on the personal characteristics, commitment and deepening of the student, but also in a self-critical way from the didactic proposal of work, to the relationship and the context within which the knowledge have been shared.

The Scaffolded Knowledge Integration approach [28] within this framework highlighted the importance of making knowledge accessible, also through different technologies but, at the same time, helping students to be aware of their thinking, to grasp the connections between ideas, to listen and learn from peers collaboratively, promoting forms of autonomous and lifelong learning.

This differentiated approach could certainly encourage the learning of deaf students and improve the quality of the educational proposal for all in inclusive terms.

Italian schools chose inclusive education at the end of the 1970s. All children attend the same educational spaces with the aim of reducing cultural, social and relational disadvantages, respecting and welcoming diversity in all its forms. Even so, staying in the same space is no guarantee of education: individualised and personalised interventions are needed to allow everyone to grow and develop their potential, regardless of certifications. Moreover, it is essential to build integrated projects between specific interventions and the ordinary proposal, between the activities of children with SEN and all the others.

The school today must assume a new responsibility in terms of recognition and action. "Responsibility is the ability to respond to various situations in life, without wasting energy blaming yourself, or blaming others for any mistakes made. It is important to be heard. Listen to what is said, the words you use, your own language. You cannot only be profoundly responsible for following a strict and constant commitment; there is also a need for genuine relaxation, a reconciliation with life. We need to be at peace with our own destiny. The most profound responsibility is not to 'be who you want to be', but to 'accept what you are'" [29].

The challenge of inclusive school is to promote opportunities for bricolage at multiple levels, which can be understood as the ability to harness the potential at the personal and contextual levels, involving the vulnerability of every individual and the system, and the agency role exercised by the individual and the community, in an inclusive system that the participants built together, beginning with the recognition of the dignity of every life project. And as part of this continuous construction, each individual "does not know exactly what will be produced, but still gathers everything that they find around them… Making do with scraps. Most of the time they are the outcome of a series of contingent events, the result of all the opportunities that present themselves to enrich their collection of odds and ends" [30].

References

1. Nussbaum, M.: Frontiers of Justice: Disability, Nationality. Species Membership. Il Mulino, Bologna (2007)
2. WHO: Deafness and hearing loss. https://www.who.int/news-room/fact-sheets/detail/deafness-and-hearing-loss.. Accessed 27 Nov 2021
3. MIUR – Ufficio Gestione Patrimonio Informativo e Statistica: I principali dati relativi agli alunni con disabilità anno scolastico 2017/201. http://www.edscuola.eu/wordpress/wp-content/uploads/2019/06/I-principali-dati-relativi-agli-alunni-con-disabilita%CC%80_a.s.2017_2018.pdf. Accessed May 2019

4. Marschark, M., Tang, G., Knoors, H.: Bilingualism and Bilingual Deaf Education. University. Press Inc., Oxford (2014)
5. Jemni, M., Elghoul, O.: Using ICT to teach sign language. In: Eighth IEEE International Conference on Advanced Learning Technologies, pp. 995–996 (2008)
6. Capitão, S., Almeida, A., Vieira, R.: Connecting families and schools of students with deafness: describing the ICT and internet use in education. Procedia Comput. Sci. 14(C), 163–172 (2012)
7. Miller, P.: Phonological, orthographic, and syntactic awareness and their relation to reading comprehension in prelingually deaf individuals: what can we learn from skilled readers? J. Dev. Phys. Disabil. **22**(6), 549–580 (2010)
8. Nikolaraizi, M., Vekiri, I.: The design of a software to enhance the reading comprehension skills of deaf students: an integration of multiple theoretical perspectives. Educ. Inf. Technol. **17**(2), 167–185 (2012)
9. Zainuddin, I., Norlidah, A.: Needs analysis for graphic design learning module based on technology & learning styles of deaf students. Cogent Educ. **3**(1), https://doi.org/10.1080/2331186X.2016.1178364 (2016)
10. European Union Employment, Social Affairs and Inclusion: Access to Quality Education for Children with Special Educational Needs, (2018.). http://www.europarl.europa.eu/RegData/etudes/STUD/2017/596807/IPOL_STU(2017)596807_EN.pd. 20 Mar 2021
11. Scataglini, C.: Facilitare e semplificare libri di testo. Adattare contenuti disciplinari per l'inclusione. Erickson, Trento (2017)
12. Maragna, S., Roccaforte, M., Tomasuolo E.: Una didattica innovativa per l'apprendente sordo. Franco Angeli, Milano (2013)
13. Baroni, F., Mostarda, M.P., Paterlini, A.: Sordità e inclusione scolastica. La prospettiva multidimensionale. Scolé, Brescia (2021)
14. Rinaldi, P., Di Mascio, T., Knoors, H., Marschark, M.: Insegnare agli studenti sordi. Il Mulino, Bologna (2015)
15. Gitti, G.: La sordità. Passato, presente, futuro. Omega Edizioni, Torino (2018)
16. Ranieri, M., Gaggioli, C., Kaschny Borges, M.: La didattica alla prova del COVID-19 in Italia: uno studio sulla Scuola Primaria/ A Didática à prova pelo COVID-19 na Itália: um estudo sobre os Anos Iniciais do Ensino Fundamental. Práxis Educativa **15**, 1–20 (2020)
17. Ranieri, M.: Country report on the impact of COVID-19 lockdown on schooling in primary and secondary education: Italy. In Carretero Gomez, S., et al., What did We Learn From Schooling Practices During the COVID-19 Lockdown, EUR 30559 EN, Publications Office of the European Union, Luxembourg, 2021, ISBN 978–92–76–28418–5, pp. 119–140. https://doi.org/10.2760/135208,JRC123654 (2020)
18. MIUR: L'inclusione via web. Didattica a distanza e accessibilità (2020). https://www.istruzione.it/coronavirus/allegati/didattica_distanza_accessibilita.pdf. 27 Nov 2021
19. European Commission: Educational inequalities in Europe and physical school closures during COVID-19. (2020) https://ec.europa.eu/jrc/sites/jrcsh/files/fairness_pb2020_wave04_COVID_education_jrc_i1_19jun2020.pdf. 27 Nov 2021
20. Ianes, D., Bellacicco, R.: Didattica a distanza durante il lockdown. L'impatto percepito dagli insegnanti sull'inclusione degli studenti con disabilità. L'integrazione scolastica sociale **19**(3) (2020)
21. INDIRE Istituto Nazionale Documentazione Innovazione Ricerca Educativa: Indagine tra i docenti italiani. Pratiche didattiche durante il lockdown. Report preliminare (2020). http://www.indire.it/wp-content/uploads/2020/07/Pratiche-didattiche-durante-il-lockdown-Report-2.pdf. 27 Nov 2021
22. OECD: School Education during COVID-19: Were teachers and students ready? OECD Publishing, Paris (2020)

23. ISTAT Istituto Nazionale di Statistica: L'inclusione degli alunni con disabilità – A.S. 2019–2020. (2020)
24. Unesco: The Salamanca Statement and Frame Work for Action on Special Needs Education. UNESCO, Paris (1994)
25. Mitchell, D.: What really Works in Special and Inclusive Education. Routdlege, London (2008)
26. Tomlinson, C.: The Differentiated Classroom: Responding to the Needs of All Learners.: Association for Supervision & Curriculum, Alexandria (SA) (1999)
27. CAST: Universal Design for Learning. Guidelines. Version 2.0. CAST Wakefield (2011)
28. Lin, M.C., Davies, E.A., Bell, P.: Internet Environment for Science Education. Lawerence Erlbaum Associates Publishers, Mahwah (NJ) (2004)
29. Callini, D.: Arcani al lavoro. Metafisica della vita organizzativa. Franco Angeli, Milano (2008)
30. Jacob, F.: Evoluzione e bricolage. Einaudi, Torino (1978)

Educational Robotics for Inclusive Design

Francesca Gratani(✉), Lorella Giannandrea, and Alessandra Renieri

Department of Education, Cultural Heritage and Tourism, University of Macerata, 62100 Macerata, MC, Italy
{f.gratani,lorella.giannandrea,alessandra.renieri}@unimc.it

Abstract. This research stems from the need to prepare future teachers to design digital inclusive teaching. The contribution thus presents a distance training course on Coding and Educational Robotics (ER) for pre-service support teachers (PSSTs). The aim was not only to enhance PSSTs' digital skills but mainly to foster their ability to design for all, using technologies in an inclusive perspective. Trainers supported them without offering predefined work packages. They stimulated PPSTs to become experimenters and researchers to identify functional paths for the introduction of coding-ER in their future curricular teaching. We investigated the evolution of PSSTs' basic knowledge and self-confidence on coding-ER tools and methodologies and their beliefs on their introduction to PSSTs' education. We finally detected their satisfaction with this training course. From the results, the training proved to be effective, despite the distance implementation and the lack of an embodied approach. The PSSTs showed a greater self-confidence and a higher awareness about the benefits of ER. They also demonstrated a conscious use of tools and a focus on inclusiveness in the design of learning paths. We can identify the following as success factors: the strong interaction between participants supported by the course structure; the continuous feedback from both peers and trainers; the possibility to experiment in groups and share successes and failures. These positive results have also led to a greater awareness of the role of support teachers in the complexity of classroom life.

Keywords: Educational robotics · Pre-service teachers · Teacher training · Inclusive didactic · Kindergarten

1 Introduction

This research stems from the need to prepare future teachers to design digital inclusive teaching. The use of robots can enable the structuring of play activities accessible to all, aimed at learning and cognitive, affective and social development, even for pupils with different types of disabilities [1]. The contribution thus presents a distance training course on Coding and Educational Robotics (ER) for pre-service support teachers

---

This paper stems from the collaborative work of the authors. Specifically, Francesca Gratani is the author of paragraphs 2 and 3; Lorella Giannandrea is the author of paragraph 1; Alessandra Ranieri is the author of paragraph 4. Abstract, conclusions and references have been written collaboratively.

M. Ranieri et al. (Eds.): ATEE 2021, CCIS 1649, pp. 185–196, 2022.
https://doi.org/10.1007/978-3-031-20777-8_15

(PSSTs). Our aim was not only to enhance PSSTs' digital skills, gaining new tools and methodologies but mainly to foster their ability to design for all. Specifically, we wanted to promote an autonomous and critical attitude in designing teaching activities using technology. Participants experienced an active training mode. Trainers supported them without offering predefined work packages. They stimulated PPSTs to become experimenters and researchers to identify functional paths for the introduction of coding and ER in their future curricular teaching. Robotics activities, indeed, are not limited to a "passive" use of the technological tool; instead, they could be a process of "production" of technology, a task that requires a conscious and critical attitude [2]. Moreover, the Covid-19 emergency led us to face the additional challenge of training teachers on these issues fully online. This has opened up research topics such as new ways of collaborating remotely and being familiar with tools that generally require an embodied/in-person approach.

We investigated the evolution of PSSTs' basic knowledge and self-confidence on coding-ER tools and methodologies and their beliefs on their introduction to PSSTs' education. We finally detected their satisfaction with the training course.

The following paragraphs will present the theoretical framework (par. 2), the methodological design (par. 3), the results (par. 4), and the conclusions (par. 5).

2 Theoretical Framework

Besides the common benefits of other ICT tools, ER is particularly well suited to create the conditions for an inclusive learning environment [3]. The variety of activities made possible by ER allows teachers to design learning opportunities for all. The inclusive force of such activities lies in the possibility of individualizing learning, implementing a path from simple to complex. The student is at the center of the learning process and can work according to its abilities, preferences, and attitudes. Coding and ER can foster problem-solving skills; attentional system and working memory; playfulness; multisensory and multilevel strategies; 'intrinsic' feedback ('low impact' regulation) [4]. In this regard, the "Istituto Tecnologie Didattiche" (ITD-CNR) has carried out several experiences in schools that show how robotics supports the development of students' computational thinking and cognition in playful contexts, through personal design, sharing and discussion [5–7]. Therefore, ER becomes a facilitator and mediator for social, emotional, and imitation skills; cognitive, visual-perceptual, and motor skills; social acceptability; attention and motivation; less stressful approach to the task in a collaborative climate; experience of self-efficacy and self-control [8, 9, 10]. Furthermore, the ability to "customize" robots can be beneficial for a genuinely inclusive approach to educational support [11].

Despite these acknowledged benefits, ER is often introduced in education from a narrow perspective due to the misconception that it is suitable only for science and technology majors and gifted children [12] and the teachers' lack of expertise and self-confidence in ICT [13]. Thus, if curricular teachers must be usually trained to use ICT effectively, there are even stronger reasons and needs to train PSSTs [3]. The aim of teacher training is primarily to enable teachers to build on the educational benefits of ER for providing a learning landscape that fosters curiosity, critical thinking, problem-solving and creativity for learners [14]. Moreover, it is essential to make the support teachers aware of the possibility of easily integrating any ER project designed for special-needs students into a project suitable for the entire class to promote collaboration between them and curricular teachers [3]. Teachers are indeed requested to design and implement activities characterized by multimodality, multidisciplinary and inclusion of students with different abilities or linguistic and cultural difficulties. Therefore, teachers need not only technical support in using robotic tools and software, but also didactic support to design activities that move away from traditional classroom teaching.

3 Methodological Design

The course was part of a specialization course to qualify as a kindergarten support teacher, provided by the University of Macerata. Specifically, it was introduced as a module within the Technology Laboratory that required compulsory attendance.

The next sub-paragraphs will provide a detailed description of the participants (Sect. 3.1), the course activities (Sect. 3.2), and the assessment instruments (Sect. 3.3).

3.1 Participants

During the course's first meeting, we administered an entry questionnaire to collect personal (gender, age) and professional information (educational qualification, employment situation, educational stage and type of teaching, previous training on the topics). The course involved 47 students, predominantly female (97.87%). Almost all of them were more than 30 years old (95.74%) and currently employed, mainly in the educational field (80.85%). The majority were teaching at kindergarten (71.05%), and 44.74% were already working as support teachers, consistent with their chosen specialization address. Data concerning personal and professional information about the sample are summarized in Table 1.

Table 1. Summary of data describing the sample.

Features	Index	Values (%)
Gender	F	97.87
	M	2.13
Age	20–25	2.13
	26–30	2.13
	31–40	25.53
	> 40	70.21
Educational qualification	Diploma Bachelor's degree Master's degree PhD	63.83 6.38 29.79 –

(continued)

Table 1. *(continued)*

Features	Index	Values (%)
Currently working	No	8.51
	Yes, in the educational field	80.85
	Yes, in other fields	10.64
Teaching educational stage	Nursery	-
	Kindergarten	71.05
	Primary school	21.05
	Lower Secondary school	-
	Upper Secondary School	2.63
	Other	5.26
Support teachers	Yes	44.74
	No	55.26

Finally, 74.47% of PSSTs reported that they had no previous training on the topics. The others stated that they had attended training courses lasting more than 5 h (6.38%), participated in basic experiences lasting less than 5 h (6.38%), or carried out individual training (books, magazines, podcasts, etc.) (10.64%). One participant reported both last two options (2.13%).

3.2 Course Description

The training course was held between March 2021 and April 2021 in fully online mode due to the Covid-19 emergency. It lasted four weeks and consisted of five synchronous meetings for a total of 23 h. We used two platforms adopted by the University: the Microsoft Teams platform for all the meetings and the OLAT LMS platform for all the asynchronous interactions (sharing of materials, notices, and tasks). Every meeting has been recorded, and every material has been shared to create a repository always accessible by participants. Considering the needs and characteristics of the sample, we decided to set the course mainly on group exercises and activities conducted during the meetings. Indeed, participants were primarily student-workers who also engaged in the weekend to attend the specialization course. Furthermore, data from the entry questionnaire showed a low level of knowledge and training related to the topics, which prompted us to provide synchronous support and promote teamwork. The group activities took place in different virtual rooms created in the Teams platform, where trainers could freely access to monitor the process and interact with the participants. Restitution then followed the teamwork in the general room. Table 2 shows the training course schedule.

The course was composed of two phases. The first phase aimed to present and familiarize with some coding and ER tools and methodologies, focusing on kindergarten. In particular, we introduced students to Cody Roby [15], Cody Feet [16], and Cody Color [17], to the Bee-Bot emulator platform [18] and Blue-Bot app, and finally to the ScratchJr software (available both in-app and desktop version) [19]. For each tool, we have shown distinctive features, potentiality, difficulties, and possible learning activities. Regarding the Cody cards, participants had to compose or apply short paths on a grid to solve the task starting from some guide-tracks. We proposed a collective exercise-guide about the Bee-Bot platform and the ScratchJr software usage in the following meetings. Then, we assigned a task to be done individually/in groups. Specifically, using the Bee-Bot simulator, they had to: choose the background (of the grid); create a short story; build a code to make Bee-Bot go through the various stages of the story; take a screenshot that includes the grid and the code; briefly describe the story created. Instead, using the ScratchJr application (from tablet or PC), we required to: customize the character; choose a background; write their name above the background; decide what to make the character do; create a script consisting of (at least) one command per color that makes the character act; take a screenshot that includes the entire ScratchJr window; describe briefly what the character must do. Finally, assignments were uploaded onto OLAT, where we subsequently provided feedback.

The second phase was then dedicated to designing an inclusive learning path for kindergarten pupils based on coding and/or ER. As a preparatory activity, we proposed the creation of a shared database of designs. Each group had to collect examples of instructional designs/activities which used coding and/or ER tools across the various fields of experience. They filled out a table with the following guide-fields: link to the video or resource; section/age of pupils (if indicated); duration; field(s) of experience; type of disability; coding and/or ER tools; annotations (why you chose it, strengths/weaknesses, etc.). Tables were uploaded onto the OLAT platform. Then, we shared the evaluation criteria and provided supporting guidelines for the design of the learning paths. Specifically, participants had to: define the context, the type(s) of disability, the competence(s), the goals and the fields of experience; explain the path highlighting the work phases, what teacher and children do, and the possible strategies, mediator, and evaluation methods; clearly explain the inclusion strategies and the coding and/or ER tools used, describing their characteristics, the reason for the choice and their use. The last meeting then focused on the restitution and evaluation of the projects.

Table 2. The training course schedule.

Meeting	Duration	Activities
I	3 h	*Preliminary Test;* Introduction to *Coding* and *ER;* Presentation of *Cody Roby, Cody Feet, Cody Color*
II	5 h	Individual exercises; Presentation of *Bee-Bot* and *Blue-Bot;* Individual exercises and group activities
III	5 h	Presentation of *Scratch Jr*; Group activities
IV	10 h	Group activity – creation of a *shared database*; Group activity – planning of a *learning path*
V	5 h	Restitution and evaluation, peer and self-evaluation; *Final Test*

3.3 Assessment Instruments

We decided to assess the evolution of three main areas: PSSTs' basic knowledge (K) and self-confidence (SC) on coding-ER tools and methodologies, and their beliefs (B) on the relevance of such training during their education, on the possible introduction of these topics in schools and the importance in terms of inclusiveness. We thus administered two questionnaires, before-course (BC) and post-course (PC), inspired by the work of Scaradozzi and colleagues [20] and reported in [21].

The basic knowledge test (Test K) uses six multiple-choice questions with three answers: correct, partially correct, and incorrect. For each type of answer, we assigned a score: 2-correct, 1-partially correct, 0-incorrect. Four questions are related to Coding, and two questions are related to ER.

The other two areas (SC and B) presented questions structured according to a 10-point Likert scale. Some of them offered an open-ended question to explore the reasons behind the given answer.

The PC questionnaire also detected PSSTs' satisfaction (SAT) with the course organization and schedule, structured like the SC and B questionnaires. We administered the test and the questionnaires through Google Form.

To assess the designed learning paths, we prepared a rubric shared in advance with the participants. This rubric focused on the following descriptors: age pertinence; time pertinence; originality; correct use of tools; conscious use of tools; inclusiveness; internal consistency. Those criteria were shared in advance with the participants. We reported the descriptors on a Google form with 5-point Likert scale questions. This form was used during the restitution meeting by the trainers and the participants themselves. In this way, we collect an "external evaluation" (made by trainers and the participants that evaluated the learning paths made by other groups) and an "internal evaluation" (each group self-evaluated its learning path).

4 Results

4.1 Course Results

Data from K-Test and SC-B BC and PC questionnaires were recorded, and statistical analysis was carried out using RStudio (v 1.4.1103).

As we reported in [21], the answers of each participant in the K-BC and K-PC tests were classified into three classes: basic (zero/one correct answer), medium (few correct answers) and advanced (all correct answers). For SC (BC-PC) and B (BC-PC), since SC and B are more complex constructs, we discretized and divided data into five classes (levels): very low level (class I), low level (II), medium level (III), good level (IV), very good level (V). We tested the difference between BC and PC to verify the training effectiveness. We decided to verify the differences by separating Coding and ER questions to analyze the improvements better.

We tested the difference between BC and PC to verify the training effectiveness, using the McNemar-Bowker test (H0: no correlation between variables, rejected with $p\text{-value} < 0.05$).

This procedure reported a statistically significant difference from all BC-PC questionnaires ($p\text{-value} < 0{,}001$ for each test) (Fig. 1).

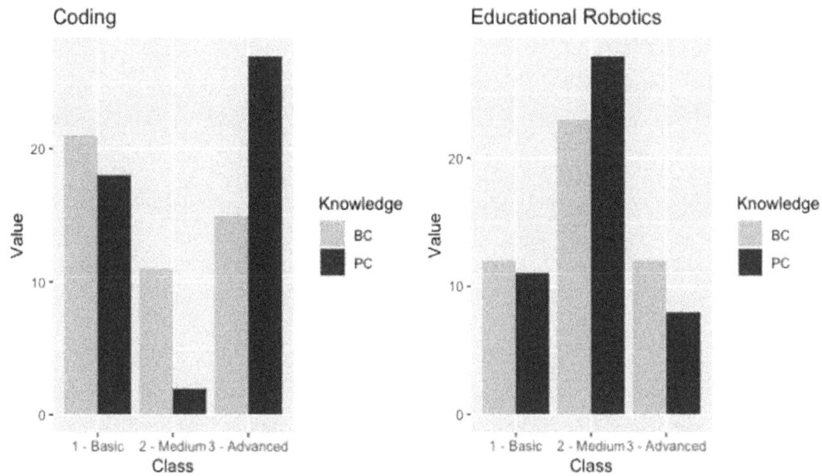

Fig. 1. Histogram reporting data from tests K-BC (light grey) and K-PC (dark grey) related to Coding and Educational Robotics.

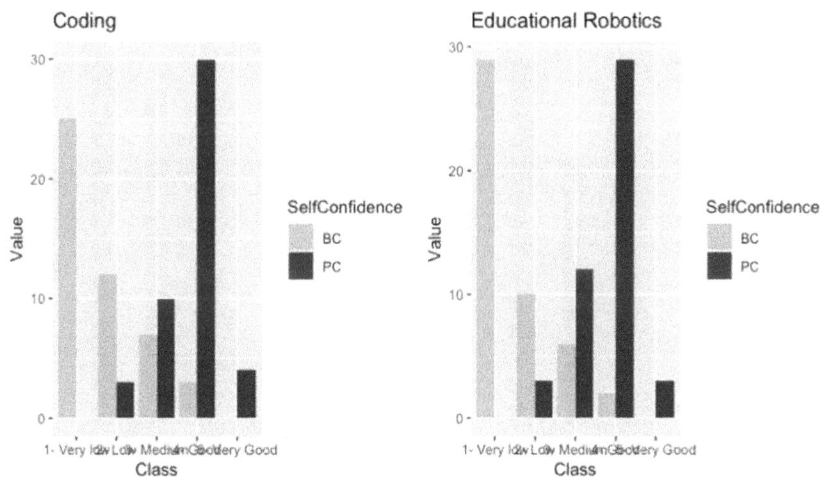

Fig. 2. Histogram reporting data from questionnaires SC-BC (light grey) and SC-PC (dark grey) related to Coding and Educational Robotics.

Unfortunately, we cannot confirm the statistically significant difference between all pairs of classes except between class I and class IV in SC-ER (BC-PC) and SC-C (BC-PC) ($p < 0{,}000274$) (Fig. 2).

In B1-BC (Fig. 3), almost all PSSTs highlighted the benefits of this kind of training during PSSTs' education (91.49%). The majority motivated the importance of setting up educational, challenging, future-oriented activities for students (36.17%) and staying updated (21.28%); only 6.38% talked about inclusiveness. In B1-PC, almost all PSSTs

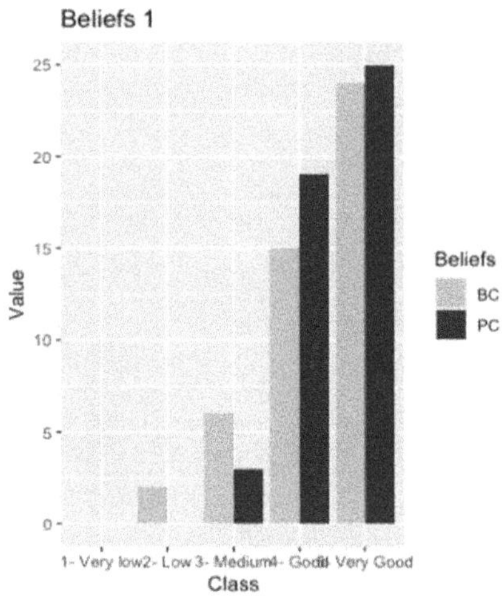

Fig. 3. Histogram reporting data from questionnaires B1-BC (light grey) and B1-PC (dark grey) related to the relevance of this kind of training during PSSTs' education.

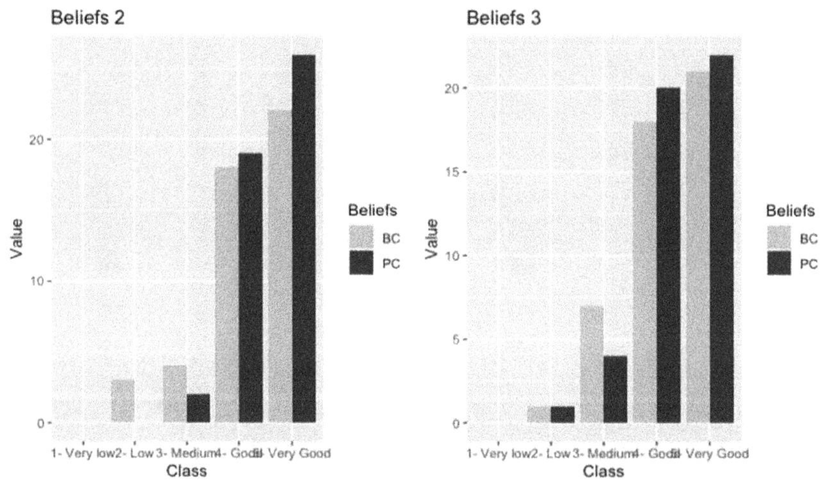

Fig. 4. Histograms reporting data from questionnaires B2-BC (light grey) and B2-PC (dark grey) related to the relevance of the possible introduction of these topics in schools and from questionnaires B3-BC (light grey) and B3-PC (dark grey) related to the relevance of these topics in schools in terms of inclusiveness.

spoke about the benefits. There was more perception of the inclusive value of these activities (19.15%).

In B3-BC (Fig. 4), PSSTs motivated the relevance by referring to coding and ER as facilitative, compensatory, and alternative tools (36.17%) or as tools accessible to all (10.64%). Only 4.25% stated that these activities support cooperative work. On the contrary, in B3-PC, 31.95% of PSSTs emphasized the importance of cooperative peer activities, and 23.40% highlighted the opportunity to learn by doing and playing.

The SAT-PC questionnaires show overall high satisfaction with the course. In particular, in SAT-Organization (Fig. 5), we detected PSSTs' satisfaction with working remotely in groups. We found that 55.32% of participants did not experience difficulty. The others mainly reported two reasons: little immediacy/direct contact or experience (27.66%) and connection/network problems (12.77%). Then, in SAT-Schedule (Fig. 6), 95.75% of PSSTs reported that it is possible to train remotely on these topics and emphasized as main favorable factors the clarity of content, materials, and organization (25,53%), team working and sharing (14.89%), and the opportunity to experiment (14.89%). However, 21.28% of PSSTs stated that in presence, it could have been even more effective.

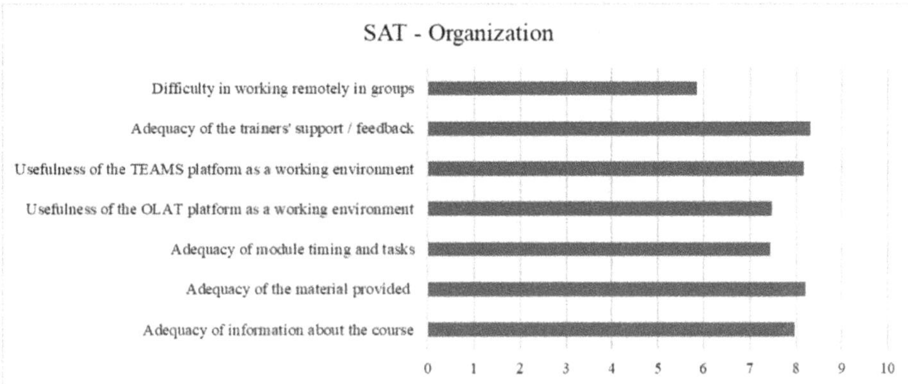

Fig. 5. Histogram reporting data from questionnaires SAT-PC-Organization.

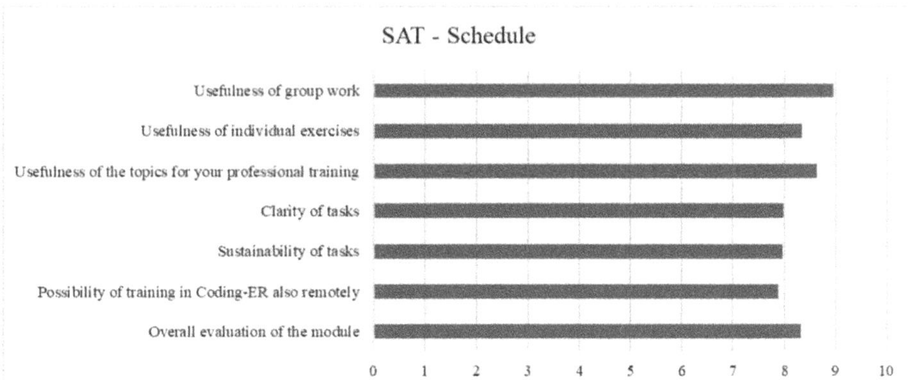

Fig. 6. Histogram reporting data from questionnaires SAT-PC-Schedule.

Finally, most of the designed learning paths proved to be original, inclusive, and consistent. Specifically, we identified as strengths the adoption of collaborative strategies to foster inclusion (e.g. peer tutoring, team working) and the promotion of authentic experiences or role-playing activities. Besides that, we suggested some areas of improvement: a more balanced use of tools in terms of quantity and time and a more conscious way of transition between the different tools.

4.2 Course Results

To assess the designed learning paths, we focus on two of the seven descriptors: inclusiveness and conscious use of tools.

Table 3. Inclusiveness.

Group	Self-evaluation	Peer-evaluation	Trainers' evaluation
G1	4.5	4.5	5
G2	4.3	4.1	4
G3	4.4	3.8	3.5
G4	4	4.1	3/3.5
G5	5	4.3	5
G6	4.5	4	3.5
G7	4.8	4.5	5
G8	4.5	4.1	5
G9	4.2	3.4	4.5
G10	4.3	3.7	4

Looking at Table 3, we can underline that there is a general consistency among the three evaluations. We can say that almost all groups have taken care of the aspect of inclusiveness. In fact, seven out of ten groups get an average score of 4/5. Specifically, we can see a higher self-evaluation for groups G3 and G6 than the peer and trainer evaluation, while we have a lower peer evaluation for G5, G8, and G9.

Table 4. Conscious use of tools.

Group	Self-evaluation	Peer-evaluation	Trainers' evaluation
G1	4.3	4.4	5
G2	4.1	4.3	4
G3	4.7	4	4
G4	4	4.2	4

(*continued*)

Table 4. (*continued*)

Group	Self-evaluation	Peer-evaluation	Trainers' evaluation
G5	5	4.15	4.5
G6	4.3	3.9	3/3.5
G7	4.6	4.2	5
G8	4.5	4.1	4
G9	4.3	3.5	4
G10	4	3.7	4

From Table 4, we can say that there was a good average level in the conscious use of the tools. We also note more minor discrepancy between the three evaluations than we saw in Table 3.

5 Conclusions

This paper describes a training proposal for PSSTs aimed at improving their digital skills and especially the ability to design for all. The course, indeed, responded to the increased current need to familiarize all teachers with technologies in an inclusive perspective. It focused the teachers' attention on the need to design in an inclusive way for the benefit of the whole section. Many of the participants were initially wary and reluctant to use technology in kindergarten. Familiarization with the proposed tools and activities changed this initial attitude and allowed PSSTs to imagine the potential of robotics in the inclusion of pupils with disabilities. The study has some limitations, such as the small sample size and the duration of the course. However, the training proved to be effective from the results of the K-test, SC, B and SAT questionnaires, despite the distance implementation and the lack of an embodied approach. We can identify the following as success factors: the strong interaction between participants supported by the course organization/structure; the continuous feedback from both peers and trainers; the possibility to experiment in groups and to share successes and failures. While the improvement of knowledge can be considered an expected and usual outcome of a training course, the improvement of self-confidence is undoubtedly less predictable. This construct is regarded as one of the main limiting factors in introducing coding-ER activities and methodologies in schools [21]. Similar results emerged in [3]. Furthermore, concerning beliefs, all questions presented show a shift from lower to higher levels of awareness. The PSSTs showed, indeed, a heightened awareness of training on these issues during university/professional education and introducing these tools at school, also in terms of inclusiveness. Almost all groups then gave centrality to inclusiveness in the planning phase of a learning pathway. Finally, the increased self-confidence gained by PSSTs is linked to a greater possibility of adopting technology in their daily teaching and learning practices. Indeed, the training has led to a greater awareness of the role of support teachers in the complexity of classroom life.

References

1. Traverso, A., Pennazio, V.: Bambini, robot: esperienze educative di gioco e relazione. RELAdEI – Revista Latinoamericana de educación infantil **3**(2), 191–207 (2013)
2. Di Luca, M., Vitacolonna, E., Papale, F., Delle Monache, R., Mammarella, F.: La robotica nella scuola delle competenze. Bricks **2**, 99–102 (2013)
3. Agatolio, F., Pivetti, M., Di Battista, S., Menegatti, E., Moro, M.: A training course in educational robotics for learning support teachers. In: Alimisis, D., Moro, M., Menegatti, E. (eds.) Edurobotics 2016 2016. AISC, vol. 560, pp. 43–57. Springer, Cham (2017). https://doi.org/10.1007/978-3-319-55553-9_4
4. Laurillard, D.: Teaching as a Design Science. Building Pedagogical Patterns for Learning and Technology. Routledge, New York (2012)
5. Chioccariello, A., Manca, S., Sarti, L.: Children's playful learning with a robotic construction kit. In: Siraj-Blatchford, J. (ed.) Developing New Technologies for Young Children, pp. 93–112. Trentham Books Limited, Stoke on Trent (2004)
6. Caci, B., Chiazzese, G., D'Amico, A.: Robotic and virtual world programming labs to stimulate reasoning and visual-spatial abilities. Procedia. Soc. Behav. Sci. **93**, 1493–1497 (2013). https://doi.org/10.1016/j.sbspro.2013.10.070
7. Bottino, R., Chioccariello, A.: Computational thinking: videogames, educational robotics, and other powerful ideas to think with. In: KEYCIT: Key Competencies in Informatics and ICT 7, pp. 301–309. University of Postdam, Postdam (2015)
8. Pennazio, V., Fedeli, L.: A proposal to act on theory of mind by applying robotics and virtual worlds with children with ASD. JE-LKS – J. e-learn. Knowl. Soc. **15**(2), 59–75 (2019)
9. Giannandrea, L., D'Angelo, I.: Bambini e Robot. La Robotica Educativa nella scuola dell'infanzia, In: Giaconi, C., Del Bianco, N. (eds.) In Azione. Prove di Inclusione, pp. 15–23. FrancoAngeli, Milano (2018)
10. Del Bianco, N.: Robotic-Lab: nuovi spazi di connessione tra Robotica e inclusione, In: Giaconi, C., Del Bianco, N. (eds.) In Azione. Prove di Inclusione, pp. 50–63. FrancoAngeli, Milano (2018)
11. Lehmann, H., Rossi, P.G.: Enactive robot assisted didactics (ERAD): the role of the maker movement. In: Moro, M., Alimisis, D., Iocchi, L. (eds.) Edurobotics 2018. AISC, vol. 946, pp. 16–26. Springer, Cham (2020). https://doi.org/10.1007/978-3-030-18141-3_2
12. Alimisis, D.: Educational robotics: open questions and new challenges. Themes Sci. Technol. Educ. **6**(1), 63–71 (2013)
13. Tondeur, J., van Braak, J., Sang, G., Voogt, J., Fisser, P., Ottenbreit-Leftwich, A.: Preparing pre-service teachers to integrate technology in education: a synthesis of qualitative evidence. Comput. Educ. **59**(1), 134–144 (2012)
14. Alimisis, D.: Teacher training in educational robotics: the ROBOESL project paradigm. Technol. Knowl. Learn. **24**(2), 279–290 (2019). https://doi.org/10.1007/s10758-018-9357-0
15. Bogliolo, A.: A scuola con CodyRoby. Il coding come gioco di ruolo. Giunti, Firenze (2020)
16. Bogliolo, A.: Coding in Your Classroom, Now! Giunti, Firenze (2016)
17. Cody Color. http://codemooc.org/codycolor/. Accessed 04 Nov 2021
18. Bee-Bot emulator. https://www.terrapinlogo.com/emu/beebot.html. Accessed 04 Nov 2021
19. Scratch. https://scratch.mit.edu/. Accessed 04 Nov 2021
20. Scaradozzi, D., Screpanti, L., Cesaretti, L., Storti, M., Mazzieri, E.: Implementation and assessment methodologies of teachers' training courses for STEM activities. Technol. Knowl. Learn. **24**(2), 247–268 (2019). https://doi.org/10.1007/s10758-018-9356-1
21. Gratani, F., Giannandrea, L., Renieri, A.: "Experience" on the screen: an online training course on educational robotics for pre-service teachers, In: Cimitile, M., Pecori, R. (eds.) Book of Abstracts HELMeTO 2021 Third International Workshop on Higher Education Learning Methodologies and Technologies Online. Studium, Roma (2021)

Teachers in a Searchable World: Findings from an Introductory Survey

Emiliana Murgia[1], Monica Landoni[2], Theo Huibers[3], and Maria Soledad Pera[4](✉)

[1] Università degli Studi di Milano-Bicocca, Milan, Italy
emiliana.murgia@unimib.it
[2] Università della Svizzera Italiana, Lugano, Switzerland
monica.landoni@usi.ch
[3] University of Twente, Enschede, The Netherlands
t.w.c.huibers@utwente.nl
[4] Web Information Systems, TU Delft, Delft, The Netherlands
m.s.pera@tudelft.nl

Abstract. In this manuscript, we discuss the findings from an introductory survey conducted with more than 50 teachers in Italy. We inquired about teachers' opinions of educational technology used in the classroom, in particular search tools. Qualitative and quantitative data inferred from collected responses provide us with a multifaceted picture of the different roles teachers perform in the classroom when interacting with technology, their preferences, skills, perceptions of the needs for training, in addition to the principles and motivations that guide them. Findings emerging from this survey serve as a foundation for an international study that would allow us to better model teachers' needs and the barriers they face when using search tools in the classroom.

Keywords: Information retrieval · Search · Classroom · Teachers · Information access

1 Introduction

The digital era we live in has led to multiple academic and commercial efforts in the form of technology meant to support learning [4]. Among the many tools available, the most salient are search tools, from search engines like Google to educational environments like Wizenoze [27]. At their core, search tools serve as a starting point towards the democratization of information [17, 23]. These tools lower the barriers to access up-to-date resources—beyond textbooks—that can complement classroom instruction by helping students connect curriculum topics with real-life facts, in addition to enabling interactions with resources once unreachable or inaccessible [3]. Chronicles about search tools and their theoretical potential to ease and improve learning are common [1, 11]. Still, little effort goes into understanding teachers' preferences on these tools, their

M. Ranieri et al. (Eds.): ATEE 2021, CCIS 1649, pp. 197–208, 2022.
https://doi.org/10.1007/978-3-031-20777-8_16

willingness to adopt them, how they use search tools to support learning[1], and teachers' efficacy to seamlessly integrate these tools to enhance learning [22].

To advance understanding of the practical implications and hurdles connected to educational technology usage, we devised a survey. We view this survey as a means to capture the behavior, preferences, modus operandi, and related concerns of a distinct user category: teachers. We ground our work on the assumption that for a productive integration of technologies at school teacher involvement is essential, as through them starts the transformation and evolution of teaching methodologies [6, 25]. Inspired by the layers of complexity defined by Murgia et al. [20], we turn to teachers of varied teaching experience and expertise on the use of technology. We do so to examine their predispositions to the use of educational technology in the classroom setting, as well as identify the traits that should guide design, evaluation, and adoption of search tools targeting children to complete tasks that are classroom-curriculum related.

Preliminary findings presented in this paper reveal insights about usual teachers' practices when adopting educational technology–particularly search tools–to complement classroom instruction. Findings also spotlight teachers' perception of students' views on search tools. Lessons learned will inform research related to the development of search tools and literacy instruction that reflect the real needs of the class. Moreover, outcomes from this work serve as a groundwork for an international, long-term study involving teachers from different countries that would help us best contextualize the needs, challenges, and expectations on technology that can support their teaching practices.

2 Data Collection

We designed a survey protocol[2] to elicit teachers' habits and perceptions on the use of educational technology in the classroom, particularly online search tools. The protocol is based on available literature and concentrates on five traits that contribute to the overall search experience for children in the classroom:

1. Different **roles** children play in the search process as discussed in [12]. The search roles introduced by Druin et al. [7] in their analysis of how children search for leisure at home were further investigated to account for the formal classroom context.
2. **Stakeholders**, beyond children, that influence adoption of search tools, as children are guided by adults both directly and by example in their choice of tools to use and strategies to adopt when searching [5, 9].
3. The concept of **relevance** when it comes to identifying resources that respond to information needs in a classroom context. Not much work exists on this topic, but it is of paramount importance to understand and describe how children measure the

[1] Here, we refer to both how teachers can turn to search tools to locate for information in preparation of classroom instruction [8], in addition to how they incorporate the use of search tools so that their students can complete inquiry assignments in the during class time or as a homework assignment [1], regardless of the teaching modality–in person or remote, as a consequence of the COVID-19 pandemic.

[2] For a copy of the survey questions, please reach out to the contact author.

performance of the search tools they are using according to their sense of relevance as discussed in [13].

4. The need for tools that foster interaction, engagement, and learning, since the level of **involvement** is essential for children to become proficient in searching for school-related topics [16].
5. The undesired and unpredictable behavior of **algorithms** that power search process, which posit ethical and social concerns as discussed in greater length in [14].

In essence, with the questions in this survey, we endeavor to capture teachers' experience with technology in general and with search tools, their attitude towards adoption, and their level of self-efficacy with such tools.

In this initial iteration of our work, we have administered this questionnaire (which was piloted beforehand) to a sample of teachers in Italy, all from a geographical region within the same educational system. We view this as a preliminary step towards a broader inquiry involving different countries around the world. It is important to note that due to the ongoing COVID-19 pandemic, the survey took place online. Moreover, teachers who completed this survey on a voluntary basis were recruited via Facebook and email. Following good practices and as instructed by the local ethics committee, we involved participants via personal contacts and asked them to reach out and invite other colleagues in education to take part in the study in a snowball approach. In the invitation letter, we informed them that data was collected for research purposes, kept anonymous and stored on a local protected server. Finally, we offered to keep participants informed on the progress of our research, and only for that purpose asked for their email contact.

From the 52 collected responses, the majority were primary school teachers (88.5%), the remaining were secondary school teachers. Teacher participants have a wide range of experience with teaching. The majority (54%) has been teaching for more than 20 years. Among the remaining teachers, approximately 17% have less than 5 years of experience, 10% between 5 and 10, and 19% between 10 and 20 years.

3 Results and Analysis

Here, we report on the findings from the responses provided by teachers; we also discuss observations and inferences emerging from collected survey data.

3.1 Teachers in a Searchable World

We live in a searchable world, one where information is a click away and every device comes with a dedicated search tool by default. To better understand teachers' view of this searchable world, we asked them to describe which tools they use when conducting online inquiries of a more personal nature, unlike tools preferred for classroom-related inquires. We also inquired about when and how they turn to these tools. Lastly, we encouraged teachers to describe their vision on the role technology can play in the classroom and include fears and concerns to be accounted for.

As illustrated in Fig. 1a, most teachers, regardless of their teaching experience, rely on educational technology both to support lesson preparation and aid classroom instruction. As for the types of tools used[3], it can be seen in Fig. 1b that teachers' choice is very broad–from interactive whiteboards (IWB) and search tools to robots. The latter, however, is not frequently adopted as an educational tool.

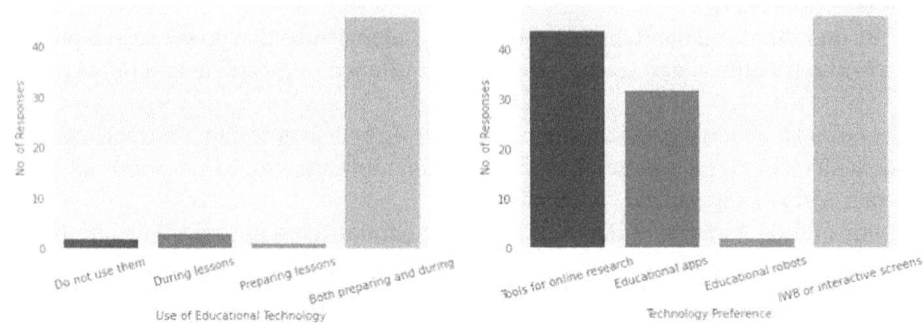

(a) When technology is used. (b) Which technology is used.

Fig. 1. Teachers' preferences on educational technology.

As previously stated, with the ubiquitous nature of search tools, we intended to understand the purpose driving teachers to these tools. From collected results, in their vast majority (75%) teachers take advantage of search tools both when preparing lessons and during their regular classroom instruction (Fig. 2a). Moreover, as showcased in Fig. 2b, close to 50% of the teachers ask their students to take advantage of search tools both during class as well as when completing homework assignments at home.

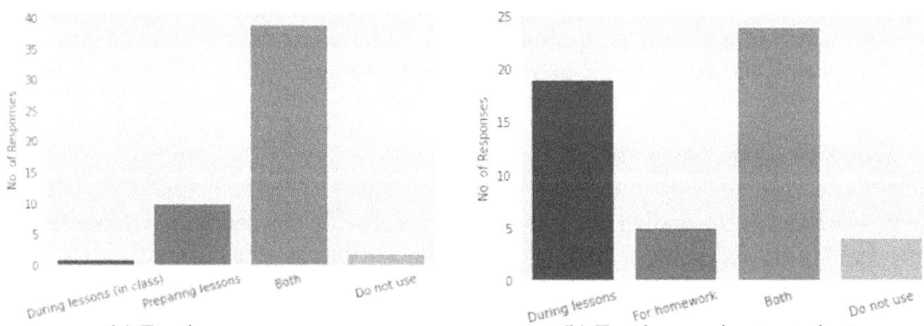

(a) Teachers usage. (b) Teachers assign to students.

Fig. 2. Teachers' reliance on search tools.

3.2 The Laundry Bucket: The Students' Side

Nowadays, students rarely organize digital resources as previous generations used to, adopting a nested hierarchy, i.e., directories, folders, and sub-folders. Instead, they are

[3] Note that as a response to this particular survey question, teachers could select more than one option or provide their own alternative.

known to create content not caring where it is stored and then pull what they need when they need it simply by searching. Students search an app or a resource in the same way: using the search tool provided on their device. This prompted us to query teachers on their preferred search tools and how they differ from those they reckon their students turn to.

From collected responses related to search tools teachers utilize, it emerges that in their vast majority, teachers use Google (90%), followed by Bing and DuckDuckGo. As for which search tool teachers believe to be regularly used by their students, Google again surfaces as the most prominent one (~94%); others mentioned include Qwant Junior, Qwant, and KidRex. In regards to the type of devices used to access search tools, very few teachers claim to not knowing or simply not using devices with their students. From those expressing their opinion on devise choice, it appears that approximately 50% of the students use Desktop computers, the rest a likely to use smartphones (~22%) and tablets (~16%).

Maintaining a focus on students, we asked teachers whether they in any way influence students' choice of tool. Collected responses from teachers who foster the use of search tools in the classroom and/or for completion of homework assignments reveal that close to 65% prefer explicitly indicating which search tool their students should use. Instead, the remaining teachers favor allowing students to turn to their chosen search tool for information discovery. Further, regardless of the search tool used, more than 93% of the surveyed teachers explicitly advise their students on how to use search tools.

3.3 Teachers' Beliefs the Use of Search Tools at School: Do We Need to Train the Trainers?

From the findings presented thus far, it is clear that search tools, among educational technology, are leaders in the classroom: these tools are more often than not, directly or indirectly embedded in the classroom setting. Emerging also from the responses is the fact that the daily use of search tools is not accompanied by an adequate knowledge and awareness on the tools themselves, both among teachers and students. This is why it is imperative to be cognizant of the level of expertise teachers' have on how to use search tools.

As captured in Fig. 3, it arises that teachers are seldom exposed to formal training on search tools. In fact, ~20% of surveyed teachers indicate receiving no training. Those seeking preparation on this area, mostly turn to colleagues and social networks for insights, with less than 30% enrolling in formal training courses. It is then unexpected that this pattern is also apparent when considering students' exposure to formal training on the use of search tools. From teachers' responses we surmise that at most, barely 30% of the students receive some sort of formal instruction on search tools, the rest depend on parents, sibling, or friends; with close to 10% receiving no tutelage at all.

To further understand teachers' perceptions on the impact search tools can have on learning, and therefore the need for more dedicated training in the future (for the teachers themselves and their students), we asked teachers three more questions. We summarize response distribution for these questions in Fig. 4. Overall, teachers agree on the fact that search tools can and do impact learning. More importantly, they strongly agree on

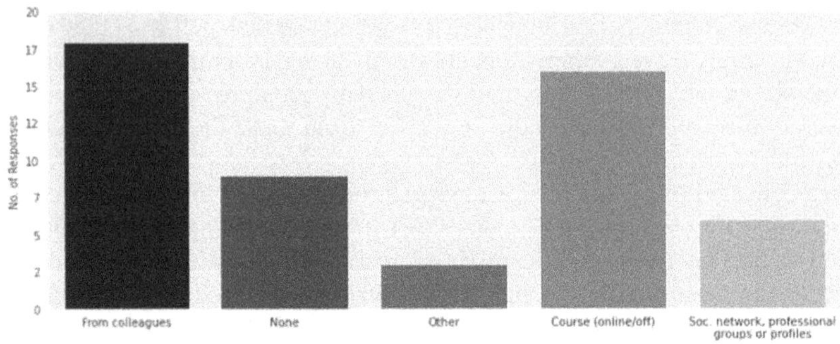

Fig. 3. Teachers' exposure to training on the use of search tools.

the need and importance of receiving training not only on the use of search tools but also on how to naturally integrate these tools to best support teaching and learning.

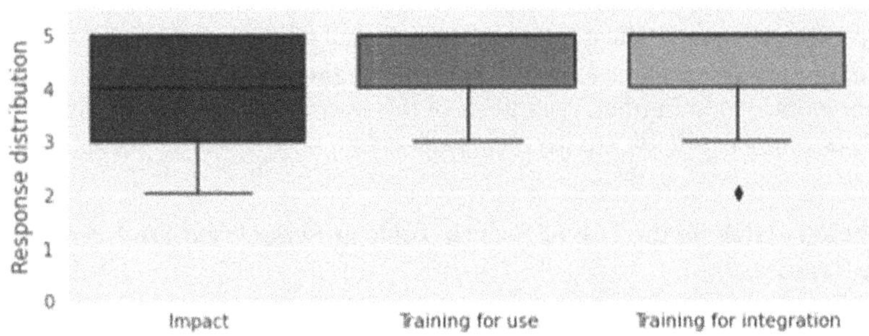

Fig. 4. Teachers' vision on the use of technology and the need for training–1 disagreement, 5 agreement.

3.4 Search Tools: Relevance, Interaction, Engagement, and Ethic Questions

We take a more in-depth look into expectations and requirements that teachers perceive as a must for search tools, if these tools are to be properly embedded to support teaching and learning.

We start by considering resources search tools retrieve and display in response to classroom-related inquiries. As captured in Fig. 5, when asked to select among a pre-defined set of characteristics, in their majority teachers expect resources to be reliable, closely followed by educational (80% and 69% of teachers selected these options, respectively). Other favored characteristics include engaging resources, written in a manner that students can read and comprehend, and that are up to date. It is noticeable that only ~20% selected "relevant" as a required characteristic in the search results.

We also inquired on primary expectations and concerns about search tools that can support learning. Teachers mention as their primary requirement the fact that in the use of search tools students have to be guided, followed by the need for them to be engaged

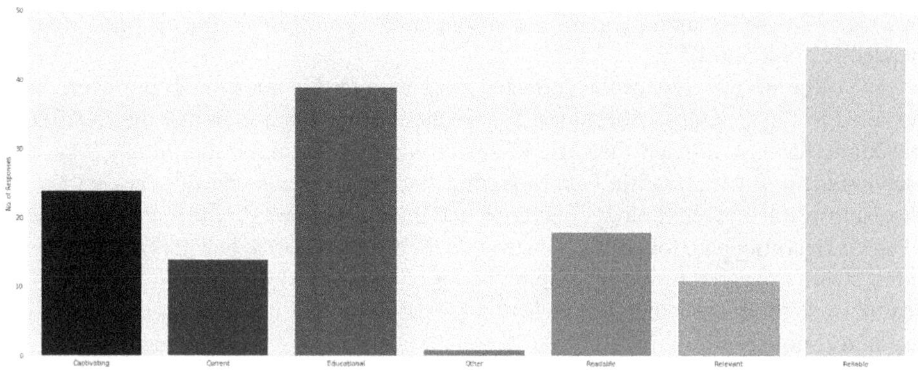

Fig. 5. Distributions of teachers' selected traits for resources retrieved and displayed by search tools for the classroom.

(see Fig. 6a). Only close to 16% indicate that students have to learn while using search tools. As for the major concerns associated with using search tools in a classroom setting, teachers indicate that exposure to unsuitable materials was without double a matter that could not be overlooked. Other emerging concerns included data privacy, interaction with fake news, and technology addiction (see Fig. 6b).

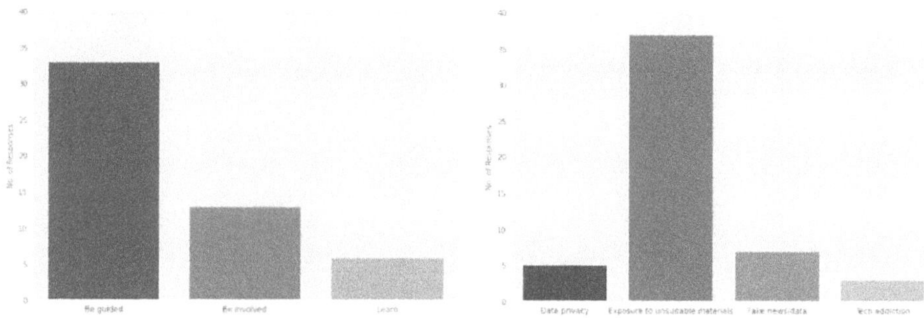

(a) Requirements. (b) Concerns.

Fig. 6. Teachers' views on search tools for the classroom.

3.5 Search Tools in a Changed World

As previously stated, data collection for this survey took place during the ongoing COVID-19 pandemic. With that in mind, we inquired on perceived changes, if any, teachers experience on their expectations and use of educational technology as a consequence of the pandemic. It was our intention to further contextualize emerging discoveries with the possible changes in common practices that could be directly impacted by the pandemic. In particular, we asked[4] teachers: Do the manner and the frequency

[4] Recall that this inquiry was presented to teachers as an open question.

in which you use technology in the classroom and/or your private life changed after the pandemic? If so, how?

We offer an overview of the collected responses to this question in the word cloud depicted in Fig. 7. Only a handful of the teachers (n = 6) mention that the COVID-19 pandemic has not affected their use of search tools in the classroom in any way. One elaborated on why that was the case by stating that this is because she does not believe "in the exclusive use of technology. The book and the teacher remain the main components of a valid learning path for pupils". Instead, in their vast majority, teachers disclose being more aware of search tools, developing better technology skills, being more reliant on search tools to locate materials for lesson preparation, and noticing an increase in the use of technology.

The general tone of the collected responses is positive, with teachers focusing on how, forced by the situation, they discovered how supportive technology could be of existing teaching practices. Teachers also appreciated that technology indeed facilitated content sharing among peers and with their students. Even so, teachers acknowledged the need for formal training–necessary to take full advantage of the potential technology demonstrated during this ongoing emergency period. Teachers also emphasized the need to revise the school curriculum to include elements for aiding the development of search skills in students. Among individual keywords in Fig. 7, DAD is quite salient. This term, an Italian acronym for distant teaching-education, often appears among teachers' comments as a flag of the effort teachers made and the opportunities they were given to keep school-related endeavors active even from remote, during the difficult lockdown period.

Fig. 7. Teachers' view on how their use of technology–particularly search tools– was affected by the COVID-19 pandemic.

4 Concluding Remarks, Limitations, and Future Work

Today's virtual world is largely a searchable one, facilitating access to a vast range of resources that are at our service using the magic wand of search tools. This remains true when considering education and specifically searching in the classroom. Integrating curriculum and technology requires "infusion of technology as a tool to enhance the learning in a content area or multidisciplinary setting" [10]. Thus, we expected the responses to the survey we designed to reveal favored tools and strategies that ease integration, in addition to gaps in technology and search literacy instruction.

Collected responses to our survey came from a sample of Italian teachers, most of them from a primary school where the research, exploration of new tools, and methodology are a constant in the history of the Italian primary school system, much more so than in the following school grades. Still, in Italy, there is no mandatory curriculum focused on media education in general, not in search literacy–the effective use of search tools to identify online resources satisfying users' information needs. Thus, we contemplated that the answers to the survey would significantly vary from school to school and even from teacher to teacher. It emerged from sample responses that teachers are aware of the importance of using online search tools in the classroom–as these account for the most used technology in preparing and administering their lessons. However, although search tools should (and often are) widely used in an educational context, it comes across that teachers feel that there is a lack of adequate tools that match the needs of students.

Another crucial issue emerging from collected responses points to the lack of specific training. This could aid teachers in taking advantage of search tools while avoiding potential risks often associated with these tools. Recall that the majority of the teachers declared they instruct students on which search tools to use and supervise how their students engage with search tools. That said, searching the Web is a scary experience for most of the interviewed teachers as they are warned more about the risks (e.g., unsuitable content and cyberbullying) than the opportunities. Even though existing works could ease this challenge by offering cues or automatically flagging possible unsuitable content [18, 24], it is still imperative to "train the trainer". In that way, teachers can become trustworthy guides for their students when they need to seek information online safely and effectively. Overall, conclusions reported in existing related literature [14, 15, 21, 22, 26], along with the results presented in this manuscript, confirm that teachers have a vital role in informing the design, development, and assessment of information retrieval tools for educational purposes. It is worth noting, however, that teachers' responses revealed that they believed that close to 30% of their students were supported at home by parents and siblings.

While out of scope, issues of inclusion and accessibility should also be probed in future versions of the proposed survey. This would enable understanding of teachers' perceptions on whether already-embedded device support (such as enlarging fonts or text-to-speech) is sufficient, or other aspects should be taken into consideration [2, 19]. Moreover, it will be of interest to the research community to deploy a similar survey among parents to also understand their views of search tools, as well as their expectations when these tools are used to support their children's learning process. Outcomes could have practical implications in designing, developing, assessing, and deploying search tools for the classroom context. The benefits of considering parents' perspectives have already been reported by Fails et al. [9] as a result of discussions taking place during an interdisciplinary workshop on children and Information Retrieval systems (i.e., KidRec).

Insights and lessons learned from the analysis of collected survey responses can serve as guidance for educational researchers to further understand how to define the training and involvement of teachers to improve the integration and productivity of technologies at school. They also inform how tools can impact, in reality, not just in theory, classroom instruction and students' learning. In the future, we anticipate recruiting teacher participants across the full primary and secondary school grades. Doing so will allow us to discern challenges and preferences that might naturally emerge by the different manners in which teachers could take advantage of search tools in different grades. We also plan to extend the reach of this survey by administering it across different countries[5]. Doing so will allow us to connect with teachers worldwide to gather different perspectives on their perceptions and needs regarding search technology for the classroom. More importantly, deploying a survey such as the one we propose on an international scale would let us showcase whether and how countries' idiosyncrasies, teachers' experience, and search tool popularity correlate with adoption. We expect the curriculum and cultural traits of each country, directives, languages, and teaching practices will yield a broader range of opinions and emerging needs that researchers and practitioners should account for when designing and deploying search technology that can explicitly support teachers and students. At the same time, extending the reach of a survey like the one we discuss in this manuscript is not an easy feat. To connect with teachers worldwide, we intend to (i) participate in international conferences focused on education and attended by teachers, such as AERA[6] and ATEE[7], (ii) join workshops like KidRec[8] or IR4K[9] co-located with computer science conferences, during which we could form partnerships with other researchers and practitioners who can also reach teachers, and (iii) continue the snowball approach adopted in this current iteration of our work, but starting with international teaching associations, beyond Facebook or local contacts.

As mentioned in the literature [9], to be of use in a real-world setting, the design of tools that enable information access to children in an educational setting, such as search tools, should simultaneously account for multiple perspectives, e.g., teachers, parents, industry, and children, to name a few. Thus, it will be necessary to juxtapose outcomes emerging from surveys like the ones presented in this manuscript with those distilled from surveying, for example, children to identify dissenting voices. Vanderschantz and Hinze [26] already reported on how teachers' views and children's views differ when it comes to information seeking. Extending the ongoing work to include perceptions on search tools would advance understanding of current gaps researchers and practitioners should account for to best support the search in an educational setting.

[5] If you are interested in taking part of this worldwide survey, please email the authors for more details.

[6] https://www.aera.net/.

[7] https://atee.education/.

[8] https://kidrec.github.io/.

[9] http://www.fab4.science/IR4C/.

References

1. Azpiazu, I.M., Dragovic, N., Pera, M.S., Fails, J.A.: Online searching and learning: YUM and other search tools for children and teachers. Inf. Retrieval J. **20**(5), 524–545 (2017)
2. Badr, N.G., Asmar, M.K.: Meta principles of technology accessibility design for users with learning disabilities: towards inclusion of the differently enabled. In: Lazazzara, A., Ricciardi, F., Za, S. (eds.) Exploring Digital Ecosystems. LNISO, vol. 33, pp. 195–209. Springer, Cham (2020). https://doi.org/10.1007/978-3-030-23665-6_14
3. Brown, C.A.: Using digital resources to support stem education. In: Handbook of Research on Learning Outcomes and Opportunities in the Digital Age, pp. 127–151. IGI Global (2016)
4. Burnett, C.: The Digital Age and Its Implications for Learning and Teaching in the Primary School. Cambridge Primary Review Trust York (2016)
5. Danovitch, J.H.: Growing up with google: how children's understanding and use of internet-based devices relates to cognitive development. Hum. Behav. Emerg. Technol. **1**(2), 81–90 (2019)
6. Davies, R.S., West, R.E.: Technology integration in schools. In: Spector, J.M., Merrill, M.D., Elen, J., Bishop, M.J. (eds.) Handbook of Research on Educational Communications and Technology, pp. 841–853. Springer, New York (2014). https://doi.org/10.1007/978-1-4614-3185-5_68
7. Druin, A., et al.: How children search the internet with keyword interfaces. In: Proceedings of the 8th International Conference on Interaction Design and Children, pp. 89–96 (2009)
8. Ekstrand, M.D., Wright, K.L., Pera, M.S.: Enhancing classroom instruction with online news. Aslib J. Inf. Manag. **72**(5), 725–744 (2020)
9. Fails, J.A., Pera, M.S., Kucirkova, N.: Building community: report on the 2nd international and interdisciplinary perspectives on children & recommender systems (KidRec) at IDC 2018. In: ACM SIGIR Forum, vol. 52, pp. 138–144. ACM, New York (2019)
10. Harris, J.: Our agenda for technology integration: it's time to choose. Contemp. Issues Technol. Teach. Educ. **5**(2), 116–122 (2005)
11. Karatassis, I.: Websail: computer-based methods for enhancing web search literacy. In: Proceedings of the 2017 Conference on Conference Human Information Interaction and Retrieval, pp. 403–405 (2017)
12. Landoni, M., Huibers, T., Aliannejadi, M., Murgia, E., Pera, M.S.: Getting to know you: search logs and expert grading to define children's search roles in the classroom. In: 2nd International Conference on Design of Experimental Search and Information REtrieval Systems, DESIRES 2021, pp. 44–52 (2021)
13. Landoni, M., Huibers, T., Murgia, E., Aliannejadi, M., Pera, M.S.: Somewhere over the rainbow: exploring the sense for relevance in children. In: European Conference on Cognitive Ergonomics 2021, pp. 1–5 (2021)
14. Landoni, M., Huibers, T., Murgia, E., Pera, M.S.: Ethical implications for children's use of search tools in an educational setting. Int. J. Child Comput. Interact. **32**, 100386 (2021)
15. Landoni, M., Huibers, T., Pera, M.S., Fails, J.A.: 5th KidRec workshop: search and recommendation technology through the lens of a teacher. In: Interaction Design and Children, pp. 658–661 (2021)
16. Landoni, M., Pera, M.S., Murgia, E., Huibers, T.: Inside out: exploring the emotional side of search engines in the classroom. In: Proceedings of the 28th ACM Conference on User Modeling, Adaptation and Personalization, pp. 136–144 (2020)
17. Makri, S., et al.: Search a great leveler? Ensuring more equitable information acquisition. Proc. Assoc. Inf. Sci. Technol. **58**(1), 613–618 (2021)
18. Milton, A., Anuya, O., Spear, L., Wright, K.L., Pera, M.S.: A ranking strategy to promote resources supporting the classroom environment. In: 2020 IEEE/WIC/ACM International

Joint Conference on Web Intelligence and Intelligent Agent Technology (WI-IAT), pp. 121–128. IEEE (2020)

19. Mulliken, A., Djenno, M.: Faculty visions for teaching web accessibility within LIS curricula in the united states: a qualitative study. Libr. Q. **87**(1), 36–54 (2017)
20. Murgia, E., Landoni, M., Huibers, T., Fails, J.A., Pera, M.S.: The seven layers of complexity of recommender systems for children in educational contexts (2019)
21. Murgia, E., Landoni, M., Huibers, T., Pera, M.S.: All together now: teachers as research partners in the design of search technology for the classroom. In: 5th International and Interdisciplinary Perspectives on Children & Recommender and Information Retrieval Systems (KidRec) Search and Recommendation Technology through the Lens of a TeacherCo-located with ACM IDC 2021, 26 June 2021. arXivpreprint arXiv:2105.03708 (2021)
22. Murgia, E., Landoni, M., Pera, M.S., Huibers, T.: When will the promises of search technology in the classroom come true? In: ICERI2019 Proceedings: 12th Annual International Conference of Education, Research and Innovation, Seville, Spain, 11–13 November 2019, pp. 10,409–10,415. International Association of Technology, Education and Development (IATED) (2019)
23. Smith, L., Hanson, M.: Communities of praxis: transforming access to information for equity. Ser. Libr. **76**(1–4), 42–49 (2019)
24. Tahir, R., Ahmed, F., Saeed, H., Ali, S., Zaffar, F., Wilson, C.: Bringing the kid back into YouTube kids: detecting inappropriate content on video streaming platforms. In: 2019 IEEE/ACM International Conference on Advances in Social Networks Analysis and Mining (ASONAM), pp. 464–469. IEEE (2019)
25. Tondeur, J., Scherer, R., Baran, E., Siddiq, F., Valtonen, T., Sointu, E.: Teacher educators as gatekeepers: preparing the next generation of teachers for technology integration in education. Br. J. Edu. Technol. **50**(3), 1189–1209 (2019)
26. Vanderschantz, N., Hinze, A.: Children's internet search behaviour in an educational context. In: Proceedings of the IR for Children 2000–2020: Where Are We Now? Workshop, co-located with ACM SIGIR (2021). https://drive.google.com/file/d/1UfSD6g3TxZEAU7YiaMjGmbXkB1qm9JT/view
27. Wizenoze: Delivering trusted digital content to learners (2021). https://www.wizenoze.com/

Teaching with Digital Conceptual Maps for the Development of Inclusive Processes

Chiara Panciroli[1(✉)], Anita Macauda[1], Laura Corazza[2], and Elena Marcato[3]

[1] Department of Education Studies, University of Bologna, Bologna, Italy
{chiara.panciroli,anita.macauda}@unibo.it
[2] Department of Industrial Chemistry, University of Bologna, Bologna, Italy
[3] Lower Secondary School, Bologna, Italy

Abstract. The research proposed here focuses attention on the development of an inclusive teaching strategy supported by digital technologies that promotes the acquisition and the creative re-elaboration of knowledge. The objective of the experimentation was to identify the educational opportunities offered by the construction of mental and conceptual maps in digital environments. With university students, future primary school teachers, we used a proprietary software to create conceptual maps: SuperMappeX. The trial, by means of the integrated use of a specific online technological instrument, SuperMappeX, led to the creation of multimedia digital maps, which were followed by the realization of artistic audio-visual products and animated presentations. They built maps about various topics and experimented with the use of maps for brainstorming, cooperative learning and group assessment.

Keywords: Conceptual maps · Inclusion · Teaching · Digital technologies · Personalization

1 Theoretical Framework

The main references are the studies relating to the use of conceptual maps to foster a process of effective teaching [1, 9, 10, 21].

A significant contribution to the research was also provided by the reflections coming from the literature referring to visual literacy. The conceptual maps, which differ from mind maps, are used in schools for the representation of knowledge domains with different aims: for reading and understanding, for memorizing, for showing what has been learned, for writing, for stimulating creative output [17, 18]. Generally speaking, they are also an effective instrument for promoting inclusive, customized and personalized didactic forms functional to the valorisation of differences.

In relation to the national and international literature, the present contribution focuses attention on the valorisation of individual differences in the learning process and on the practices of cognitive flexibility and constructivism, for the development of mental processes of a superior order in relation to inventiveness and creativity [1, 8]. The application of visual and multimedia methods, from digital conceptual maps to the production of

M. Ranieri et al. (Eds.): ATEE 2021, CCIS 1649, pp. 209–218, 2022.
https://doi.org/10.1007/978-3-031-20777-8_17

video presentations, stimulates different perceptive channels and overcomes the need for schematization and representation, traditionally associated with the use of the maps in teaching, to develop competencies useful for more complex practices, such as change and innovation [3, 15].

Visual codification is generative of concepts and meanings in every field of knowledge, for communicative, creative use as well as memorization and personal re-elaboration. Architects and engineers visualize before building and this is functional to the design; scientists use systems of visualization of the data to highlight concepts bonds. Students create conceptual maps to clarify and memorize facts and ideas, relating them to one another to interpret, re-elaborate and convey knowledge visually.

A map has a hierarchical structure that involves all the elements of the object of communication: the pivotal concepts, the ties between these and the overall path of the reasoning. But it can also have a reticular structure, rich in connections. It is, indeed, the visual architecture that makes the map a creative product, thanks to which knowledge is enriched with new stimuli and elements: each graphic image rendered by the map, with its foregrounds, the colours, forms, equilibriums, aesthetic criteria, identifies a new structure inside concepts that are already known.

Indeed, for the same contents, different people are able to create different visual and meaning architectures, overcoming the simple idea of a chart [19]. In a map thus conceived, the visual organization of the elements corresponds to the logical and functional structure of one's own knowledge; indeed, different architectures allow one to explore the many standpoints from which one same phenomenon can be analyzed and to highlight diverse, simple or complex structures, with different levels of expositional clarity and communicative efficacy. Constructing a map reduces the likelihood of mechanical learning in favour of an active/meaningful learning, stimulating the process of learning to learn. Giving knowledge a personal organization, different from who presented it previously, allows for an awareness of different learning styles, reflecting on one's own mental processes and allowing for reciprocal remediation [16–18, 20].

The repercussions on learning are well-known and multiple and are particularly evident when the maps created in different educational contexts are analyzed. The students' age, the diverse capacity for learning and for managing complex knowledge, the different styles of learning and organization of knowledge are expressed very well by the kind of structure chosen to construct the conceptual map. Digital maps differ from one another in many ways, like the style chosen on the grounds of the target audience, aspects of trait and colour, complexity of the connections, adequacy of the choices in relation to the objectives. In this regard, a study conducted in 2015 drew attention to the learning results in relation to the use of various instruments for the digital presentation of the contents [5], showing how dynamic systems of representation positively influence the acquisition of knowledge by the students. These aspects show how visual communication is composed of multiple levels, variable in relation to the typology of support/medium through which the information is diffused, and showing the specificity of the visual language, comprising formal and chromatic elements, which variously arranged on a surface determine oppositions and transformations of values contributing to constructing the semantic content of an image [2, 3, 11, 14, 15].

2 Methodological Design

The research proposed here focuses attention on the development of an inclusive teaching strategy supported by digital technologies that promotes the acquisition and the creative re-elaboration of knowledge. In this regard, a trial is presented conducted at the Department of Education Sciences of Bologna University, within the six laboratories of the single cycle Post-Graduate degree in Primary Education Sciences in the academic year 2018–2019. The experimentation involved 180 students, future primary school teachers, enrolled in the fourth year of the course, almost all women. From a preliminary survey, it emerged that with regard to work experience, 8% have taught at school for several years with fixed-term contracts; 10% had occasional teaching experience. As for the use of maps, only 30% said they use maps as a study tool; all students declare that they have never used maps to support specific teaching strategies, either as a teacher or as a learner. The experimentation led to the design and the creation of digital conceptual maps, through the use of multimodal and flexible formats, adaptable to the perceptive characteristics of the individual students and capable of reducing the obstacles to the process of text comprehension or to the personal production of knowledge.

The objective of the experimentation was to identify the educational opportunities offered by the construction of mental and conceptual maps in digital environments.

2.1 First Phase: Active Learning Laboratories

With university students, future primary school teachers, we used a proprietary software to create conceptual maps: *SuperMappeX*. The trial, by means of the integrated use of a specific online technological instrument, *SuperMappeX*, led to the creation of multimedia digital maps, which were followed by the realization of artistic audio-visual products and animated presentations. They built maps about various topics and experimented with the use of maps for brainstorming, cooperative learning and group assessment.

Brainstorming. The map was created by the teacher during the brainstorming process to collect the ideas in a large group.

Cooperative Learning. Students in small groups searched for information and created a map to organize content and to expose to peers.

Collaborative Assessment. Teacher and students evaluate together the maps (student's written test) and the oral presentation.

Before starting the laboratory activities, the students watched a video made in Elena Marcato's class with 12-year-olds, to identify some elements of cooperative learning and collaborative assessment.

2.2 Second Phase: Data Collection and Analysis

After experimenting and creating the maps, we asked each student to analyze SuperMappeX through the SWOT tool. Specifically, students, future primary school teachers, were asked to reflect on the strengths and weaknesses and on the risks and opportunities of the software used for the creation of digital concept maps in an inclusive teaching context.

180 SWOT analysis sheets were collected. We carried out a qualitative analysis of the content of the responses by identifying the textual data assumed as a unit of observation and the definition of two specific macro-categories.

3 Classroom Teaching Strategies (First Phase)

All four teachers who conducted the laboratories used the software to build maps in similar educational situations, designed together by identifying three strategies: brainstorming, cooperative learning and shared evaluation, the same strategies that teacher Elena Marcato uses with its lower secondary school classes.

3.1 Brainstorming

The teacher can introduce a work in the classroom with concept maps, when facing a new didactic activity. It is a brainstorming which involves all the pupils, and which activates the participation of the class group. In this case it is the teacher himself who co-constructs the concept map with the verbal help of the students, and it is then the teacher himself who uses the dedicated software and guides the students in mapping ideas. The topic to be discussed has never been addressed, but the students may have previous knowledge about it, so they will bring their personal contribution to the drafting of the map in question. The role of the teacher is to guide the final production through stimulating questions to the class, in such a way as to involve all the participants. The intent is to carry out a common basic work, where each member of the class will be able to enrich the map with personal contributions and at the same time recognize themselves in the chorality of the information expressed.

The key words that emerge from the teacher's stimulus questions are transformed from narration to nodes of the map, which in turn can be related to the link phrases. Once the map has been created in the classroom, it can be shared with all students.

Producing a map and learning a dedicated software, especially if it has accessibility and easy-to-use characteristics such as reading and writing, are no longer two diversified moments, but merge into a synchronous learning, which activates different skills.

3.2 Cooperative Learning

A second use involves a group of students already experienced in producing maps. This is the final part of a cooperative activity, where the final delivery is to exhibit your digital artefact to classmates via the LIM (or Smart TV): the map created by the students will help them summarize the topics addressed. Students work in a small group and have both the textbook and digital resources selected by the teacher and uploaded to a dedicated e-learning platform, such as Moodle. Groups have the possibility of using personal and/or school devices connected to the Internet. The cooperative activity concerns the creation of an artifact, for example a presentation, to be exhibited to classmates following precise instructions provided by the teacher: view the materials on the platform and those present in the textbook; write short texts with keywords for presentation; accompany the work with relevant thematic papers and enrich the work with relevant images.

The final part of the work is to create one or more clear and legible concept maps: once the presentation is finished, the students jointly create one or more maps that summarize the topics addressed and deepened together. The map becomes a verification of the work already done, allowing for any reworking of the artifact, but at the same time a moment to better memorize what is sought.

The map also becomes a graphic summary for the companions who attend the group's exhibition. Also in this case, the presence of guide colours, for single topics, and/or internal images will help classmates to better follow the oral presentation of the small group.

The function of the teacher is that of tutor: after indicating the instructions, he assists the working groups, corrects where necessary and checks that the drafting of the maps is relevant to the topics covered and easy to use for the entire class group.

3.3 Collaborative Assessment

A third use, closely related to the second, concerns the analysis of the maps that the individual working groups have drawn up together in the previous activity, in order to be able to express an assessment of the group's artefact [4].

Evaluation and self-evaluation of the individual groups include a rubric that is made explicit to the class at the time of delivery. The map or maps are made visible to everyone via the LIM (or Smart TV) and, after the oral presentation of the group, together, under the guidance of the teacher, the work presented to the entire class is evaluated. In this case, the map becomes the graphic (multimedia) guide to be able to conduct an informed evaluation, following a specific rubric, which the students already know and which they actively discuss together with other classmates. The rubric indicators are: clarity in presentation, clarity in presentation, consistency in work and harmony in teamwork. The map becomes a highlight of the activity, as the teacher, as a mediator, is able to tell the entire class group whether the cooperative work strategies implemented by each group have been functional and profitable. Individual students express their opinion based on the rubric indicators, without forgetting the relational element, which is highlighted as an added, but essential, value to team activity.

The function of the teacher in this last case is that of mediator who leads the class towards a conscious evaluation of the activity.

4 Data Collection and Analysis (Second Phase)

The students responded more broadly in the sections of the SWOT dedicated to strengths and opportunities, while few elements of risk were identified.

As for the positive aspects, we collected the answers by assembling them into two categories: technical aspects, didactic aspects. Among the technical aspects we have identified the sub-categories relating to multimedia and multimodality, on the one hand, and usability and accessibility, on the other.

From a technical point of view (see Table 1), the students particularly appreciated the fact of being able to add visual and audio-visual content, animations, colours and even tables to the map, considering the graphical interface to be excellent. Furthermore, a strong point of the software that has been highlighted is the speech synthesis in many languages and the possibility of voice typing. Another key feature is the fact of being able to work remotely even in a collaborative way, building the same map with several hands.

Table 1. A summary of the technical opportunities offered by the software and detected by the students.

Summary of the answers – Technical Opportunities	
Multimedia and Multimodality	Usability and Accessibility
Visual content	Excellent graphical interface
Audio and audio-visual content	Upload images
Animation	Upload video
Customization of nodes with texts, images, colours and shapes	Speech synthesis
Multimedia presentation function	Voice typing
Speech synthesis in multiple languages	Web app
Building tables	Spell check
	Sharing
	Use in multiple languages
	Export in many format

The same functions can be considered as educational opportunities (see Table 2). Thanks to sharing, for example, the map can be built in a group in class or in distance learning. Everyone is responsible for the same job. Thanks to the images and audio-visual contents, to voice typing and speech synthesis, the software is a help for children with disabilities. In addition, the tool can be used in an interdisciplinary approach and with students of all ages.

Table 2. A summary of the educational opportunities offered by the software and detected by the students.

Summary of the answers – Educational opportunities		
Interdisciplinarity - The tool can be used for all subjects in multidisciplinary and interdisciplinary approach	Collaborative writing – The map can be built in a group in class and in distance learning. It is mandatory to interact, everyone is responsible for the same job	Inclusion – The students can "speak with images". The software has voice typing and speech synthesis
All scholastic levels – The tool and the method can be used with students of all ages	Individualization and personalization – The tool allows you to use many languages. You can choose to follow the paths you want	Motivation and engagement – The group control promotes engagement

There are a few weaknesses and threat (see Fig. 1). You need internet to use the software and this can be a weakness. The software is also subject to a fee.

And even, maps can get too complicated. In fact, the students need to learn how to build maps, respecting for example the rules in the choice of nodes and colours.

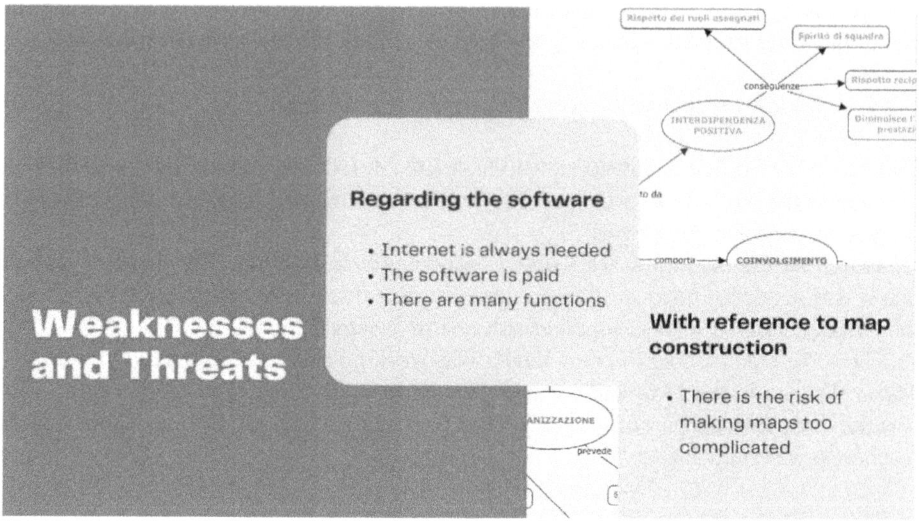

Fig. 1. The main weaknesses encountered by the students.

We also report below some dialogues taken from the video that the students watched before starting the activities, to observe how a teacher, in this case with 12-year-olds, conducts the final phase of cooperative learning, which corresponds to the moment of collaborative assessment. The transcription of the dialogues was the subject of analysis by the students who, in a phase of conducting a dialogue by the teachers of the laboratory, were able to collectively reflect on the strategy used thanks also to the intermediation of the software.

Teacher: So you listened to the other guys. Let's start with Sofia
Sofia: I'd say that her Map was excellent. Because it was good. There were only a few grammar mistakes. It was very clear. Maps sum up all the topics. So I'd say that her Map was excellent. And the presentation as well, because they didn't just look at the board. Speaking clearly.
Giorgia: Just I'd rather divide the texts into shorter parts instead of having a full text.
Teacher: For a better comprehension of the text?
Giorgia: Yes.
Teacher: Are the concepts, colors and linking phrases clear?
All: Yes.
Teacher: Do you think that it summarizes what the guys have said?
All: Yes.
Teacher: Do you agree that the job of each member of the group was excellent?
All: Yes … No …
Teacher: I mean the written part, not the oral presentation. I'd like to ask the group who made the map if, in your opinion, you all have worked the same way.
All: Yes … yes …
Teacher: Mattia, let's think about how your ability of talking in front of the class has changed. Do you agree that you all improved a lot? And that Maria - who was anxious and didn't want to speak - Is now good both in making the maps and in speaking?
All: Yes … yes …
Teacher: It took a whole school year but we're very satisfied.
< … >
Teacher: Now I'd like to ask those who have talked. He said that to him it was difficult to organise the work. I ask everyone: For you it was difficult to organise the work? How did you arrange the group work?
Giovanni: At the beginning we worked individually from home. But then we realised that it was better for us to work in groups of two or three from home. So we've divided the work and we've worked together at home in groups of three.
Teacher: Ok. I'd also like to know how it was working at school. What did you do?
Maria: We made the Map and we add more images at home. The written part – that was the most difficult part of the work – has been done at school. Because there was the teacher so we could ask for help.

5 Conclusions/Findings

The digital conceptual maps created using SuperMappeX have confirmed, in the students' opinions, their efficacy for the organization and the formalization of knowledge and for the learning and memorization processes. Particularly relevant was the evidence concerning the development of metacognitive processes of personal re-elaboration of knowledge and creative output. The possibility to valorize differences and to foster personalized learning pathways was also observed by the students, along with the creation of original products characterized by a high visual impact and a strong multimediality.

With respect to the use of maps and the risk that they are too complicated and therefore not very useful, it is necessary to introduce some reflections. The creation of the maps, in the educational actions described above, is always accompanied by a group reflection and a collaborative dialogue based on explicit and shared criteria. The focus of the work is the school experience in its breadth and evaluation is one of the steps in the learning process. The purpose of the assessment is to help pupils reflect on their learning and give each other feedback, to critically reflect on what they have done and what they have learned during the process [6, 7, 12, 13]. Students therefore learn to build complete and clear maps thanks to the feedback of their peers and recognize the value of the evaluation criteria. The great flexibility of the software, which could lead to the error of constructing maps that are too complicated, also allows you to review the structure of the map itself following the comments and suggestions of fellow recipients of the presentation in the classroom. Furthermore, it is perhaps superfluous to specify that software evolves over time and others are launched on the market.

Currently, SuperMappeX is also associated with some active and inclusive teaching projects and therefore offered free of charge if included in larger packages; also for this reason its use is spreading, in addition to the fact that it has many functions that make it particularly flexible and easy to use. Its development could be an example for free software that requires some new functions to be implemented. Finally, the experimentation presented here highlights how this technological device, when inserted within a specific didactic design that involves the use of active strategies, is particularly significant for the development of inclusive learning processes. Specifically, there are some educational dimensions, such as interdisciplinarity, collaboration and cooperation, individualization and personalization, multimedia and multimodality, motivation and engagement, as privileged lines of research and training intervention in an inclusive context.

References

1. Agudelo, O.L., Del Rosario Atuesta, M., Echeverry, L.M.: Itinerario Flexibles de Aprendizaje (IFA). Como Propuesta de Flexibilidad y Autonomía Escolar. Una Experiencia desde el "Plan Digital Itagüí". In: Proceedings of the Eighth International Conference on Concept Mapping 2018, Colombia, Medellin, pp. 162–170 (2018)
2. Calabrese, O.: Il linguaggio dell'arte, Bompiani, Milano (1984)
3. Cañas, A.J.: What are my students learning when they concept map? In: Proceedings of the Eighth International Conference on Concept Mapping, Colombia, Medellin, pp. 290–300 (2018)
4. Cooper, S.: A collaborative assessment of students' placement learning. Assess. Eval. High. Educ. **42**(1), 61–76 (2017)
5. Damini, M., Surian, A.: Cooperative learning e valutazione in contesti multiculturali. Giornale italiano della ricerca educative **5**(9) (2012). https://ojs.pensamultimedia.it/index.php/sird/article/view/214/202. Accessed 21 July 2022
6. Del Pilar Toro, R., Esteban Buitrago Ropero, M.: Organizadores graficos para afianzar competencias lectoras en estudiantes universitarios de primer semestre. In: Proceedings of the

Eighth International Conference on Concept Mapping, Colombia, Medellin, pp. 192–199 (2018)
7. Emili, E.A., Reggiani, A.: Le mappe concettuali come mediatori di cambiamento. In: Panciroli, C. (ed.) Educare nella città. Percorsi didattici e interdisciplinary, pp. 267–283. FrancoAngeli, Milano (2018)
8. Fogarolo, F., Guastavigna, M.: Insegnare e imparare con le mappe. Strategie logico-visive per l'organizzazione delle conoscenze. Erickson, Trento (2013)
9. Greimas, A.-J.: Sémiotique figurative et sémiotique plastique. In: Fabbri, P., Marrone, G. (eds.) Semiotica in nuce. Teoria del discorso, Roma, Meltemi, pp. 196–210 (1984)
10. Hargreaves, E.: The validity of collaborative assessment for learning. Assess. Educ. **14**(2) (2007)
11. Ioannou, A., Artino Jr., A.R.: Learn more, stress less: exploring the benefits of collaborative assessment. Coll. Stud. J. **44**(1), 189 (2010)
12. Martinez Gomez, I.: Mapas conceptuales: una estrategia para evidenciar aprendizaje significativo. In: Proceedings of the Eighth International Conference on Concept Mapping, Colombia, Medellin, pp. 360–364 (2018)
13. Marzano, A.: Mappe concettuali dinamiche e processi di rimediazione in ambienti di apprendimento in rete. Formazione Insegnamento **15**(3), 245–278 (2017)
14. Novack, J.D.: Learning, creating and using knowledge: concept maps as facilitative tools in schools and corporations. J. e-Learn. Knowl. Soc. **6**(3), 21–30 (2010)
15. Novack, J.D.: Costruire mappe concettuali. Strategie e metodi per utilizzarle nella didattica. Erickson, Trento (2012)
16. Panciroli, C., Corazza, L., Macauda, A.: Visual-graphic learning. In: Cicalò, E. (ed.) IMG 2019. AISC, vol. 1140, pp. 49–62. Springer, Cham (2020). https://doi.org/10.1007/978-3-030-41018-6_6
17. Pellegrini, M., Mensuali, A.: L'efficacia delle mappe concettuali per l'apprendimento: analisi critica di evidenze empiriche. Form@re - Open Journal per la formazione in rete **15**(3), 129–141 (2015)
18. Scocco, A.: Costruire mappe per rappresentare e organizzare il proprio pensiero. Strumenti fondamentali per professionisti, docenti e studenti. FrancoAngeli, Milano (2008)
19. Simper, N., Reeve, R., Kirby, J.R.: Effects of concept mapping on creativity in photo stories. Creat. Res. J. **28**(1), 46–51 (2016)
20. Trentin, G.: Mappe concettuali, flussi di conoscenza e sviluppo professionale continuo. Form@re - Open Journal per la formazione in rete **15**(2) 4–18 (2015)
21. Vlachopoulos, P., Jan, S.K., Buckton, R.: A case for team-based learning as an effective collaborative learning methodology in higher education. Coll. Teach. **68**(1), 69–77 (2020)

Teacher Professional Development on Social Inclusion: The PLEIADE Approach

Donatella Persico[1(✉)], Marcello Passarelli[1], Francesca Dagnino[1], Andrea Ceregini[1], Flavio Manganello[1], Francesca Pozzi[1], Nikolina Nikolova[2], Krassen Stefanov[2], Kleio Anagnostou[3], Tsvetelina Georgieva[4], Christos Kyriakides[5], and Marilina Lonigro[6]

[1] Consiglio Nazionale delle Ricerche, Istituto per le Tecnologie Didattiche, Genova, Italy
persico@itd.cnr.it

[2] Sofia University St. Kliment Ohridski, Sofia, Bulgaria

[3] Avgoulea-Linardatou School, Athens, Greece

[4] 144 Secondary School "Narodni Buditeli", Sofia, Bulgaria

[5] Neapolis Gymnasium, Limassol, Cyprus

[6] Scuola secondaria di 1° grado Rocca Bovio Palumbo, Trani, Italy

Abstract. This paper presents some preliminary results of an intervention case-study intended to improve the ability of an international community of 75 teachers to design collaborative and inclusive activities for their students. The study is carried out in the framework of an Erasmus+ project adopting a long-term, participatory, and gamified approach to teachers' professional development. This comprises a preparatory phase, followed by one-year training phase and a one-year enactment phase. During the training, the teachers design collaborative learning activities for inclusion, while during enactment they carry them out with their students. This paper focuses on the training phase, presenting the approach adopted and preliminary results in terms of its feasibility, discussing enabling factors and barriers to its application. Among enablers, the previous experience of the teachers, the careful and systematic design of the training, and the availability of motivated team leaders who coordinate the activities in their schools deserve being mentioned. Among the barriers, it should be noted that the pandemic situation preventing teachers' mobility and the linguistic issues were an obstacle to straightforward peer interactions. Additionally, low familiarity with practice sharing behaviors and scarce digital competence hindered effective practice sharing.

Keywords: Teachers' professional development (TPD) · Social inclusion · Collaborative learning · Gamification · Learning design

1 Introduction

Conflict, poverty, and social displacement beyond and within Europe's borders are currently having a strong, sometimes disruptive impact in many areas of its social system, including its education. As European society becomes increasingly diversified - due to intensifying migration flows but also increased inequality and social disadvantage

M. Ranieri et al. (Eds.): ATEE 2021, CCIS 1649, pp. 219–229, 2022.
https://doi.org/10.1007/978-3-031-20777-8_18

- Europe's education systems face an urgent need to address the inclusion of all their students, which is the key to achieve inclusive societies [1–4]. School teachers play a pivotal role in facilitating the inclusion of students [5], but many of them feel they are ill-prepared for the task and express a strong need for more Teacher Professional Development (TPD), especially for dealing with multicultural settings [6]. As a consequence, inclusive education has long been a European Commission's priority when it comes to teacher training [7], and is still one of the main focuses of the Erasmus+ program.

However, developing teachers' skills for promoting an inclusive climate and culture is not, itself, an easy task; beyond simple recommendations, teachers typically need practical, context-relevant knowledge and good practice examples that can inspire their daily practice. This translates into a demand for TPD opportunities that support teachers in the longer term, enhancing their design abilities with relevant methods and technologies [8].

The traditional training models – short workshops or courses in which teachers are trained in an expert-driven process – are unsuitable for preparing teachers for such a complex task [9]. These approaches to TPD, in fact, tend to be disconnected from classroom practice, and don't align with current theories of teachers' professionalism [10, 11]. TPD should, instead, be grounded in reflective practice and involve the formation of professional learning communities that could evolve into communities of practice [12]. Collaboration in virtual communities facilitates practice sharing by establishing important inter-cultural connections among teachers, provides opportunities for collective reflection on practice and enables access to a multicultural range of perspectives, extending the community beyond the physical boundaries of the school or the local context [13, 14]. In addition, when teachers belong to an international community, they can more easily find colleagues with whom they can design international collaborative activities for their students, which is the first step towards getting students used to see children from other Countries as peers that can contribute to their own personal and cultural development and foster their positive attitude towards inclusion.

This paper presents an intervention case study of a TPD pathway focused on improving teachers' ability to foster social inclusion. Context of the case study is an Erasmus+ project called PLayful Environment for Inclusive leArning Design in Europe (PLEIADE[1]), aimed at supporting the efforts of primary and lower secondary teachers working in four different European Countries to cope with issues of educational inclusion, especially where that is rooted in cultural diversity or socio-economic disadvantage.

As the case study is still in progress, providing evidence of its effectiveness is beyond the aims of this contribution. Rather, the paper intends to showcase the approach by presenting how it can be used to design a pathway and by exploring enablers and impediments to its application.

2 Theoretical Framework

This study lies at the crossroads of several research fields, as it draws from current research in TPD, Learning Design (LD), and gamification.

[1] More details can be found on the project website at https://pleiade-project.eu/.

In particular, the approach to TPD proposed in the study [15] relies on three pillars: (a) long-term collaborative activities among teachers oriented to self-regulated learning and reflection on practice; (b) Learning Design practices that lead to the formation of communities of practice [16]; (c) teachers' continuous engagement in the learning community.

Firstly, (a) TPD research advocates for a move away from short-term initiatives focused on specific competences and skills, often delivered by experts away from school premises [9, 17]. Effective TPD has to be grounded on learning theories, intertwine with teaching practice and promote self-regulated learning through participatory and collaborative approaches [18]. Additionally, having the pathway be collaborative can help teachers directly experience the effectiveness of collaborative learning in a multicultural environment. For these reasons, in PLEIADE teachers are proposed collaborative activities (at school, as well as at international level) and a framework for self-regulated learning is implemented [11, 19] to support practice sharing behaviors.

Secondly, (b) LD research focuses on the complex decision-making process through which teachers design students' learning activities. Aim of research in this area is to develop methods and tools to ensure that such a process is systematic and informed by pedagogical theory. In PLEIADE, teachers need to build upon inclusive education principles to make sure they design effective inclusive learning activities, where all their students have an opportunity to develop their skills [20]. However, studies in LD [21, 22] indicate that teachers cannot face complex LD challenges in isolation, as the adoption of new and effective educational strategies is very much dependent on practice sharing among educators. In other words, LD competence can only be developed if teachers embrace a participatory culture and take control of their own professional development [17]. This is particularly true when the target is practicing teachers and the field of knowledge is one where they have already developed a significant amount of tacit knowledge through practice, such as social inclusion in education. Hence, research in LD and in TPD converge on the idea that fostering practice sharing is an essential component of the training of teachers in complex domains.

Of course, such a TPD approach requires long term engagement of participants (c), which need to rely on a cheerful and relaxed atmosphere. Thus, gamification is the third pillar underpinning the PLEIADE approach. Gamification has been defined as the use of game elements in non-game contexts [23]. In our case, the TPD pathway relies on a gamified *narrative*, where "story, world, and aesthetic presentation tightly bind mechanics to purposeful tasks and vice versa" (p. 229, [24]). A playful narrative can alleviate the burden of complex tasks and foster motivation, engagement, and task performance. In particular, in the case of teacher training initiatives, the adoption of a journey metaphor may facilitate reflection on practice and meta-reflective thinking in a relaxed and safe shared space [24]. In PLEIADE, the chosen metaphor is that of a space journey. Hence, the terminology used and the graphical layout of the learning environment hosting participants' interactions are coherent with this choice. As a second gameful element, LD activities of the TPD pathway will make use of a game, the I4Ts game [26, 27], expressly developed to support teachers in systematic design practices.

3 Methodological Design

The PLEIADE TPD approach is the object of an international intervention case study [28], involving about 75 teachers belonging to 4 different European schools. The study is still in progress, as the PLEIADE project started in September 2020 and should last approximately three years, entailing 4 main phases:

- a "preparatory phase" devoted to the needs analysis and detailed design of the TPD pathway, the set-up of the gamified learning platform and the development of the I4Ts game to be used in the pathway;
- a "training phase" lasting about one year, during which the TPD approach is put into practice with significant scaffolding from the project's academic institutions;
- an "enactment phase", lasting approximately 12 months, during which TPD goes on in a more self-regulated way as the scaffolding fades and the teachers' community members will support each other in a less structured way in implementing collaborative inclusive teaching in their classrooms;
- a "conclusive phase", devoted to analyzing the data collected during the training and enactment phase, in order to understand the TPD dynamics and outcomes, as well as fine tune the tools developed in the preparatory phase. The impact of the adopted approach on participants will be evaluated according to Guskeys's model [29], by collecting data concerning teachers' reactions, teachers' learning, institutional support and change, teachers' use of the new knowledge and impact on their students.

At the time of writing, the preparatory phase has been thoroughly carried out, while the training phase is still under way (currently at month 8 out of 12).

4 The Training Pathway

According to the needs analysis performed in the preparatory phase [30], the involved teachers already have some experience concerning LD and educational inclusion, while they don't regularly share their practices. For this reason, a participatory approach involving the teachers in the design of inclusive activities can leverage their prior experience while fostering their interaction.

The experts' contribution to the training is mainly focused on getting the PLEIADE teachers used to view design as a systematic decision-making process, in line with LD research results, and to facilitate reflection on practice and practice sharing through a gamified approach. This is done by providing extensive scaffolding at the beginning of the training phase, and then fade this scaffolding gradually as teachers gain autonomy.

In particular, during the training, the teachers are guided to collaboratively design good practice examples of collaborative, inclusive activities. Following the training, they will enact some of these activities in their own classes, with lighter support on the part of experts. At the end of the project, a selection of these designs will be made available through an Open Access repository, for other teachers to reuse them after adapting them to different contexts.

Additionally, during the training phase participants are involved in a collective reflection on the criteria for designing inclusive collaborative learning activities, and practice sharing is fostered so as to facilitate the development of a community of practitioners that can survive beyond the time span of the project.

To these ends, the pathway is built from the ground up to be participatory and engaging, to encourage the sharing of participants' own experiences, beliefs, challenges, and solutions.

To facilitate teachers in the adoption of a systematic process to LD the 4T model has been adopted [31], so as to provide teachers with a common framework for describing and designing inclusive collaborative activities. This model allows teachers to formally describe an activity in terms of the Task, Team(s), Time and Technology it considers, which facilitates both sharing and adaptation to a novel context.

4.1 Structure of the Training Pathway

The PLEIADE training phase lasts about one year and comprises 7 modules, as indicated in Table 1. The pathway alternates intensive, face-to-face events of about one week at the premises of one of the schools (called "space rendez-vous", in accord with the journey metaphor)[2] with lighter online work. The intensive events, in turn, alternate plenary sessions with experts' presentations of content or participants' presentations of their work with collaborative activities in smaller groups (sometimes international, some time national groups). Online work is always collaborative, based on asynchronous interactions on the platform.

Table 1. Structure of the PLEIADE training pathway (PS = plenary sessions; IC = international collaboration; NC = national collaboration). Module titles follow the 'space journey' metaphor.

Module title	Module type	Aim	Content
M1 - Countdown	Online Non intensive PS + IC	Playfully breaking the ice among participants	Participants self-introductions of their competences and emotions
M2 - Take off	Face-to-face Intensive IC	Getting to grasps with inclusive teaching strategies and the 4Ts model to design collaborative learning activities	Inclusive teaching strategies collaborative learning learning design
M3 – Leaving the Earth's atmosphere	Online Non intensive NC	Peer reviewing examples of previous practices	As above

(*continued*)

[2] The Erasmus + programme provides funds for teachers' (or students') mobility.

Table 1. (*continued*)

Module title	Module type	Aim	Content
M4 – Rocket men and women working together	Face-to-face Intensive NC + IC	Reflecting on importance of self-regulated learning and practice sharing	Models of Self-regulated learning in academic contexts and in informal learning
M5 – Space oddities taking shape	Online Non intensive NC + IC	Bootstrapping the design of activities for enactment	Design principles for inclusive teaching from literature
M6 – Orbit calculations	Face-to-face Intensive NC + IC	Advancing the designs of activities for enactment Reflecting/improving the design principles for inclusive teaching	4Ts model in practice Design principles for inclusive teaching amended
M7 – Outer space	Online Non intensive NC + IC	Finalizing the designs of activities for enactment	As above

While in the early phases of the training, after some playful ice-breaking activities (M1), participants are asked to share with colleagues their previous experiences of collaborative learning for inclusion (M2-M3), in the subsequent phases they reflect on the role of practice sharing in their self-regulated professional development and on the features that make a learning activity more or less inclusive (M4, M5). The last two modules (M6, M7) are the most creative ones, as the teachers start to design the activities they will subsequently enact in their classes. The design is supported by using the I4T game, which makes learning design of collaborative activities a more playful, scaffolded process. Additionally, in these final stages of the training, teachers and experts build a rubric for the assessment of the inclusive potential of their designs, starting from a draft derived from a literature review and integrating it on the basis of their experience. This rubric will further help teachers engage in a systematic LD process, in which they carefully plan their collaborative activities.

5 Preliminary Results: Barriers and Enabling Factors

The training pathway is being implemented starting from May 2021, involving about 75 primary and lower secondary teachers from four countries (Italy, Bulgaria, Greece, and Cyprus) which are either experiencing a recent surge of immigration or are facing other inclusion challenges.

One of the main issues faced during the pathway implementation was that, due to the COVID-19 pandemic, the face-to-face modules could not be held in presence, but had to be carried out online. This was perceived by the teachers as a major problem, hindering their motivation to participate in the training and in the enactment. For the PLEIADE teachers, not being able to meet in person means not being able to achieve the necessary sense of trust in their colleagues for a productive collaboration. In addition, the shift to online mode of the intensive events added further effort to a period of very hard work, characterized by internet fatigue and high levels of stress. While this barrier has to be considered an exceptional event, it certainly tells us that the original design in blended mode was the right choice and would have probably motivated the involved teachers to make a bigger effort to overcome the other problems. For teachers, the mobility funds made available by the Erasmus+ programme are an important contribution to their professional development, as their job is otherwise very much anchored to the local context.

A second barrier to practice sharing was the lack of fluency in the chosen interaction language (English), that especially concerned Italian and Bulgarian teachers. The approach chosen to overcome this barrier was diversified: some educational content of the pathway was localized, participants were encouraged to use automatic translators to translate their messages, some presentations were automatically subtitled, others were professionally translated by interpreters, and participation in collaborative activities was facilitated by Italian and Bulgarian tutors. Moreover, early identification of participants with advanced English skills informed the formation of groups for the collaborative activities, so that these teachers could act as 'bridges' to relay critical information to their peers and facilitate their participation. In spite of all these measures, linguistic issues remained one of the main barriers to international collaboration, especially during the first intensive event. Therefore, during the second intensive event, an alternative approach was adopted to tackle this problem. Teachers were invited to carry out the collaborative part of their work in national groups, while the international exchange was delegated to representatives, whose linguistic skills were good enough. This solution undoubtedly hindered the spontaneity and richness of interactions, but at least allowed all participants to feel "represented" and to contribute to the collective work.

Additionally, stark differences between the four involved schools in terms of inclusion challenges they face emerged, although in some cases they could be turned into enablers. For example, the Cypriot teachers' experiences with refugees were seen as especially important to address one of the needs expressed by Greek teachers, i.e. fostering empathy and awareness of social disadvantage in their own students. This, together with the fact that linguistic barriers do not exist between Cyprus and Greece, is probably an important facilitating factor for collaboration. Another important difference between the PLEIADE schools concerns uneven technological equipment and digital competence of the teachers. This was not a major concern during the training, but could turn out to be a barrier during enactment.

Lastly, many teachers had relatively low familiarity with some concepts related to practice sharing and some of them had low digital competence. The first information led to the decision of dedicating one of the intensive events to this concept, so as to provide teachers with the tools for effective practice sharing throughout their professional life. The second pointed to the need to provide continuous technical support to the use of the training platform, even in the form of video tutorials.

While the long duration of the training helps make it more relevant and effective, it should be noted that, in a project lasting three years, the core activities (i.e. the training and enactment phases) are interrupted by the summer holidays at least twice. In some Countries, summer is a period of intense teacher turnover. In PLEIADE, the 2021 summer holidays produced a significant change in the cohort of participating teachers, with obvious difficulties deriving from the need to update and include in the community the new teachers.

As for enabling factors, a key one is that the teachers are not new to the field of inclusive design and implementation. They have previous experience in this area and, although their approach to LD is not systematic and their theoretical knowledge about collaborative learning for inclusion is not always solid, they have a layer of preliminary competence they can build upon in a self-regulated way.

A second enabling factor is the availability of funds for the teachers' mobility (even if this was – so far – frustrated by the travel difficulties created by the pandemic). In order to replicate a similar approach without the Erasmus+ funds, it would be necessary to rely on a local network of schools, whose teachers can occasionally meet face-to-face. Although this would mean losing the international dimension typical of international projects, it would take advantage of the fact that the linguistic issues would no longer apply. Alternatively, international communities can be built at no cost within EC community platforms like eTwinnings[3], but these communities are entirely online and do not usually involve academic institutions. This means that the level of self-regulatedness of the community should be rather high from the start. However, building a community bottom-up, starting from interested teachers who are already active on the platform is a guarantee of interest and motivation, which is not necessarily the case for all teachers when the school is involved in a top-down manner. This is actually a two-sided factor: the formal commitment of the schools in the project, typical of funded projects, is not just useless bureaucracy: it is an important enabling factor. It may not ensure intrinsic motivation of all participants, but it does entail that the organization will support the initiative and make sure there is recognition for participating teachers.

The significant duration and the systematic approach of the training pathway are another enabler. Even if some of the teachers involved in the PLEIADE training did not have the digital skills needed to participate from the start, in a few weeks they got acquainted with the learning environment and started to feel more confident in its use.

On the other hand, the usage of a playful approach [25] – both in the underlying journey metaphor and in the use of a full-on game for supporting learning design – was greatly appreciated by the teachers, and helped bring some levity in an otherwise long and demanding training pathway.

Another important asset of the project is the presence, in each school, of at least one "Team leader", that is, a teacher who acts as a contact person inside the school and coordinates the activities of his/her colleagues. Without the Team leaders acting as bridges between the coordinating institution and the participating teachers, carrying out the training and enactment phases would be almost impossible.

Last but not least, another important element for the feasibility of the approach is the strict collaboration between the academic institutions and the schools, both during

[3] https://www.etwinning.net/it/pub/index.htm.

the training and during the enactment. This is a major learning opportunity for all participants. On the one hand, teachers will be able to act as action researchers and will be provided with tools to assess the effectiveness of their teaching. At the same time, the academic partners of the project will receive from the teachers a wealth of feedback thanks to which they will be able to fine tune the tools used both during the training and the enactment.

6 Conclusive Remarks

In spite of the difficulties and barriers mentioned in the above section, the PLEIADE project is well under way and will hopefully lead to identify further elements that may help others to replicate the chosen approach in different contexts. To further improve the replicability of the PLEIADE approach, even in contexts where suitable funding may not be available, PLEIADE is strongly committed to making its results accessible to a wider international community. Besides the publications documenting the approach and its further developments, the project intends to develop a number of open and reusable "intellectual outputs": the TPD pathway design, with indications of how to tailor it to different TPD aims, contexts and countries involved [30]; the I4Ts game, which is intended to support the design of socio-constructivist learning activities for inclusion [32]; the gamified platform, which is a customization of the Moodle platform and is thus Open Source and reusable in different participatory TPD contexts [33]; a toolkit for assessing inclusive features of learning designs; an open collection of good practice designs for inclusion, produced collaboratively by the PLEIADE partners; and finally a toolkit intended to amplify and disseminate the above outputs, by providing indications on how to reuse and repurpose them.

Acknowledgements. Co-funded by the Erasmus+ Programme of the European Union The PLEIADE project is co-funded by the Erasmus+ programme of the European Union (Agreement number 2020-1-IT02-KA201-080089). The European Commission's support for the production of this publication does not constitute an endorsement of the contents, which reflect the views only of the authors, and the Commission cannot be held responsible for any use which may be made of the information contained therein.

References

1. Dronkers, J., van der Velden, R., Dunne, A.: Why are migrant students better off in certain types of educational systems or schools than in others? Eur. Educ. Res. J. **11**(1), 11–44 (2012). https://doi.org/10.2304/eerj.2012.11.1.11
2. Guðjónsdóttir, H., Cacciattolo, M., Dakich, E., Davies, A., Kelly, C., Dalmau, M.C.: Transformative pathways: inclusive pedagogies in teacher education. J. Res. Technol. Educ. **40**(2), 165–182 (2007). https://doi.org/10.1080/15391523.2007.10782503
3. OECD: Immigrant students at school: Easing the journey towards integration. OECD reviews of migrant education. OECD Publishing, Paris (2015). https://doi.org/10.1787/9789264249509-en
4. UNESCO: Policy Guidelines on Inclusion in Education. UNESCO, Paris (2009)

5. OECD: Teachers matter: Attracting, developing, and retaining effective teachers. OECD Publishing, Paris (2005)
6. OECD: TALIS 2018 Results (Volume I): Teachers and School Leaders as Lifelong Learners. OECD Publishing, Paris (2019). https://doi.org/10.1787/1d0bc92a-en
7. European Commission: Joint Report of the Council and the Commission on the implementation of the Strategic framework for European cooperation in education and training (ET2020) (2015). http://ec.europa.eu/education/documents/et-2020-draft-joint-report-408-2015_en.pdf
8. Dukuzumuremyi, S., Siklander, P.: Interactions between pupils and their teacher in collaborative and technology-enhanced learning settings in the inclusive classroom. Teach. Teach. Educ. **76**, 165–174 (2018). https://doi.org/10.1016/j.tate.2018.08.010
9. Trust, T., Carpenter, J.P., Krutka, D.G.: Moving beyond silos: professional learning networks in higher education. Internet High. Educ. **35**, 1–11 (2017). https://doi.org/10.1016/j.iheduc.2017.06.001
10. Trust, T.: Professional learning networks designed for teacher learning. J. Digit. Learn. Teach. Educ. **28**(4), 133–138 (2012)
11. Persico, D., Milligan, C., Littlejohn, A.: The interplay between self-regulated professional learning and teachers' work-practice. Procedia Soc. Behav. Sci. **191**, 2481–2486 (2015)
12. Lave, J., Wenger, E.: Legitimate peripheral participation in communities of practice. In: Supporting Lifelong Learning, pp. 121–136. Routledge (2001)
13. Vescio, V., Ross, D., Adams, A.: A review of research on the impact of professional learning communities on teaching practice and student learning. Teach. Teach. Educ. **24**(1) (2008). https://doi.org/10.1016/j.tate.2007.01.004
14. Delfino, M., Dettori, G., Persico, D.: An online course fostering self-regulation of trainee teachers. Psicothema **22**(2), 299–305 (2010). https://reunido.uniovi.es/index.php/PST/article/view/8905
15. Passarelli, Dagnino, Persico, Pozzi, Manganello: Gamification and support to self-regulation as a means to promote practice sharing for teacher professional development. Cult. Edu. (2022). https://doi.org/10.1080/11356405.2022.2102291
16. Persico, D., Pozzi, F.: The role of representations for the development of a participatory culture of Learning Design among educators. In: Proceedings of the ATEE-SIREM Winter Conference - Learning & Teaching with Media & Technology, pp. 365–372. Association for Teacher Education in Europe, Brussels (2013)
17. Persico, D., Passarelli, M., Manganello, F., Gewerc Barujel, A., Rodriguez Groba, A.: The participatory dimension of teachers' self-regulated professional learning about learning design: beliefs versus behaviours. Prof. Dev. Educ. 1–13 (2020). https://doi.org/10.1080/19415257.2020.1787193
18. Osterman, K.F., Kottkamp, R.B.: Reflective Practice for Educators: Professional Development to Improve Student Learning. Corwin Press (2004)
19. Littlejohn, A., Milligan, C., Margaryan, A.: Charting collective knowledge: supporting self-regulated learning in the workplace. J. Workplace Learn. (2012)
20. CAST: Universal Design for Learning Guidelines version 2.2 (2018). http://udlguidelines.cast.org
21. Laurillard, D.: Teaching as a Design Science: Building Pedagogical Patterns for Learning and Technology. Routledge (2013)
22. Asensio-Pérez, J.I., et al.: Towards teaching as design: exploring the interplay between full-lifecycle learning design tooling and teacher professional development. Comput. Educ. **114**, 92–116 (2017)
23. Deterding, S., Dixon, D., Khaled, R., Nacke, L.: From game design elements to gamefulness: defining "gamification". In: Proceedings of the 15th International Academic MindTrek Conference: Envisioning Future Media Environments, pp. 9–15 (2011)

24. Lane, N., Prestopnik, N.R.: Diegetic connectivity: blending work and play with storytelling in serious games. In: Proceedings of the Annual Symposium on Computer-Human Interaction in Play, pp. 229–240 (2017)
25. Saban, A.: Functions of metaphor in teaching and teacher education: a review essay. Teach. Educ. **17**(4), 299–315 (2006)
26. Pozzi, F., Ceregini, A., Persico, D.: Designing networked learning with 4Ts. In: Proceedings of the 10th International Conference on Networked Learning, pp. 210–217 (2016)
27. Ceregini, A., Persico, D., Pozzi, F., Sarti, L.: The 4Ts game to develop teachers' competences for the design of collaborative learning. In: Burgos, D., et al. (eds.) HELMeTO 2019. CCIS, vol. 1091, pp. 192–205. Springer, Cham (2019). https://doi.org/10.1007/978-3-030-31284-8_15
28. Merriam, S.B.: The case study in educational research: a review of selected literature. J. Educ. Thought (JET)/Revue de la Pensée Educative 204–217 (1985)
29. Guskey, T.R.: Evaluating Professional Development. Corwin, Thousand Oaks (2000)
30. Passarelli, M., Dagnino, F.M., Persico, D., Pozzi, F., Nikolova, N.: Blended Teachers' Professional Development (TPD) Pathway (PLEIADE Intellectual Output No. 1) (2021)
31. Pozzi, F., Persico, D.: Sustaining learning design and pedagogical planning in CSCL. Res. Learn. Technol. **21** (2013)
32. Bicocchi, M., Ceregini, A., Persico, D., Polsinelli, P., Pozzi, F., Sarti, L.: The Hybrid I4T Game (PLEIADE Intellectual Output No. 2) (2021)
33. Manganello, F., Persico, D., Georgiev, A., Mihnev, P., Peltekov, M.: Gamified Platform for the Blended Training Activities (PLEIADE Intellectual Output No. 2) (2021)

Educational Technologies, Social and Emotional Learning and School Inclusion: Challenges and Opportunities

Alessia Signorelli(✉)

Department of Philosophy, Social and Human Sciences and Education, University of Perugia, Piazza Ermini 1, 06123 Perugia, Italy
alessia.signorelli@unipg.it

Abstract. The paper explores the connections between social emotional learning and the use of technologies for inclusion while also providing an assessment model for the quality of social and emotional technologies.

Keywords: Social-Emotional Learning · Inclusive education · Technologies

1 Introduction

1.1 Social and Emotional Learning, a Key to Inclusive Education

This research was carried out as part of a PhD course, and it was a first attempt at both investigating the relations intercurrent between inclusion, technologies and social emotional learning and providing an assessment model for social emotional learning (SEL) apps and platforms to highlight their inclusive potential.

This initial study on the opportunities and challenges posed by the interaction between inclusion technologies and social and emotional learning was part of a doctorate research that lasted three years, from 2017 to 2020.

The research was carried out selecting and analyzing a sample of apps and platforms for social and emotional learning using inclusion and exclusion criteria gathered from the intersection of the literature on educational technologies and social emotional learning with a special attention to the levels of inclusiveness (usability, accessibility, customization). Further, to investigate the possibility of use of platform or apps for social emotional learning in educational settings, a MOOC was designed and launched in November 2019.

Inclusive education is still a highly debated topic; to these days, even though the main, founding principles are widely shared, there is no univocal, internationally agreed upon definition both in "practical" and philosophical terms. These differentiated ways of understanding inclusive education reflect both cultural and structural aspects and tend to also impact the ethical principles at stakes, calling them into question, especially while arguing whether a fully inclusive model such as the one existing in the Italian education context, for example, is acceptable or even if it is really working.

M. Ranieri et al. (Eds.): ATEE 2021, CCIS 1649, pp. 230–240, 2022.
https://doi.org/10.1007/978-3-031-20777-8_19

However, it is still possible to broadly identify inclusive education as a "process" [1–3], that is created daily through the different and often complex interactions occurring between teachers, school staff, students, communities, but also context and curricula [4]. In this sense, inclusive education calls for, and entails, an increase in the social and educational participation of **all** learners [5]; therefore, in addressing the issue of inclusion, it is necessary to go beyond the more narrow vision that associates inclusive education only with disabilities (regardless of their severity) while leaving out all other special educational needs (whether they are of social, cultural, economic, emotional, gender-related, or learning nature, and so on).

Inclusive education is closely linked to the concept of quality education. This connection has been highlighted also in UNESCO' Agenda 2030, especially in Goal 4, "Ensure inclusive and equitable quality education and promote life-long learning for all." Furthermore, inclusive education overcomes and dismantles the idea of "traditional special education" which "[...] consists in segregating students with special needs from mainstream students within separate and typically smaller classrooms or educational settings" [6].

Damiani [7] states that the new inclusive competencies of teachers should be "transversal", encompassing also the social and emotional development aspects of learning. This falls within the framework known as Social-Emotional Learning [8], that originates from the works of Daniel Goleman on Emotional Intelligence [9]. Social – Emotional Learning (SEL) as well as inclusion, can be defined as well as a process through which children, teenagers and adults alike can acquire and put into practice a series of social and emotional competencies fundamental for their personal, working, and social well-being [10].

Cefai et al. [11] defined social and emotional learning as "[...] the educational process by which an individual develops social and emotional competence for personal, social, and academic growth and development through curricular, embedded, relational and contextual approaches. The definition implies developing and applying the attitudes, knowledge and skills required to understand oneself and others, to express and regulate emotions, to develop healthy and caring relationships, to make good, responsible, and ethical decisions, and to make use of one's own strengths and overcome difficulties in social and academic tasks".

A further definition of this framework comes from The National Conference of State Legislators, which describes social emotional learning as "[...] a wide range of skills, attitudes, and behaviors that can affect a student's success in school and life. Critical thinking, managing emotions, working through conflicts, decision making, and teamwork are all skills not necessarily measured by tests, though they are crucial components of a student's education. These skills may impact his/her academic success, employability, self-esteem, relationships, as well as civic and community engagement" [12].

The ability of recognizing one own's emotions and other people's, valuing them, being able to understand other people's point of view, thoughts, and actions, are considered key elements in inclusive educational processes since they promote open, warm, welcoming attitudes and behaviors [13].

In turn, these attitudes and behaviors are pivotal in the creation of an educational context that can welcome all individual differences, thanks to the resource represented by peers [8, 14]. Within the classroom's microcosmos, peers can become fundamental in supporting, valuing and appreciate the differences of each and all. However, such social and emotional skills are not "innate" but can be developed and improved. If, starting from a very young age, children are exposed to an education encompassing social and emotional competencies, an education that will help them develop what Gerard Hüther [15] calls "compassionate brain", or what Damasio and Immordino – Yang [16] call "emotional thought", they will be able to relate to others in a healthy and well-balanced way.

An early and systematic exposure to social emotional learning becomes an essential feature for improving inclusive processes inside and outside the school environment. Hüther's discourse is also connected to several studies in the field of developmental psychology that highlight how emotional and social development and growth starts at birth and continues during infancy, through adaptive or maladaptive responses towards primary emotions such as anger, fear, and sadness [17]. Growing up, children begin to correctly identify and use emotions to understand the many perspectives of everyday life that could vary from each other; children, therefore, start to understand other people's thought and actions and begin to form empathic connections [18, 19].

Much research, literature review and meta-analyses have been produced in the past 12 years to collect and provide evidence on SEL's efficacy. The first and most notable is the Durlak et al. [20] meta-analysis, which collected and analyzed 213 evidence – based studies on the effects of SEL development programs on a total sample o 270.034 students from United States – from kindergarten to high school. The data from this meta-analysis showed good outcomes in social and emotional skills, in appropriate social behaviors, and in academic achievement compared to those students who did not take part in any SEL program or activity [21].

Taylor et al. [22] analyzed the follow-up of randomized, semi-experimental studies, highlighting how the results obtained via the implementation of social emotional learning programs during school time did not fade with time, but they would persist between six months and three years after the end of the intervention [13].

Further studies [23, 24] highlighted a positive correlation between social emotional learning interventions and academic achievement and between social emotional learning interventions and a reduction in behavioral problems.

2 Social Emotional Learning and Technologies: A State of the Art

2.1 Affective Computing: A Starting Point

The concept of emotion linked to technologies has been explored in depth starting from the mid – 1990s through the works of Rosalind Picard of the Massachusetts Institute of Technology (MIT), who first coined the term "affective computing" as a branch in the HCI (human-computer-interaction) field of research. Affective Computing's main goal is to develop a "[…] computing that relates to, arises from, or influences emotions" [25].

While was not Picard's intention to investigate and provide answer to the questions about the nature and origin of emotions, nor was to create "emotional computers", her work focused on developing models that would foster affective recognition and innovative applications in the field of computer-assisted learning, of recovery of perceptual information, and of human interactions [25].

Starting from Picard's formulations, Affective Computing has seen, in time, an exponential growth in research and implementation; many tools have been developed such as games, diagnostic tools, tutoring systems, emotional monitoring systems, personality simulators for virtual characters and so on.

Landowska [26] reminds us that whenever we interact with computers, with digital devices, we remain "emotional beings" and our emotions, in relation to the use of such "mechanical" tools, are, however, still real.

2.2 Technologies for Social and Emotional Learning: Issues and Open Questions

Even though the field of social emotional technologies is somehow still young, there are some interesting examples of virtual spaces, apps, and devices that, although limited and often unique, can provide starting points in envisioning future developments.

In 2016, the World Economic Forum [27] published the document "New vision for education: fostering social and emotional learning through technology", where the connection between SEL and technologies has been addressed in the following terms: "To thrive in the 21st century, students need more than traditional academic learning. They must be adept at collaboration, communication, and problem-solving, which are some of the skills developed through social and emotional learning (SEL).

Coupled with mastery of traditional skills, social and emotional proficiency will equip students to succeed in the swiftly evolving digital economy [...] education technology has the potential to play a pivotal role in fostering SEL efficiently and cost-effectively. We see technology as a tool that a parent, educator or caregiver can use to complement and extend the learning experience – especially given the host of emerging technologies that go beyond traditional screens. These innovations can mix the physical and virtual worlds and facilitating forms of human interaction impossible a decade ago." [27].

The World Economic Forum report, even though it focuses more on the economic than the pedagogical aspects, points out an element which should be considered; in the document only two examples of social emotional learning technologies are cited, Minecraft Education Edition and ZooU, which have been specifically developed with social and emotional learning objectives.

This is reflected also by scientific literature, which outlines a paucity of studies for what concerns the pairing social emotional learning and technologies [13, 28–30] and how the existing research is limited – so to say – to the use of technologies to help develop social and emotional learning mainly in individuals with autism spectrum disorders [31–34].

A further analysis of the literature and of the projects carried out in the past 10 years, allowed for the outlining of two main "voids":

- The lack of an updated mapping of the apps and online platforms which are specifically designed of the development of social and emotional skills.

- The lack of an evaluation system of the quality of such apps and platforms able to assess outcomes in terms of learning, while such systems exist for other educational apps.

In addition, it must be pointed out that, currently, the market is overflowing with apps that claim to fall in the category of social and emotional development while, when closely examined, they only use the tags "social and emotional learning" or "social and emotional development" while their content does not provide any educational aspect and are aimed to an adult audience.

As the importance of the development of social and emotional skills in children is constantly growing in the field of education, this background calls for the creation of a taxonomy of social and emotional learning apps and digital platforms to help teachers choosing the right device for supporting kids' social and emotional growth and thriving.

3 Assessing the Quality of SEL Apps and Web Platforms: A Perspective Model

3.1 A First Survey of the App for Social Emotional Learning: Research Results

Taking stock from what outlined in the previous chapter, the research's focus was twofold: on one hand, it wanted to investigate how many SEL apps and online platform are currently available and, starting from this, to create an assessment system for such devices, following the examples already set for the general educational technologies. The first part of the PhD research, therefore, was to carry out a survey and a mapping of such apps and platforms.

To collect apps and platforms, three main channels were used:

- iOS App Store
- Android Google Play
- Google search engine for web research.

Research in this phase was further «refined» by considering web platforms and apps specifically recommended by the main organizations for research and diffusion of social-emotional learning.

The keywords used in all three channels were the following: social emotional learning, emotional intelligence, emotional development, children social emotional learning, inclusive social emotional learning. This first survey collected a total of 350 between apps and platforms.

A further refinement was carried out, using the following inclusion criteria:

- Development of one or all SEL skills presented by the CASEL 5 framework
- Age ranges from early childhood to high school (5 to 18)
- Accessibility and usability (voice-over, clear tasks, easy to navigate, possibility to use either alone or with the help of an adult)
- Possibility to be used to in school and at home

The exclusion criteria were the following:

- Exclusive focus on meditation and mindfulness
- Adult age range
- Complex tasks
- Complex design and navigation, overload of visual and other sensory cues

The application of inclusion and exclusion criteria led to the selection of a final sample of 64 between apps and web platforms.

To gain a further insight of the final sample selected (what was the most target age-range, what kind of SEL skills they were addressing and if they were only "entertaining" or could be connected to school learning), another analysis was carried out extracting additional information from the apps/platforms' presentations and synopsis.

Following, a final set of criteria was decided:

- Type (app or platform)
- Age range
- Connection to school subjects
- Specifically designed for disabled/special educational needs subjects
- Targeted SEL skills

48 were apps for mobile devices, 15 were web platforms and only 1 presented a "mixed" modality (both web and mobile).

17 were aimed at pre-school aged children, 18 were designed for kids aged 6 to 10 years and 29 addressed kids aged 10 to 18. Only 12% of the selected sample showed some connection to school's subjects such as science, math, literacy. Only 6% of the 64 apps and platform analyzed were specifically designed to address the specific needs of users with disabilities (autism spectrum disorder).

The targeted social emotional learning skills were self-awareness (26 out of 64), social awareness (18 out of 64), self – management (3), problem – solving (3). 14 out of 64 focused on developing all five core skills: self-awareness, self-management, social awareness, relationship skills, responsible decision making/problem-solving.

Based on existing systems for assessing the quality of the learning cycle of general educational apps, a Digital SEL Cycle taking stock from the one proposed by Garris & Driskell [35] for the assessment of educational games app and from the one proposed by Ak [36], based on Kolb's Experiential Learning Cycle was designed (ELC).

Garris and Driskell's cycle is based on the analysis between learning outcomes and use of digital learning games, particularly on the positive effects that they can have on students' motivation according to what stated by Kolb [37], namely that learning is a process through which knowledge is created by transforming experiences.

The Digital SEL Cycle differs from the Garris & Driskell's model in these aspects: firstly, Garris & Driskell's model is focused on the correlation between students' engagement and outcomes with the aim of improving the engagement aspect.

The Digital SEL Cycle, on the other hand, is structured around a series of specific outcomes (increase of emotional granularity, improvement in the social emotional learning skills area, creation of an inclusive brain frame) resulting from the interaction between

3 input elements (contents, usability and social emotional learning skills) and the use of social emotional learning apps or digital platforms borne from the intersection of a literature review on the three fields of interest (inclusion, social and emotional learning and technologies) and the analysis of the apps and online platforms selected.

Furthermore, the Digital SEL Cycle aims at helping students becoming not only engaged but also able to understand their own and other people's emotional states in a more refined way, therefore working on their emotional granularity [17] while also acquiring or boosting their social and emotional skills and developing and inclusive brain frame thanks to the use of the SEL app or online platform.

3.2 The MOOC "DIGItal Competences for the Development of Social Emotional Skills for Inclusion"

In order to understand the impact of the use of social – emotional learning apps and platforms within educational contexts, the PhD research envisaged the creation and distribution of a MOOC, which ran for 5 months, from November 2019 to April 2020 and was distributed through the EDUOpen platform[1], the first Italian portal for free and open to all university courses, created by a consortium of universities, and supported by the Italian Ministry of Education, University and Research.

The MOOC was structured in three main units and a fourth one which allowed the download of the certificate of attendance. The units were consequential and each one touched a different topic: Unit 1 – Inclusive Education, Unit – 2 Social Emotional Learning and Unit – 3 Technologies. To access the following unit, the attendees had to complete a short test.

Of the 1212 total initial participants, 582 completed the whole course, going through the three learning areas, undertaking the final test, and getting their certification of attendance. 39% of the participants lived in Northern Italy, 28% in Central Italy, 26% from Southern Italy, 6% did not state their geographical area, and 1% lived in other European countries (Serbia and Greece) and extra European Countries (Brazil, Columbia, Ecuador). The age range of participants varied from 18 and 65 years (Fig. 1).

14,17% was male, 85, 56% female, and 0,27% did not state their gender. Teachers were the majority (46.29%), followed by educators (27.26%) and by users that worked in other non – educational fields (23.75%). Psychologists were only 2.70%.

The MOOC was designed to allow participants to choose and evaluate the impact of an app/platform on social emotional learning of their choice, selected from the previously identified sample of 64 (the chosen ones were: Positive Penguins, GoStrengths! and Minecraft Education Edition[2]). At the end of the course, the participants were asked to answer a final questionnaire.

Amongst the questions concerning their user experience (connected with workload, use of specific language, previous knowledge of the topics explored), users were asked to reflect on how they perceived their knowledge on inclusive education, technologies and SEL after completing the MOOC.

---

[1] https://learn.eduopen.org/eduopenv2/course_details.php?courseid=393.

[2] www.positivepenguins.com; www.gostrengths.com; https://education.minecraft.net/en-us.

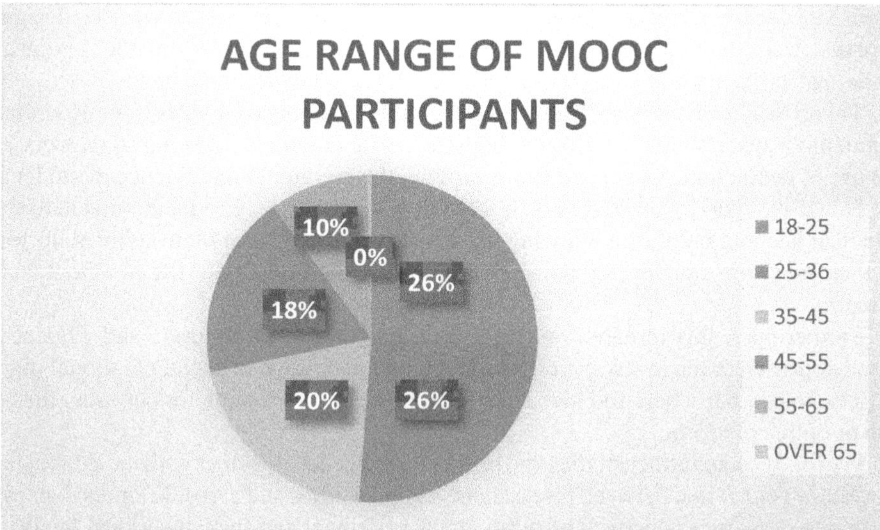

Fig. 1. Age range of MOOC participants.

58.08% felt more confident in their knowledge and in their ability to implement it in their daily work; 35.91% declared they felt more confident in the knowledge but still felt unsure about how to put it into practice, while 2.23% stated that they did not perceive any change with respect to their initial situation.

63.75% claimed that it was highly likely they would apply their new knowledge in their daily work; 32.30% said that it was likely; 1.55% quite unlikely, and 0.17% unlikely. Generally, responses were positive, showing also good points for refining the MOOC, especially for what concerned providing users with more practical examples.

4 Conclusions

The emotional life of individuals and technologies now share a momentum and are two of the main topics (and maybe trends) of the current educational debate concerning innovation and inclusive education.

The research carried out as part of a PhD course, showed that even though there is a keen interested in connecting social emotional learning and technologies, this match is still to be properly implemented.

The charting of apps and platforms related to social emotional learning showed how fragmented and sometimes unclear is the same concept of "social and emotional learning", sometimes overlapping with aspects that lie outside the perimeter of the framework, causing a risky "cloudiness" that could lead those teachers or educators who are however willing to give it a try, to either get lost in a such a wide offer to apps and platforms or choosing those whose design and contents could revealed to be ineffective for children and teenagers in school.

The results obtained from the implementation of the MOOC, on the other hand, showed the keenness of teachers and educators and other key actors involved in the inclusive education, in learning and applying those technologies that have been designed with the clear intention of helping children and adolescent in developing their social and emotional skills, particularly with students with special educational needs.

This clearly calls for a re-thinking and possibly updating of teacher training courses, where more space should be given to both the social emotional learning framework and the use of technologies designed for improving the emotional intelligence of students.

However, overall, the study highlighted how technologies in education, due to their role, can become helpful in allowing all students, regardless of their abilities, to work on their inner life and develop the skills to improve their quality of life at school and at home.

Furthermore, this research outlined the need for a more accurate and evidence – based approach to the investigation, classification, and usage of social emotional digital devices, to equip teachers and kids alike with the right information for choosing the best app or online platform.

For this reason, further studies and research are needed, together with the establishing of a closer connection between researchers, teachers, kids, and app developers to expand the scope of learning opportunities for social emotional and the educational quality of the devices made available.

What should be done in the future:

- Designing further research pathways through which systematically testing and validating the perspective model here introduced for its further revising/adjusting through the collection of evidence
- Broadening the research horizon for what concerns the triangulation of inclusion – technologies – social emotional learning applied to all learners
- Planning training pathways for teachers and educators on using SEL technologies as tools for fostering the development of inclusive attitudes and skills.

References

1. Ainscow, M.: Developing inclusive education systems: what are the levers for change? J. Educ. Change **6**, 109–124 (2004)
2. UNESCO: Policy guidelines on inclusion in education. UNESCO, Paris (2009)
3. Cottini, L.: Didattica speciale e inclusione scolastica. Carocci, Roma (2017)
4. Hollenweger, J., Pantič, N., Florian, L.: Tool to Upgrade Teacher Education - Practices for Inclusive Education. Council of Europe, Brussels (2015)
5. Hick, P., Ainscow, M., Dyson, A., Kalambouka, A., Izzidien, S., Francis, A.: Inclusive learning with ICT. University of Manchester, Coventry (2005)
6. Dalgaard, N., Bondebjerg, A., Viinholt, B., Filges, T.: PROTOCOL: the effects of inclusion on academic achievement, socioemotional development and wellbeing of children with special educational needs. Campbell Syst. Rev. **17**(2), 1–20 (2021)
7. Damiani, P.: Tra innovazione e inclusione: il bisogno di formazione alle "nuove competenze inclusive" dei docenti. Basi teoriche per un modello formativo coerente. Formazione & Insegnamento **13**(2), 297–302 (2015)

v.ingramcontent.com/pod-product-compliance
am Content Group UK Ltd.
eld, Milton Keynes, MK11 3LW, UK
IW021020050925
?611UK00012B/1341
9 7 8 3 0 3 1 2 0 7 7 6 1 *

8. Morganti, A., Signorelli, A.: Insegnanti alle prese con programmi educativi evidence-based: l'esperienza italiana del Promoting Alternative Thinking Strategies (PATHS®). Ital. J. Spec. Educ. Incl. **2**(4), 121–136 (2016)
9. Goleman, D.: Intelligenza Emotive. BUR, Milano (1996)
10. Oberle, E., Domitrovich, C.E., Meyers, D.C., Weissberg, P.R.: Establishing systemic social and emotional learning approaches in schools: a framework for schoolwide implementation. Camb. J. Educ. **4**(3), 277–297 (2016)
11. Cefai, C., Bartolo, P.A., Cavioni, V., Downes, P.: Strengthening Social and Emotional Education as a core curricular area across the EU. A review of the international evidence, NESET II report. Publications Office of the European Union, Luxembourg (2018)
12. Katzman, N.F., Stanton, M.P.: The integration of social emotional learning and cultural education into online distance learning curricula: now imperative during the COVID-19 pandemic. Creat. Educ. **11**, 1561–1571 (2020)
13. Morganti, A., Pascoletti, S., Signorelli, A.: Index for Social Emotional Technologies – Challenging Approaches to Inclusive Education. Routledge, Abingdon (2019)
14. Signorelli, A.: Inclusione scolastica ed educazione socio emotiva: risultati di una ricerca europea. Ital. J. Spec. Educ. Incl. **5**(2), 53–70 (2017)
15. Hüther, G.: Il cervello compassionevole. Come percezioni, emozioni e conoscenza possono trasformare le nostre capacità intellettive. Castelvecchi, Roma (2017)
16. Immordino-Yang, M.H., Damasio, A.R.: We feel, therefore we learn: the relevance of affective and social neuroscience to education. Mind Brain Educ. **1**(1), 3–10 (2007)
17. Feldman Barrett, L.: How Emotions are Made: the Secret Life of the Brain. Pan Macmillan, London (2017)
18. Decety, J.: The neural pathways, development and functions of empathy. Curr. Opin. Behav. Sci. **3**, 1–6 (2015)
19. Connolly, P., Miller, S., Mooney, J., Sloan, S., Hanratty, J.: Universal school based programs for improving social and emotional outcomes in children aged 3–11 years: a systematic review and a meta-analysis (2016). https://campbellcollaboration.org/media/k2/attachments/Connolly_Universal_Schoolbased_Programmes_Title.pdf. Accessed 09 Aug 2022
20. Durlak, J.A., Weissberg, R.P., Dymnicki, A.B., Taylor, R.D., Schellinger, K.B.: The impact of enhancing students' social and emotional learning: a meta-analysis of school-based universal interventions. Child Dev. **82**, 405–432 (2011)
21. Durlak, J.A., Mahoney, J.L.: The Practical Benefits of an SEL Program (2019). https://casel.s3.us-east-2.amazonaws.com/Practical-Benefits-of-SEL-Program.pdf. Accessed 09 Aug 2022
22. Taylor, R., Oberle, E., Durlak, J.A., Weissberg, R.P.: Promoting positive youth development through school-based social and emotional learning interventions: a metanalysis of follow-up effects. Child Dev. **88**(4), 1156–1171 (2017)
23. Barnes, T.N., Smith, S.W., Miller, M.D.: School-based cognitive- behavioral interventions in the treatment of aggression in the United States: a meta-analysis. Aggress. Violent. Beh. **19**, 311–321 (2014)
24. Corcoran, R.P., Cheung, A., Kim, E., Xie, C.: Effective universal school-based social and emotional learning programs for improving academic achievement: a systematic review and meta-analysis of 50 years of research. Educ. Res. Rev. (2018)
25. Picard, R.W.: Affective Computing M.I.T Media Laboratory Perceptual Computing Section Technical Report No. 321 (1995). https://affect.media.mit.edu/pdfs/95.picard.pdf. Accessed 09 Aug 2022
26. Landowska, A.: Affective computing and affective learning – methods, tools and prospects, EduAkcja. Magazyn edukacji elektronicznej **1**(5), 16–31 (2013)
27. World Economic Forum: New Vision for Education: Fostering Social and Emotional Learning through Technology WEF, Geneva (2016)

28. Clare, J.: Social-Emotional Apps for Special Ed (2015). https://www.edutopia.org/blog/social-emotional-apps-special-ed-jayne-clare. Accessed 09 Aug 2022
29. Stern, R.S., Harding, T.B., Holzer, A.A., Elbertson, N.A.: Current and potential uses of technology to enhance SEL. What's now and what's next? In: Durlak, J.A., Domitrovich, C.E., Weissberg, R.P., Gullotta, T.P. (eds.) Handbook of Social and Emotional Learning, pp. 516–531. The Guilford Press, New York (2015)
30. Slovák, P., Fitzpatrick, G.: Teaching and developing social and emotional skills with technology. Hum. Comput. Interact. J. **22**(4), 1–34 (2015)
31. Lozano, J., Ballesta, J., Alcaraz, S.: Software para enseñar emociones al alumnado con trastorno del espectro autista. Comunicar **36**(18), 139–148 (2011)
32. Chua, L., Goh, J., Nay, Z.T., Huang, L., Cai, Y., Seah, R.: ICT-enabled emotional learning for special needs education. In: Cai, Y., Goei, S.L., Trooster, W. (eds.) Simulation and Serious Games for Education. GMSE, pp. 29–45. Springer, Singapore (2017). https://doi.org/10.1007/978-981-10-0861-0_3
33. Walker, G., Weidenbenner, J.V.: Social and emotional learning in the age of virtual play: technology, empathy and learning. J. Res. Innov. Teach. Learn. **12**(2), 116–132 (2019)
34. Signorelli, A.: Affective computing e intelligenza emotiva: stato dell'arte e prospettive di sviluppo. QTIMES **13**(1), 94–108 (2021)
35. Garris, R., Ahlers, R., Driskell, J.E.: Games, motivation, and learning: a research and practice model. Simul. Gaming **33**(4), 441–467 (2002)
36. Ak, O.: A game scale to evaluate educational computer games. Procedia Soc. Behav. Sci. **46**, 2477–2481 (2012)
37. Kolb, D.A.: Experiential Learning: Experience as the Source of Learning and Development. Prentice-Hall, Hoboken (1984)

Author Index